Engaging Education

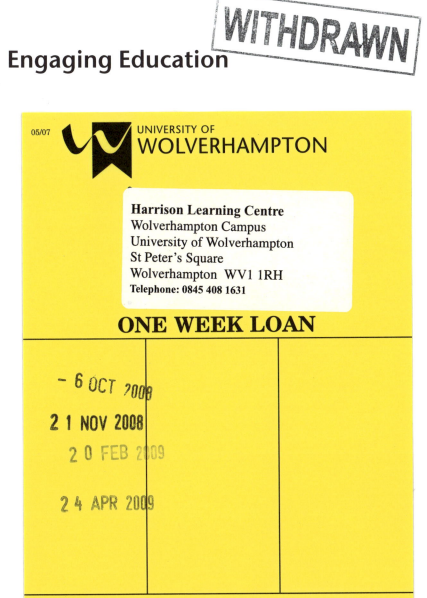

05/07

UNIVERSITY OF
WOLVERHAMPTON

Harrison Learning Centre
Wolverhampton Campus
University of Wolverhampton
St Peter's Square
Wolverhampton WV1 1RH
Telephone: 0845 408 1631

ONE WEEK LOAN

‑ 6 OCT 2008

2 1 NOV 2008

2 0 FEB 2009

2 4 APR 2009

Telephone Renewals: 01902 321333 or 0845 408 1631
Please RETURN this item on or before the last date shown above.
Fines will be charged if items are returned late.
See tariff of fines displayed at the Counter. (L2)

D0302074

Engaging Education

Developing Emotional Literacy, Equity and Co-education

Brian Matthews

Open University Press
McGraw-Hill Education
McGraw-Hill House
Shoppenhangers Road
Maidenhead
Berkshire
England
SL6 2QL

email: enquiries@openup.co.uk
world wide web: www.openup.co.uk

and Two Penn Plaza, New York, NY 10121-2289, USA

First published 2006

A catalogue record of this book is available from the British Library

ISBN-10 0 335 21579 3 (pb)   0 335 21580 7 (hb)
ISBN-13 978 0335 21579 9 (pb)   978 0335 21580 5 (hb)

Library of Congress Cataloging-in-Publication Data
CIP data applied for

Typeset by RefineCatch Limited, Bungay, Suffolk
Printed in the UK by Bell & Bain Ltd, Glasgow

Contents

Acknowledgements

I owe a debt of gratitude to many people over a long period of time. This book has grown out of my experiences as a child, teacher, lover, father, family man, lecturer and from life in general. Numerous friends and colleagues have helped me in the writing of this book. I would in particular like to acknowledge Carrie Paechter, John Head and Michael Reiss for their encouragement to write the book in the first place, and for their constructive criticism as my drafts emerged.

I owe a huge debt of thanks to John Jessel, Liz Morrison and Richard Ford who took over my work so that I could have the time to write, while also providing invaluable insights on my writing. Other people gave unstintingly of their time in reading and making excellent comments on the chapters, and my thanks go to: James Park, Wendy Riddle, Lesley Jones, Lyn Matthews, Susan Sidgwick, Pauline Boorman, Rosalyn George, Elena Silva, Carole Lee, Kass Aldred, Mark Matthews, Robert Matthews and Spencer Broughton.

I would also like to thank Tim Kilbey, Caroline Doneghan and Suzanne Harrison who skilfully carried out the original classroom research on which much of this book is based.

The final views expressed are mine, but without all the above people this book would never have been written.

And finally to my partner, Lyn, and to Louisa and the rest of the family, whose support enabled me to keep going, while reminding me of the true reasons for, and importance of, an emotional life.

Introduction

The origins of this book

Some books come to people in a flash, but not this one! The views I express in this book evolved over a number of years and grew out of my teaching experiences. I taught for 19 years in co-educational and single-sex secondary comprehensive schools. During this time I was interested in trying to make lessons more engaging. However, as I taught I became increasingly interested in how to enable pupils to get on well with each other. It seemed to me that the subjects taught in schools focused too much on cognitive ability. Certainly, the subject I taught, science, did not allow enough time for teachers and pupils to be able to pursue interesting topics, and develop their critical and creative faculties. Additionally, I wanted to have space to enable pupils to learn the social and emotional skills needed to appreciate each other. I used collaborative group work and introduced problem-solving exercises to aid pupils' emotional development, and to make the subject more interesting. I found ways of getting all pupils to work together, and although at the time I did not know the terminology, I was developing their emotional literacy through dialogue. Education, I believe, should include a celebration of the child, and help adolescents become adults with a strong social and emotional connectedness.

Also as a science teacher I was interested in equality – or equity – and trying to get more girls to take up science as a subject. These three themes – dialogue, emotional literacy and equity – are the themes of this book. The integration of emotional literacy and equity is novel and has not been explored before as it is in this book. I recognize that at present the pressures on schools are to focus almost exclusively on getting pupils through examinations. Change is difficult with a governmental or state control of education that results in a loss of freedom for teachers in what they can teach. This makes it even more important that teachers and other educators try and effect change. In society there is a recognition of the importance of emotional literacy and this is resulting in an increasing pressure on schools to develop emotional literacy programmes. This book is one of the calls for a change in emphasis.

Engaging the emotions

Growing up to become healthy and happy adults in our society has less to do with earning large amounts of money and more to do with having strong relationships of all kinds, and feeling that one has some control over life. While we recognize that being happy is connected with our emotional states, many of us are scared of emotions. This can be in part because we are sometimes afraid that our feelings don't conform to those of the society in which we live. It is also the case that feelings of high emotion can make us feel vulnerable, as they show sides of ourselves to others. We can be ridiculed for laughing so much; we can fear a person may leave us if we show we are dependent on them. People can find emotions difficult to deal with and so avoid talking about them or expressing how they are feeling. One indication of this is how schools, rather than helping young people face up to these difficulties, focus on subject learning in ways that exclude the emotions to a great extent. There can be a strong emphasis on testing the individual pupil with little time put aside for pupils to be able to talk together, let alone time for pupils to learn how to handle the complex emotions they experience as they go through schooling and adolescence. Yet many people will say that social and emotional development is essential for leading a happy life, and that pupils need help, advice and time to discuss and develop in these areas. There is now a plethora of books for adults on why and how they should enhance their emotional connectedness. Similarly, there are calls for schools to attend to pupils' emotional, social, moral and physical development, which will enable them to contribute to society. However, to attend to these needs pupils need to be engaged in the educational process, not be remote or disconnected emotionally from it.

I have used the word 'engaged' in the title with two meanings in mind. The first is that pupils should be involved in their learning; be active and absorbed and not just passive recipients of a set curriculum. Additionally, they should feel engaged in the processes of education and have some input into creating their own agendas for learning. In practice, this would mean that teachers and pupils have a degree of flexibility to create a common vision for learning. Second, to engage, in its emotional sense, means that people have an emotional commitment to each other, will support and nourish each other while facing up to difficulties in their relationships. I interpret emotional engagement in this book to involve people in groups and communities. This second meaning of to 'engage' is my main focus and in this book I argue that pupils' emotional development should be central to education, while alerting educators to some difficulties in its inception. To facilitate pupils' emotional development, though, means finding ways of engaging their emotions.

Outline of the book

Part 1. The Need for Emotional Literacy: Background Issues

Part 1 of the book develops the background issues to emotional literacy in the classroom. The first chapter, *Educating the whole person*, argues for an education that will engage pupils so that they are more prepared to become active thinkers and take their place in society while being open to considering how it might change. However, to help pupils enter the fast-changing technological world, they would be helped if they were emotionally equipped to handle uncertainty and change. Hence schools could help pupils develop an emotional maturity. In this chapter, I argue that developing pupils' social and emotional abilities is an essential element in enabling pupils to become active thinkers and democratic citizens. The theme of equity and social justice is developed in Chapter 2, *Equity and social justice: getting to know each other*. Ideas on how to achieve equity now include a consideration of how people differ from each other, and that those differences generate diverse wants and visualizations of need. To take account of people's diversity of views, it is argued that they have to meet to discuss their differing perceptions of social and political situations. Yet genuine understanding of each other would be important and to do this people should be able to accept themselves, while also being able to understand and empathize with people of differing sexualities, cultures and religions. Hence, I argue in this chapter that the development of pupils' social and emotional abilities, their emotional literacy, is required for them to make a contribution to society and to be engaged in a democracy that involves genuine discussion. This is called a deliberative democracy.

The meanings of the key terms 'emotional literacy' and 'emotional intelligence' are explained in Chapter 3, *'Emotional literacy', 'emotional intelligence' and dialogue*, while Chapter 4, *Emotional literacy and education*, is concerned with how schools can approach emotional literacy and draws attention to some of the key issues. Two key themes emerge in these chapters. First, that pupils can improve their emotional literacy through pupil–pupil dialogue. Second, that the development of both emotional literacy and equity should be integrated. The interconnection between the two is a theme of the book that is not evident in either the literature on emotional literacy or that on equity.

It is common for educators to consider a pupil's emotional literacy as if it were purely the property of the individual. Yet emotions and feelings occur because of interactions with others. Pupils can both learn and share their subjective feelings through their social interactions. It is through these communications that equity issues can surface and a more inclusive atmosphere is generated. Chapter 5, *Groups and power*, discusses evidence that people being brought together and working under certain conditions can reduce stereotypes. One key point is that supposed differences between people are in part generated through the psychological process of projection. The 'differences' between groups of people are emphasized over similarities to 'justify' power differences and discrimination. For people to maintain these differences, and justify their ways of acting, psychological boundaries have to be maintained. Since these boundaries are based to some extent on denial of similarities and a belief in clear, certain differences, the boundaries are fragile and require emotional work to maintain them. One way to change the boundaries is to help people accept that categories like masculine, feminine, Asian and European contain ambiguities, uncertainties and incorporate many similarities. In essence, psychological, social and cultural aspects of communities are all interwoven and overlapping. The chapter ends by drawing out some principles for educational practice such that pupils can be made conscious of power in the contested spaces of classroom dialogue. Figure (i) summarizes the structure of these chapters.

Part 2. Emotional Literacy and Equity in the Classroom: Communication Between the Sexes

The second part of the book is concerned with emotional literacy in practice and how the individual and group aspects of development could be combined. Chapter 6, *Approaching emotional literacy and equity in the classroom*, provides details of my research into how to enable pupils to develop their emotional literacy in science lessons through dialogue, while also addressing equity issues with a focus on gender. The strategies developed are widely applicable to most curriculum areas. Chapter 7, *Emotional literacy and equity: some possible outcomes*, explains what was achieved in the classroom. While there are many complexities, and pupils did not find it easy to work collaboratively, they changed and realized the importance of getting to know each other. The results indicate that pupils can learn to support each other in their learning, get on better together and to cultivate their social and emotional skills. One issue that emerges is the importance of *not* studying boys or girls as if they were in isolation from each other, but of exploring their views and feelings in an integrated way. Figure (ii) summarizes this section of the book.

Chapter 8, *A new saying for old*, is a short interlude and is a chapter that stands on its own but focuses on developing an alternative pedagogic saying to Confucius. Confucius' well-known saying that applies to cognitive learning is:

I hear and I forget,
I see and I remember,
I do and I understand.

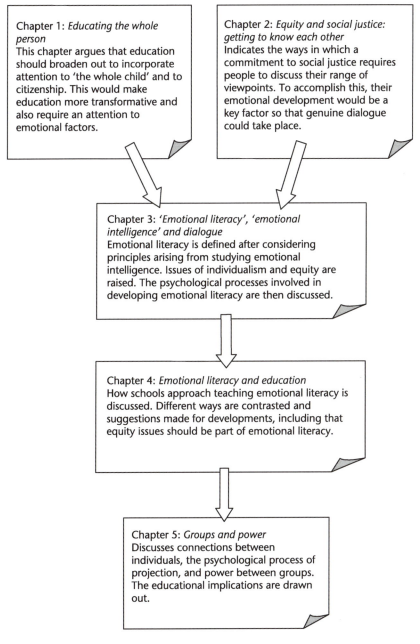

Chapter 1: *Educating the whole person*
This chapter argues that education should broaden out to incorporate attention to 'the whole child' and to citizenship. This would make education more transformative and also require an attention to emotional factors.

Chapter 2: *Equity and social justice: getting to know each other*
Indicates the ways in which a commitment to social justice requires people to discuss their range of viewpoints. To accomplish this, their emotional development would be a key factor so that genuine dialogue could take place.

Chapter 3: *'Emotional literacy', 'emotional intelligence' and dialogue*
Emotional literacy is defined after considering principles arising from studying emotional intelligence. Issues of individualism and equity are raised. The psychological processes involved in developing emotional literacy are then discussed.

Chapter 4: *Emotional literacy and education*
How schools approach teaching emotional literacy is discussed. Different ways are contrasted and suggestions made for developments, including that equity issues should be part of emotional literacy.

Chapter 5: *Groups and power*
Discusses connections between individuals, the psychological process of projection, and power between groups. The educational implications are drawn out.

Figure (i) Structure of Part 1.

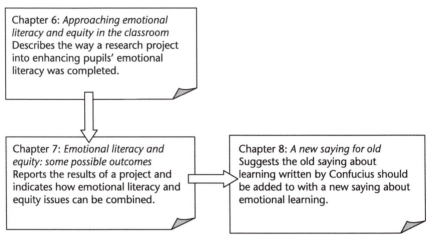

Figure (ii) Summary of Part 2.

Imagine that Confucius had written a saying that was on emotional development, what might it look like? This chapter asks what would be in a new saying that placed emotional learning at its heart.

Part 3. Moving Forward

This part of the book is concerned with how education systems may progress. One theme that has grown through the book is how integration, or inclusion, can be a vital factor in creating greater social justice, emotional literacy and equity. Against this background Chapter 9, *Single-sex and co-educational schools*, argues a case for co-educational schools. This reflects my original interest in enabling boys and girls to relate well together, with dialogue as one of the techniques.

However, even if schools do become committed to introducing schemes to develop pupils' emotional literacy, there are pressures from society that may thwart its intended effectiveness. Chapter 10, *Broadening the emotional context*, considers the increasing level of anxiety in societies, the promotion of the individual and the changing nature of work against the background of the theory that societies may be moving towards an increasing emotional control of its citizens.

Schools have a difficult task of deciding on priorities, which almost always involve balancing different demands. One example is the balance in the time spent on cognitive learning as opposed to developing emotional literacy, while acknowledging that the two can be integrated. The final chapter, 11, *Ways forward*, overviews the book, outlines the key features to be achieved in schools, with suggestions for teachers on how these might be achieved. Figure (iii) summarizes this section of the book.

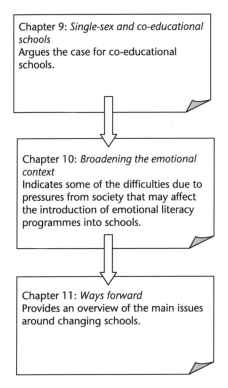

Figure (iii) Summary of Part 3.

In writing this book I have been in awe of the ideas and creativity of so many writers and colleagues. I know I have not done justice to them, and at times I have wanted to write, 'and now go and read so and so's article'. I finish this Introduction with an acknowledgement of my debt to them.

PART 1
The Need for Emotional Literacy: Background Issues

1 Educating the whole person

In this chapter, I consider two broad aims for education. The first is that schools should produce pupils who will be able to contribute to the economic stability of the country. The second is that education should enable pupils to be able to question society and to play a part in changing it. I will consider both aims and discuss how schools could change to achieve the second aim.

Schooling for industry

There are many problems facing society and education is being called on to help solve them. Societies are becoming more multi-faith and diverse, which can cause conflict. There is a continuing world migration where refugees are often not welcomed, causing tensions in society. Unemployment is an issue in many societies, and can contribute to an unacceptably high proportion of pupils living in families who are below the poverty line. The gap between the rich and the poor is often wide. There is an increasing influence of corporate capitalism that transcends national boundaries. The growth of globalization and the intensification of market competition are resulting in a fast-changing world where the nature of employment is altering. Pupils are staying on at school to acquire higher qualifications to get jobs: 'The United Nations predicts that in the next thirty years more people will be looking for qualifications in education than since the beginning of civilisation' (National Advisory Committee on Creative and Cultural Education 2001: 20). There are also concerns about pupils leaving school without the skills that are required by a changing industry (Sheerman 2004; Cabinet Office 2005; ContractorUK 2005; Dhingra 2005).

Some governments have responded to these competitive pressures by making the main aim of education to serve industry through producing pupils who can adapt when new skills are required and so create successful businesses. These changes have placed a greater emphasis on education for wealth production (Bacon and Eltis 1976). The impact of this shift can be seen in the nature of the debates on education, which, in Britain and the USA, have become increasingly infused with the language of the neo-liberal Right, namely, 'choice', 'freedom', 'competition' and 'standards' (Brown 2000; Ball 2003). While there is variation between many countries, there has been a trend towards centralized education systems under government control. These changes have been accompanied by an emphasis on pupils' academic achievements rather than, for example, their emotional and social develop-ment. The emphasis on quantifying and measuring the outcomes of education through exams is consistent with the view of the individual pupil as a con-tainer of knowledge that can be used to serve market forces. This view of the pupil has been accompanied by a focus on competitiveness and the culture of self-interest. Personal motives have been given a systematic preference over values that apply broadly and so produced a new individualistic moral environment (Ball 2003). One purpose of education is for pupils to be prepared 'for the differing tasks they would perform in the modern capitalist economy' (Benn and Chitty 1997: 278). In an interview with a UK government represen-tative, it was made clear that the state was developing modes of control in education which permit closer scrutiny and direction of the social order. The representative stated that: 'if we have a highly educated and idle population we may possibly anticipate more serious social conflict. People must be edu-cated once more to know their place' (Ranson 1984: 241).

This traditional approach to education can be characterized as the trans-mission model, where certain people select the important knowledge that has to be 'transmitted' or 'delivered' to the pupil, who is an empty vessel for filling. The 'important knowledge' is selected to ensure the continued economic prosperity of the country in an increasingly competitive world. To ensure that there is little deviance from the delivery of the curriculum, a series of centrally controlled tests (SATs) and exams are put in place, which in turn help to control what teachers can cover. The centralization of the core curriculum is concerned with controlling what is taught and making teachers accountable – that is, controlling teachers. 'Whereas the professional approach was con-cerned with individual differences and the learning process, the bureaucratic approach was associated with the norms of bench-marks, norm-related criteria and judgements based on the expectations of how a statistically-normal child should perform' (Chitty 1996: 23). One key aspect of this bureaucratic approach is that people who are not teachers largely decide schooling, and this has important implications. Here is an example to illustrate my argument.

> Imagine a government that decided to tell architects what buildings they were to design and how to design them. Why would a government do this and what would be the result? Clearly, to dictate to architects would indicate that the government did not like the buildings being

completed, and that they wanted to control architecture to make it respond to the government's needs. This process would inevitably lead to a reduction in professionalism and make creativity less likely (precisely because the governmental control was intended to remove changes in direction that were not compatible with their desires). Since architects are professional people who have been trained and learnt on the job for many years, it makes no sense for the government to tell them what to do. Such a decision would reflect a deep-seated desire to ensure that architects' power was taken away. There would be a danger that buildings would be sub-standard and architecture would suffer as a result. Consultations would likely be a sham because the professionals have a greater knowledge and understanding. Substitute 'teachers' for 'architects' and you have a mirror of the position in education.

As a result of centralization, teachers can become de-professionalized. An illustration from the UK is of the extent to which primary teachers have lost confidence in their basic pedagogic abilities. Primary teachers were asked to vote on whether or not to abandon the government-set tests that restrict the curriculum. The teachers voted to keep the exams because they did not know what their lessons would look like without the tests. 'There was a widely stated dislike of the tests, but a nervousness of what might happen on a day-to-day basis' if they were stopped (Mansell 2004). This demonstrates the extent to which teachers had lost confidence and undervalued themselves. Overall, the educational approach taken tends to combine a centralized curriculum with the controlling of teachers. In essence, schools present a fixed body of knowledge to be learnt to prepare students for society as it is now.

Education for a changing society

The above traditional approach has been criticized for a long time and a social-critical approach advocated which accepts that society is changing. Postman and Weingartner (1971) and Freire (1972a, 1972b) attacked the education system and its traditional approaches, which Freire calls the 'Banking concept of education', as it involves pupils filing and storing deposits of knowledge. Their wish, along with that of Illich (1973), was to try to change education so that it could respond to the changing nature of society and help to liberate rather than enslave pupils. Postman and Weingartner indicate that the extent to which science is used in society means that change is inevitable and that this renders traditional approaches to education irrelevant. The ways that these writers suggest changing education differ, but all of them realize that the transmission model has to be replaced if pupils are to become capable of dealing effectively with uncertainty and change in their personal and public lives. Postman and Weingartner stress that the message received by pupils is inseparable from the way that it is taught. They argue for an inquiry approach to education where pupils are taught to question and:

> The new education has as its purpose the development of a new kind of person, one who – as a result of internalising a different series of concepts – is an actively inquiring, flexible, creative, innovative, tolerant, liberal personality who can face uncertainty and ambiguity without disorientation, who can formulate viable new meanings to meet changes in the environment which threaten individual and mutual survival.
>
> (Postman and Weingartner 1971: 204)

Freire argues that education should be concerned with *conscientization*, where one learns to perceive the social, political and economic contradictions and to take action against the oppressive elements of reality. Education is seen as a process of problem-solving where people develop their power 'to perceive critically *the way they exist in the world with which* and *in which* they find themselves; they come to see the world not as a static reality, but as reality in process, in transformation' (Freire 1972b: 56, my emphasis). Reflection and dialogue are essential components of this educational process. Pupils are in the search for self-affirmation. This is not the type of affirmation that comes externally from the praise of teachers for passing exams. Both Freire and Illich are concerned with the ways that society could change. Illich (1973: 11) argues for a 'convivial society', where conviviality means the 'autonomous and creative intercourse among persons, and the intercourse of persons with their environment; . . . [and] to have individual freedom realised in personal interdependence and, as such, an intrinsic ethical value'.

There are two aspects of change within these ideas. The first is that society is changing and pupils should be able to accept change. The second is that pupils should be prepared for entering society in ways that enable them to critically reflect on it, and to have some control over the direction the changes should take. At heart, a flexible approach to education is required that is responsive to pupils and their needs. This in turn requires professionally confident teachers who are trained to make decisions about their pupils' needs and requirements and adapt the classroom as necessary. Watkins *et al.* (2000) call for teachers to reject the factory approach to education and to teach with integrity and uncertainty to equip pupils to contend with the changing nature of society. Similarly, Hart *et al.* (2004), working from the assumption that ability is not fixed, evolved teaching methods that are based on responding to pupils. The focus on the needs of pupils is part of a call to educate the many wider aspects of the learner (Best 1996; Erricker *et al.* 1997; Kessler 2000; Lamb 2001).

Educating the whole person

One approach to educating pupils for a changing and unknowable world is to try to cover a wide range of aspects of the human condition. Pring (1994), for example, suggests that educating the whole person would include: knowledge and understanding; intellectual virtues; imagination; intellectual skills; self-reflection; moral virtues and habits; social and political involvement; integrity and authenticity. The difficulty with the approach of trying to encompass all aspects of the human condition is that it can lead to schools trying to cover everything, often based on a fractured curriculum that accepts division between, for example, the cognitive and the affective. Also, as McLaughlin (1996) argues, there are many aspects of life that are not the realm of education. Each person must be allowed to define for themselves many aspects of their lives, including their politics, religion and types of relationships (sexual and non-sexual). One should not impose one's 'truths' upon pupils; rather, education can help pupils by presenting a non-evaluative curriculum and set of experiences.

McLaughlin (1996) and Lamb (2001) argue that a different meaning should be attached to the term 'whole child'. This is one where the aim of education is to help children become 'whole' in the sense of being integrated and coherent as a person. This includes developing to become integrated and happy with oneself, to be able to assume responsibility for oneself and one's actions, while recognizing the preferences and independence of others. Pupils would also be encouraged to attain autonomy and be reflective about their choices. Another way of putting this is to help them become 'rooted'. This can be contrasted with pupils who are at 'war with themselves', unable to control their desires, needs and actions. Erricker *et al.* (1997) were surprised at the numbers of children in Britain who had fragmented lives due to loss and conflict. Lamb argues that 'continuity' and 'adequacy' should be added to McLaughlin's 'integration' and 'coherence'. She argues that pupils' history must not be ignored, and that the development of the whole child in schools should be continuous.

> First it means that the educator has to recognise that the child has a personal history that she brings to the learning situation ... Secondly, the education of the whole child obliges the educator both to recognise and, to some appropriate degree, address cases of discontinuity and distinctiveness in children.
>
> (Lamb 2001: 212)

Adequacy means 'treating the child as intrinsically worthwhile and aiming to foster the kind of educational development that issues in genuine creativity.

"Wholeness" here again means "unconditionally adequate" and "intrinsically worthwhile" and gives an insight into the psychological preconditions of productive learning' (Lamb 2001: 214). However, the development of emotional maturity has been left out of Lamb's analysis. For pupils to become increasingly rooted, they should be enabled to handle their emotions and relationships.

Yorks and Kasl (2002) argue for the importance of affective aspects of life and the integration of cognition and affect, mainly through seeing learning in a social and emotional context. They use the term '*learning-within-relationship*, a process in which persons strive to become engaged with both their own whole-person knowing and the whole-person knowing of their fellow learners' (p. 185). Indeed, I would argue that pupils develop a secure sense of themselves through their experiences with others. All experiences have cognitive and emotional aspects. Further, what we call experiences are what we make/construct of the events that occur to us. That is, experiences are not what happen to us, they are the meanings we ascribe to what happens to us. Each person is a meaning maker and our 'truths may be related to the personal narratives constructed out of personal experience' (Erricker *et al.* 1997: 9). This means that for teachers the conditions under which pupils engage with each other are of the essence, while accepting that the family is the greatest influence. People who have very varied views and lived experiences can learn together through dialogue and because of the variations their emotional receptivity can be increased. Through developing empathy and trust, commonality can be engendered. This is not easy and Yorks and Kasl (2002) point out that the more diverse people are, the more likely they will challenge each other's habits of being, thus holding out the possibility of growth and transformation. At the same time, the greater the range of diversity present, the more the emotional strain of trying to comprehend them. Having to learn together can help 'learners bridge differences by affording glimpses into the other's world of felt experience, thus creating pathways for empathic connection' (p. 187). Pupils also have to be able to hold up for inspection their own views and feelings.

The integration of the cognitive and emotional sides of education are echoed in Lewis's (2000) view of the spiritual. He argues that children bring with them their own spiritual aspect and that this should be considered and drawn out together with the cognitive and emotional aspects. There are many differing views on what constitutes an education of spirituality, and it is beyond the scope of this book to go into detail here. In brief, commentators draw attention to the importance of the spiritual in considerations of the whole person, stressing that while spirituality conjures up religion and religious attitudes, they wish to define it in a broader sense and to include considerations of the ethical, personal and self-feelings, such as wonder and awe (Best 1996; Erricker *et al.* 1997; Bigger and Brown 1999; O'Sullivan 1999). The conceptualization of spirituality can take different forms:

1   Spirituality can be seen as about self-discovery and discovery of others (Best 1996).
2   Spiritual can refer to anything that might be regarded as a source of inspiration, wonder and joy to a person's life and is connected to ideals, goals, sense of purpose and identity (O'Sullivan 1999).
3   Spiritualization is the process whereby teachers and pupils employ and develop unique combinations of positive qualities from within all domains of being human (Prentice 1996).
4   Rodger (1996) argues for spirituality as *awareness* in contrast to seeing spirituality as something that should be imposed as a set of beliefs or a response and argues that we still do not understand what spirituality is!

Spirituality can be seen broadly as how one responds reflectively in thought, physically and in feelings to events and experiences, and is part of a curriculum that recognizes the range of aspects pupils bring to school. Through considering an integrative model of 'the whole child', he or she can be helped to work out a coherent narrative of their beliefs and lives. As Erricker *et al.* (1997) found, children developed quite complex explanations of their experiences. What is required is an education that enables reflections, subjective review and consideration of possible transformations in society (Askew and Carnell 1998; O'Sullivan 1999). Yet, to educate the whole child in the sense described above requires a development in education processes that is far from the preoccupation with league tables, measurement of cognitive knowledge, a market mentality and predefined outcomes that goes with a technocratic view of teaching. And, of course, this requires a body of teachers whose professional judgement is trusted.

Each choice of teaching method is value-laden and fits particular views of what education should be about. If the whole person is to be educated, then all aspects of a person will be helped to develop in an integrated way. Lee (2003) argues that this would include four aspects: touching the affective, working with experiences, strengthening the cognitive and enhancing the social. These can all be approached through collaborative learning. Lee argues that education should include ' "the practice of freedom", the means by which men and women deal critically and creatively with reality and discover how to participate in the transformation of the world' (p. 88). As Freire (1997: 3) puts it: 'To be is to engage in relationships with others and with the world. Human communication involves the exchange of meaning, even if not fully understood. Meaning making is an activity that involves feelings as well as knowledge'. Biesta and Miedema (2002: 180) use traffic lights as an example: one can experiment and understand the electronics involved, but the meaning of traffic lights does not exist in scientific understanding but in cultural practices – that is, 'in between' human beings. The extent to which this is true means that pupils must participate in cultural practices to understand them; a child cannot just 'receive' them. Biesta and Miedema go on to argue that participation should be accepted as a process in which the whole person is involved. The process should be open enough to encourage reflection on feelings, beliefs and values. All of the above require a pedagogy and curriculum that values pupils' identity and promotes unknown outcomes as much as known ones. It would be a transformative and creative education (Askew and Carnell 1998; O'Sullivan 1999; National Advisory Committee on Creative and Cultural Education 2001). Transformative education 'involves change in the way we perceive ourselves and our experiences' (Askew and Carnell 1998: 1) and emphasizes the integration of the emotional, cognitive, spiritual and social domains. Pupils can then be prepared to cope emotionally with change and to have some input into the direction of those changes.

At present, there is a tension between educating for a competitive industrial complex and for the whole person. One approach uses a centralized and exam-orientated system, the other advocates a fluid curriculum with some outcomes unknown. The tension, which is also about seeing pupils as recipients of selected knowledge and skills, or as being actively engaged in the educational process, emerges in attending to civic purposes in education, which is one component of educating the whole person (Laitsch *et al.* 2005).

Citizenship and civics

The introduction of 'citizenship' or 'civics' is a consequence partly of pressure from educators and partly of governmental concerns about the lack of people voting in elections and of being uninterested in local issues. This is a worldwide phenomenon (International Idea 1999). Writing about the USA, Jenny Smith (2003: 1) states: '[Youth] are at risk of entering adulthood lacking the commitment necessary to sustain relationships and the responsibility to participate in a democratic society. When asked about their goal in life, many students say it is simply to make money'. There are tensions between seeing citizens as passive or active participants in democracy, between individual and collective definitions, and the balance between rights and duties (Pearce and Hallgarten 2000). The more that responsibilities are stressed, the more it reinforces the idea that citizens are passive in that they have to respond to those responsibilities, rather than argue for their rights. There is also a tension between inducting pupils into an acceptance of the systems of government that exist as compared with ensuring they engage in critical debate for change. Furthermore, citizenship in a democratic society implicitly, or explicitly, enshrines the idea that all citizens are equal, and must be treated equally, that everyone's vote matters the same amount. Hence ideas on equality could be central to citizenship. Many inequalities have a structural component and are built into the fabric of society, such as those due to class and 'race' (Hall 2000). There are clear divisions in society and Gamarnikow and Green (2000) argue that 'social capital' can be used in citizenship to help solve some of society's problems. 'Social capital' refers to the connections that people have that can be present in networks and are based on trust and cooperation, although there are variations on this definition (Print and Coleman 2003). Social capital can be positive or negative. For example, a church group can have high social capital in that they support, trust and help each other. However, they can do so to the exclusion of others in society and define others as outgroups. In extreme circumstances, this can result in hatred and violence towards other groups.

Alderson (2000) argues that there are two ways of theorizing citizenship. The first is to see children as not yet competent citizens who need to be taught a set of ideas that are selected by adults. This splits theory from practice. The second accepts that children are already engaged in practical citizenship and consequently believes that schools should engage in practical critical democracy, for example in Schools Councils. 'It is illogical to expect students to understand lessons about rights and democracy yet expect them not to notice denials of their own rights, or discrepancies between what school staff practise and preach' (p. 132). Hence, for pupils to be prepared for citizenship, they have to be actively involved in decision making, not passively learn that, for example, it is important to vote (Deuchar 2003). To enable pupils to engage in democracy in schools requires a great degree of teacher autonomy and openness. Additionally, it would appear that one element of citizenship is to be able to discuss the ways in which, for example, surveillance in schools and society are a danger to democracy. There are many debates over the use of information technology and surveillance in society. Peissi (2003) argues that security and surveillance have been mixed up and that the reduction of people's privacy through governmental action is already leading to a change in democracy. Surveillance is being introduced that affects society at individual and societal levels (Salusbury 2003; Liberty 2004). While some people support the introduction of surveillance (Dorman and Hudson 2003), others argue that its impact can be very negative and requires greater regulation (Graham and Wood 2003). Marx (2002: 25) warns that 'Powerful forces work against any easy assumption that a decent society is self-perpetuating or that once set in motion, progress must continue'. Warschauer (2000) argues that information technologies can help free pupils in education, but that it will take vision and struggle; Kelly (2003) believes that young people are being targeted so that surveillance is institutionalizing the mistrust of youth. Hassan (2001), in his article on university students, goes further and argues that it:

> could debilitate the function of critical thinking in student generations to come. Society's loss of a critical faculty may turn out to be something akin to dementia in the individual: the worse it gets, the

less it matters to the victim. He or she becomes gradually oblivious to the personal catastrophe that has befallen them . . . When we reach a certain point in this process we will . . . become almost unaware of it, and our once healthy, pluralistic society and civic-democratic culture may have ceased to function as it should.

(Hassan 2001: 100)

I believe that the same principles apply to school pupils.

Marx (2002: 25) argues that 'Liberty and individualism are fragile and historically the exception rather than the rule. There is no guarantee that hard won rights will stay won or be extended, in the face of continual social and technical challenges. But vigilance, knowledge and wisdom are likely to help'. Teachers and policy makers can ask if their education system is engaged in protecting and preparing its pupils in these three areas, or if it is denying the need for vigilance while ensuring that certain controversial issues are not on the curriculum, limiting knowledge to 'acceptable knowledge' and replacing wisdom with information learning. It seems to me that pupils should be given the opportunity to enter fully into these debates so that they can decide the extent to which such views are valid. This also means a degree of flexibility and autonomy for professionally confident teachers, which, under centralized government control, are unlikely to be exercised.

Emotional development

There are calls for pupils to be able to think and reflect on themselves and society, engage with pupils from diverse backgrounds, consider inequalities, problem-solve, be creative with others and be tolerant and face ambiguity. Yet clearly for pupils and adults to engage in these aspects of life requires an attention to their ability to be self-aware, self-confident, show empathy for others and to be able to cooperate in dialogue with others. This requires that attention be paid to the emotional development of pupils to enable them to enter into communications effectively so that they feel less threatened by difference and new ideas.

Yet what is written about developing the whole person, or citizenship, contains little or no discussion of the need for pupils to develop their emotional literacy.

At present, many countries have a static curriculum based on selected knowledge and skills that are seen as important in the present cultural situation and which only require an emotional maturity that equips pupils to take their place in society as it is now. This is clearly an important aim for schools. However, additionally, emotional maturity is needed that enables pupils to cope and contribute to life that will contain uncertain and unknown challenges. It includes giving pupils a strong enough sense of themselves so that they can face whatever life casts at them. It would be part of a transformative curriculum: education in knowledge, questioning, critical and creative thinking, with emotional development that enables pupils to contribute positively to transforming society (O'Sullivan 1999).

Summary

There are demands on teachers to prepare pupils to take their place in a competitive world market. It appears that a consequence of this is an instrumentalist view of education, which values a traditional emphasis on exams and testing. It is possible to cast serious doubt on the extent to which reforms that encourage testing and grading are in the interests of, or address the needs of, children at all (Bullough and Krudel 2003). In contrast to this approach, people are arguing for an education system that addresses the changing nature of society and prepares pupils to take their place in a moving world where there are many uncertainties. To do this with integrity means engaging the whole pupil as active learner, encouraging them to be a critical thinker and enabling them to become a participative citizen, as well as passing exams. It is, however, noticeable that most of the discussion on developing the whole child, while acknowledging the importance of the affective, under-emphasizes developing pupils' emotional growth and maturity. The affective is discussed only in general terms, rather than being placed centrally within the curriculum. To engage meaningfully in dialogue, and to be a critical thinker, requires being able to reflect, have a degree of self-esteem and being able to engage emotionally with others without being threatened. This crucial area I will return to in Chapter 3. Finally, teachers are needed who are confident in their abilities to transform the classroom in response to both the curriculum and their pupils' needs.

2 Equity and social justice: getting to know each other

In this chapter, I will consider some of the debates about social justice and explain some of the terminology used. It will be argued that a concern for social justice leads to a form of democracy that requires people to meet, discuss and to engage in dialogue. Finally, I will argue that progress towards social justice and deliberative democracy requires an emotional maturity.

Conceptions of social justice

Distributive justice

Rawls' (1971) theory of 'justice as fairness' has been influential in recent debates on social justice. He is concerned about the social, economic and political arrangements we should choose to achieve a fair distribution and he suggests two principles of justice. The first is that each person is to have equal rights and liberty to the extent that it is compatible with the freedoms of others. The second is that there should be distribution of economic and social goods so that the least advantaged should benefit the most: 'All social primary goods – liberty and opportunity, income and wealth, and the bases of self-respect – are to be distributed equally unless an unequal distribution of any or all of these goods is to the advantage of the least favoured' (Rawls 1971: 303).

But who will decide if this is the case? Rawls' (1971) answer is a person who is 'situated behind a veil of ignorance' (p. 136), in that they do not know their social class, wealth, abilities or intelligence. They would then have to decide on the ways that social primary goods would be distributed. Rawls' point is that if a person does not know whether they may benefit from a particular socio-political organization, the outcome of a distribution is likely to be fair. Further, that different people are likely to agree, since 'everyone is equally rational and similarly situated, each is convinced by the same arguments' (p. 139). Hence, the individual is at the heart of Rawls' approach and there is a search for universal truths, although, according to Kukathas and

---

Box 2.1   The Matthews form of distributive justice!

When I was a child, my brother and I would fight over who had the biggest piece of cake, and would ask to cut it. My mother (and so I call this the Matthews version of distributive justice, although this is unfair to all the other parents who did the same) would let us, but under the condition that whosoever cut the cake took the last piece. I feel that this is a stronger form of distributive justice, as there is no 'veil of ignorance' – which I do not believe is possible – but a recognition of the social situation and that if we cut it unfairly we would get the smallest bit.

Pettit (1990), his later writings incorporate a more social view. Rawls' approach is called *distributive justice*, as at its core are ways of distributing social opportunities and material resources.

Rawls' approach has been criticized on a range of grounds, although most accept that distributive justice is necessary (Sandel 1982; Walzer 1983; Young 1990; Fraser 1997). One disagreement is with the basic premise that there can be a dispassionate person. Other people argue that each person, by their very identity, incorporates a set of socio-political viewpoints (Sandel 1982; Walzer 1983). Additionally, Rawls sees free individuals agreeing to form a community through agreement on the principles of 'justice as fairness'. This is a key point to which I will now turn.

Politics of difference or recognitive justice

I was born an English male in a city. How might my views be different if I had been born a female in a Thai village? Most people would agree that my identity, how I saw myself and related to others, would be very different. The community into which we are born and raised has a great impact on our identity and political views: we are *not* individuals who then come together to form a community as Rawls postulates. Individuals, while they are highly flexible and open to change, bring their community with them when they meet other people. Consequently, it is not possible to have a dispassionate person who can review from behind a veil of ignorance, so much broader approaches to social justice are needed. As people bring their communities with them, they will view issues through the veil of a set of cultural assumptions and modes of thinking. These give rise to a set of categorizations of other people. These categories – often including ideas on in-groups and out-groups – can be accepted as positive differences, but are often the source of oppression and dislike. Young (1990), in *Justice and the Politics of Difference*, argues that the difference between social and ethnic groups has to be central to social justice; hence the term the *politics of difference* within her title. She argues that groups in society suffer at the hands of others through *oppression* and *domination* and identifies five different forms of injustice. These are: exploitation (economic and social), marginalization (preventing people from being fully involved in social life), powerlessness (including the lack of being listened to), cultural imperialism (a dominant culture being imposed on you, and your experiences and interpretations being ignored), and violence. The experiences of different forms of oppression can give rise to different concepts of justice. For example, people experiencing racism have felt-oppressions and therefore have needs that only they can define. For this reason, while distribution may be important, an essential component of equity is that people's voices can be heard and taken account of.

Young (2000) argues that differences have to be acknowledged and attended to, not ignored. For example, gay people do not wish to be assimilated in a way that denies their difference, but to have their difference recognized and accepted. This is, of course, central to their self-identity and self-esteem. Young wants to affirm difference but this means having to avoid the usual situation where minority or oppressed groups are defined as 'different' as part of a way of oppressing them. Also, difference can be known but not acknowledged, for example the use of 'he' to mean both men and women, hence denying difference. As Phillips (1993: 46) says; 'Categories presumed to deal with both men and women, without even noting if it was more one than the other, necessarily wrote the experience of one sex as if it automatically embraced the other'. Difference can also operate in the reverse way by excluding people who could be included. For example, the word 'feminist' excludes men, yet can be used when some men and women have comparable views.[1] For example, 'Feminist approaches to pedagogy' often suggest methods that are very similar, if not the same, as those written about and used by men.

Young argues that all groups should be able to participate and have a voice in solving society's problems, a key element being that they are listened to. Other people use differing terms to mean similar things; for example, Yeatman (1994) argues for a *politics of representation* to enable people to express their needs in freedom. Consequently, people have to be able to empathize with each other; Taylor (1994: 25) uses the term a *politics of recognition* where people can recognize and understand how others feel. People have to come together in collective communication in a spirit of cooperation and feelings of mutual tolerance to have an adequate representation of identities. The way that people can feel their identities are accepted is to feel comfortable with both the differentiation that occurs because of the varied cultural practices, but also the communality they feel for each other across the boundaries (since people are more similar than they are different).

Fraser (1997), while taking issue with some aspects of Young's work, sees it as making an important step forward in political theory as she 'encompasses claims of both redistribution and recognition, both equality and difference, of both culture and political economy' (p. 190). Fraser points out that there are various forms of difference to be acknowledged in others. Some differences are to be welcomed, but some should be fought against, for example a group that supports and propagates racism. Fraser, like Taylor, uses the term 'recognition' to emphasize that people need to have their identities accepted. She argues that a framework is required that integrates both distribution and recognition so that the two are intertwined (Fraser and Honneth 2003). On the other hand, Honneth argues that recognition should be the single framework through which distribution is subsumed, since groups constantly change the meaning of their identity and so what they need materially also changes (Fraser and Honneth 2003).

Overall, the argument put forward by the different writers is that social justice must take account of difference, but how can that be done practically?

Deliberative democracy

A commitment to social justice, therefore, has to involve people in meeting with recognition and respect for difference and have equality of participation in social and political life. This would entail mutual listening, expressing feelings, learning, dealing with uncertainty, resolving problems and participating in decision making. In other words, democracy is a necessary condition for the political governance of people. Democracy rests on assumptions of equality. As Phillips (1999: 2) says, 'Democracy is never just a system for organising the election of governments. It also brings with it a strong conviction about the citizens being of equal intrinsic worth'. While there are many forms of democracy, the term 'deliberative' has been used to emphasize the importance of communication and public discussion in order to understand cultural differences: 'Deliberation is most likely to arrive at a fair distribution of resources, just rules of co-operation, the best and most just division of labour and definitions of social position, if it involves the open participation of all those affected by the decisions' (Young 1990: 93).

Many writers disagree over issues such as how far deliberative democracy should extend into local politics and the workplace (Gould 1996). However, there is wide agreement on:

The Inclusive constraint: that all members should be equally entitled to vote on how to resolve relevant collective issues.

The Judgemental constraint: before voting all members should deliberate on the basis of common concerns.

The Dialogical constraint: members should conduct this deliberation in an open and unforced dialogue with one another.

(Pettit 2003: 139)

One slightly tongue-in-cheek suggestion for ensuring deliberation is to have a public holiday to do it (Ackerman and Fishkin 2003). Many writers subscribe to the importance of dialogue and participation, but have different emphases. For example, Phillips (1995) argues that in many countries party politics is based on a discussion of ideas and that this needs to be replaced with a *politics of presence*, which would give voice to marginalized groups on matters that concerned them. Gewirtz (1998: 470) uses the term 'relational' to 'refer to the nature of the relationships which structure society', while Young (1996) sometimes uses the term 'communicative democracy' to emphasize the importance of the exchange of ideas.

However, whatever the method, through its emphasis on ensuring people are engaged in democracy, the core of social justice shifts from the primacy of having (resources) to the primacy of doing (self-development and determination). The ability to participate, listen to voices with empathy, and forge recognition with understanding is part of the education of the whole person. This requires an integration of emotional, cognitive and social areas to develop the skills of personal and group whole-person knowing-within-relationships.

Problems with the difference approach

The approach to equality through acceptance of difference means that differences have to be acknowledged. However, an emphasis on difference can lead to problems. Suppose you have three groups going to a pub, one is all female, one equally female and male, and one male only. Should the conversation in each group turn to discussion of relationships, how might the discussions be different? The single-sex groups are more likely to vent feelings against the other sex. In other words, they might emphasize difference over similarity. This can have a good cathartic effect and allow exploration of communality, but it does so by sealing the borders. Fraser and Honneth (2003: 92) call this the problem of reification, where separatism, group enclaves and intolerance can be encouraged. However, as both Young and Phillips point out, similarities between groups are often greater than their differences. For example, men and women are much more similar than they are different. Additionally,

> The group 'men' is differentiated by class, race, religion, age and so on; the group 'Muslim' differentiated by gender, nationality, and so on. If group identity constitutes individual identity and if individuals can identify with one another by means of group identity, how do we deal theoretically and practically with the fact of multiple group positioning?
>
> (Young 2000: 88)

Also, there are occasions when one does not want differences to enter into the equation. For example, a person going for a job or being sentenced for a traffic offence would be unlikely to feel that their religion, sexuality or ethnic background should be taken into consideration. On the other hand, in many situations people want their individuality recognized. Many children have an intuitive feel for these complexities. They state that one of the main attributes they want from teachers is 'fairness' – that is, being treated the same. At the same time, they want to be valued for who they are.

These complexities of difference can enter into group discussions. Cooke and Kothari (2001) highlight the psychological process of group dynamics that can undermine participation through producing 'risky decisions, with which no-one really agrees, or that rationalise harm to others' (p. 102). I know that I have been in meetings where the dynamics of the group have influenced the final decision to the extent that the evidence presented for discussion has been overridden. It would be easy to imagine that deliberative democracy means that groups can come together and deliberate in a peaceful way to reach joint decisions. This is very similar to the idea of a 'reasoned' debate that was objected to with Rawls. Karst (1990) reiterates that expression is power, and that freedom of expression is the freedom to contribute to the social definition of other people, and to contribute to our own self-definition as well. However, when people object to the way they are treated, they are often from a sub-ordinated group. When their cries are heard and understood, they will often challenge the dominant community of meaning. Hence, the identity of the dominant group, who have accepted those meanings, can be emotionally challenged and they can feel that their identity is threatened through 'fear of the unknown, fear of our own negative identities and fear of loss of position' (Karst 1990: 111).

Clearly, deliberative democracy requires the participation of different groups or communities. There is, however, a debate about the meaning of community as well as what it means to participate in the political process (Cooke and Kothari 2001; Amit 2002; Little 2002). Community can be seen through its institutions and social practices. The reality of community can also lie in its members' perceptions of what makes its culture different from that of others. 'People construct community symbolically, making it a resource and repository of meaning, and a referent of their identity'. It is also possible for a community of people to join together for some specific reason, for instance to oppose a shopping centre or to raise financial resources. One problem is that the term 'community' can mask the very varied power and cultural differences (like class, caste, age, ethnicity) within it and over-emphasize people as harmonious with common interests and needs. Cooke and Kothari (2001) raise the question as to how one can ensure that participatory approaches recognize the different, changing and multiple identities of individuals.

One approach to getting more participation is to encourage people to vote. There is an argument that modern technologies can help everyone to vote more easily, and so be more involved. This may have some truth in it, but it only involves them in expressing ideas (and this expression could be in isolation and without thought). 'In spite of the discourses of inter-activity which underlie most "electronic democracy" initiatives, most of them have in practice been executive-initiated, top-down and mostly based on giving more information' (Tsagarousianou *et al.* 1998: 174). More electronic voting does not necessarily equal more understanding of diversity; for example, voting about maternity rights without talking to women who have had children or men who have taken the primary role in looking after children.

However, for deliberative democracy to be authentic, people would also have to *mould* their ideas together. Interaction helps enable us to get behind the abstraction of the 'other' and to recognize them as people, but body language and nuance contains much of what is being communicated. Additionally, groups in deliberation are characterized by emotional dynamics that can destroy, contain or sustain communication. Hence it is essential that we understand these emotional processes as well as we can (Thompson and Mintzes 2002), especially since all significant positive changes in society have been due to small groups of people who have been prepared to think the unthinkable and take unpopular positions (e.g. those who argued for democracy in the first place). These people challenge the emotional security of the dominant group. I now turn to issues of emotions and discussions.

Emotions and the 'other'

It is easy to assume that people can simply meet and discuss together to reach informed conclusions. However, people may feel threatened, insecure, angry or over-confident, and so be unable psychologically to enter fully into discussion. As a result, they can misunderstand or mis-recognize other people. To engage in deliberative dialogue is not a simple process and it means that we have to be committed to learning and understanding 'the other'; the phrase Young uses is an 'ethics of unassimilated otherness'. I will now explain some of the background to the term the 'other'.

We gain in infancy a sense of self through separating out from our parents (Chodorow 1978; Kegan 1982). Young (1990: 143) says that fear and anxiety 'arises from the primal repression which the infant struggles to separate from the mother's body that nourishes and comforts'. That is, the infant struggles to accept himself or herself as having a separate identity from the parents. This means separating ourselves from those who care for us and so is ambivalent because it involves the child in disavowing parts of loved ones (Moore 2005). The child has to develop a sense of 'I' or 'self' and a sense of 'not-me' or 'other'. However, this does not stay at the personal level but is part of forming in-groups and out-groups, as Paechter (1998: 6) argues:

> The subject is defined in opposition to and through the exclusion of the Other; this means paradoxically, that without that which is denied, the Other, there can be no Subject. The Other is, as a result, simultaneously feared, loathed and desired, this is why the Subject/ Object relationship contains so much power.

Hence other groups can threaten one's identity, while also consolidating it. Similarly, theories of human development indicate that our internal picture of the 'other' is influenced by the interactions we undergo. It is more common for women to be referred to as the 'other' than for men, but the term applies equally to both sexes: women see men as the 'other' just as much as the other way round. The social, cultural and psychological are strongly entwined. Walkerdine *et al.* (2001) explore the psychosocial basis of gender and class and explore how the mechanisms of 'otherness' can become a repository of fantasies:

> At the conscious level anxieties may be named and talked about. But at the level of the unconscious, rather than being 'out of sight, out of mind', anxieties continue to wield their considerable power beyond the rationalising influence of language. Object relations theorists such as Klein and Bion suggest that recognising that this is an indwelling fear that makes sense of our constant striving but fundamental inability correctly to represent it.
>
> (Walkerdine *et al.* 2001: 90)

These processes occur in many ways but some mark a psychological boundary, as the out-group can become a repository for unconscious anxieties. These anxieties come from inside us, and so in a sense it is similarity that divides us, we see ourselves in the 'other' (Moore 2005). The association between groups and what attributes are accepted as 'us', and what is 'other', is socially constructed: once the link is made, however, these associations lock into the subject's identity and anxieties. 'They represent what lies just beyond the borders of the self, the subject reacts with fear, nervousness and aversion to members of these groups because they represent a threat to identity itself' (Young 1990: 145).

The fears and anxieties that are conscious and unconscious can have a strong negative impact on us when we communicate/interact with others. Strong emotions can emerge that hold us at ransom unless we learn to develop emotionally so that we can self-reflect, inspect our feelings and learn to move forward. Clearly, emotional maturity and development of psychodynamic process are central to being able to deliberate effectively (Thompson and Hoggett 2001). Thompson and Hoggett argue that emotions cannot be excluded from deliberation, and so it is important to understand the processes involved, which can otherwise be destructive. They explore the possibilities of a democracy of the emotions. Young, while drawing attention to psycho-dynamic factors, does not indicate that it would be central to address and develop these psychodynamic factors in order to enable people to engage in participation, for without emotional development it may not be possible to recognize other communities. Taylor (1994: 25) argues that recognition is linked to identity, where 'the latter term designates something like a person's understanding of who they are, of their fundamental defining characteristics as a human being'. Mis-recognition can cause people damage, especially when a demeaning picture of themselves is reflected back to them from other people. This is because people gain a sense of themselves in dialogical relationships with other people 'sometimes in struggle against the things our significant other want to see in us' (p. 33). So, one's identity does not appear individually, but is worked out through negotiation in dialogue with oneself and others. Our relationships with loved ones, and one's partner in particular, are import-ant as they are 'crucibles of inwardly generated identity' (p. 36). Young makes a similar point when she says that desire – meant broadly – involves the movement out from the self to the person or object.

Everybody has, to varying degrees, unconscious aversions, so why do only some people react very strongly to out-groups? One explanation is the strong influence of the way in which infants go through the stage of separation from the parents, and the extent to which the infant is positively helped to form a secure sense of 'self' and 'other'. The infant-to-child-to-adolescent can be enabled to come to terms with difference and be relatively unthreatened by the transgression over the border of 'self' and 'other'. Indeed, the transgression of the border can be a source of creativity, interest and emotional progress. Similarly, difference can be a resource of creativity, as it helps to enable one to think outside of one's cultural assumptions. However, it is not just a case of healthily presenting one's self-identity in political situations. A very influen-tial factor is the extent of the power difference between the group that the person identifies with, and other groups.

Young (1990: 260) finishes her book thus:

> Only psychological dispositions, cultural expressions, and political institutions able to loosen but not dissolve borders, make them per-meable but un-decidable, at the same time that they create guarantees of group self-definition and representation in the public, can hold the hope of a more peaceful and just future for the world.

Hence she ends by stressing the importance of psychological, cultural and political levels to move towards a just world. At the psychological level, she is saying people have to develop emotionally to change their borders so as to be able to accept contingency and vagueness. One implication of this for schools is that they could help pupils develop their emotional literacy so they can deal with ambiguity and recognize the 'other'.

Emotional literacy and social justice in schools

The importance of psychodynamic processes in enabling people to be able to discuss, recognize the 'other' and feel unthreatened by difference in order to engage in a politics of presence indicates that we should be enabling pupils to develop emotionally. Consider a school trying to help its pupils avoid getting a drugs or drink problem. A common way is for teachers to provide information about the dangers, often in a form that is intended to scare. This is an approach that has been found to be limited in its success. One reason is that there are unaddressed psychological factors at work. A person who drinks, and most of us do, is normally able to keep the amount in proportion. Those who do become alcoholics do so because they are trying to compensate for factors like stress, feeling isolated in life, an inability to form good relationships, or feeling that life is not worth living. In brief, underlying psychodynamic factors are involved. Similarly, information about other cultures, sexes or classes can help pupils understand across boundaries, but also attention should be paid to the underlying emotional difficulties that hinder open minds, for example fear of the 'other'. This chapter has drawn attention to in- and out-groups and the importance of the psychodynamic processes involved. These are the same processes required for pupils to become reflexive, tolerant, creative and able to face uncertainty in a changing world, as discussed in Chapter 1. Social justice and deliberative democracy are supported by a transformative education with teachers who are able to adapt and change lessons and the curriculum as necessary. This is difficult within a rigidly defined subject-based curriculum.

Social justice is something to be done-in-action and so requires an active participation, a theme that runs throughout Griffiths' (2003) book *Action for Social Justice in Education*. The pedagogy required to promote social justice coalesces with that raised in Chapter 1, namely, inclusion of open, critical thinking and a move to a participatory conception of citizenship with a transformative component as one of its aims. In so doing, three strands are brought together: education for deliberative democracy, social justice and a transformative education. One focus of such an education is to 'analyse social life through a lens of diversity and social justice and to prepare students to be transformative democratic agents' (Nagda *et al.* 2003: 167). Clearly, central to this educational endeavour are reflection and dialogue, along with an active engagement with the world-as-is.[2] This can be contrasted with the approach to citizenship where there is 'an almost total absence of concern for structured inequalities, especially economic ones; a mis-recognition of the political, social and educational hierarchies embedded in social relationships, networks and associations; and the invisibility of inequalities of power as an issue for social justice' (Lawton *et al.* 2000: 107). Clearly, such a pedagogy will help as a preparation for participation in a deliberative democracy, but there are unequal power relationships that lie beneath multiple voices and viewpoints. Pupils have to be helped to learn about each other across cultural, psychological and power boundaries. However, we as teachers may want social justice, but have to recognize that in some cases people are not actually concerned with justice. They are disturbed about *injustice to them* and how they feel they have been affected by it.[3] It can be through a sense of being individually unjustly treated that people will consider and act for justice as an overarching concept. Life is full of injustices, and provides a rich ground for schools to openly make these explicit, inspect power relations and so link individual injustices to a concern for justice as a whole. These include those due to culture, gender, class, sexuality and those arising between teachers and pupils. The latter is often forgotten. It will help the educational process if pupils' voices are made audible.

In general though, as Griffiths (2003) points out, pupils are helped by refusing to accept simple descriptions of identity, along with learning to accept difference/differentiation as normal. One necessary condition for pupils to be able to achieve this is for groups to be empowered through representation and voice. However, not all are present. For example, schools have become increasingly segregated by class (Gewirtz *et al.* 1995; Tomlinson 2001). Lynch and Lodge (2002) show how social class divisions occur through a combination of 'market'-type approaches to education, and through streaming and ability grouping. Therefore, one aspect of social justice is to comprehensivize (Benn and Chitty 1997) and change to mixed-ability classes. Lynch and Lodge (2002) explore social justice issues in schools and provide a useful analysis of equity, power and democracy, while Griffiths (2003) gives an account that focuses on classroom and personal detail. She discusses the importance for pupils of having self-expression, a sense of being validated by others and of feeling a sense of solidarity.

However, in all the above texts there is no structured focus on emotional development to help pupils with their psychological boundaries. The assumption seems to be that such improvement would only occur by chance. There are, however, other factors to consider, and I will now briefly discuss Dweck's research to illustrate this.

Dweck and self-theories

According to Dweck (2000), a pupil's view about how people learn, and how much they can adapt socially, can affect the extent to which the pupil is likely to change. In essence, Dweck argues that children have two implicit basic beliefs or theories about themselves (self-theories) that give meaning to their experiences. One is called the 'entity' theory, in which factors are seen primarily as fixed traits that dwell within us and are unlikely to change; for example, that they are due to biology. In contrast, other children see 'intelligence' or personality as something that is not fixed but that can be cultivated and is open to change, and Dweck calls this the 'incremental theory'. In other words, the incrementalists recognize the importance of social and cultural factors. Dweck shows that holding the entity theory can make pupils vulnerable, because if they fail at a task or test they see it as a refection on their own intelligence and so their self-image is lowered. They can find it more difficult to deal with failure than those pupils who are incrementalists. Incrementalists are also more likely to work harder when confronting a problem, as they believe that achievement is affected by social factors.

Dweck goes on to establish that there is a relationship between implicit theories and a contingent self-worth. In other words, pupils who hold entity theories can feel down or depressed about themselves if they do not succeed. Further, Dweck argues that people can believe that personality is fixed (entity/ biological) while others believe that it is malleable (socially open to change). She argues that students who believe in fixed personality and hold an entity theory are more likely to feel vulnerable and to have helpless responses when rejection occurs, thus negatively affecting their self-esteem. In contrast, those pupils who hold the incremental theory are more likely, in their relationships with people, to do something about problems and learn or grow from the experiences. They are less likely to make snap judgements about people, and be more likely to reflect on a range of social experiences. This means that since entity theorists believe in fixed traits that can be judged quickly, they believe they can know what people are like from a small sample of their behaviour, and this forms a basis of their stereotyping. Of course, this stereotyping can be good or bad. On the other hand, incrementalists can see variability in groups and explain negative behaviours in ways that leave room for growth and change.

Therefore, psychodynamic process and the 'other' are only one part of enabling emotional development, and how we educate children is important. In the classroom, we can reinforce either the entity or the incrementalist view of pupils through the way we interact and treat them. For example, the more we treat some pupils as 'thick' or 'intelligent' (e.g. through streaming), the more we reinforce the entity model. The more we encourage children to interact socially and take responsibility for their learning, the more they will see learning, as a social, incremental, process.

Pupils can be helped if ways can be found to allow their inner turmoils and conflicts to surface. Then they can be confronted and worked on. But teachers in schools cannot also be therapists – although it is possible to have some available in schools – and it would not be ethical to have children opening up in front of classmates. However, schools can help by systematically enabling pupils to develop emotionally. This is the focus of the next two chapters.

Summary

The term 'social justice', which includes both distributive and recognitive justices, has been discussed. Social justice, which is linked to deliberative democracy, requires people to be able to understand cultural and personal differences. Social justice is linked to self-identity and emotions. However, to be able to participate in dialogue, it is helpful for people to have developed emotionally. Hence schools could have emotional literacy programmes for their pupils. The issues raised reinforce those broached in educating the whole person to be integrated, coherent, tolerant, self-reflective and able to handle uncertainty.

Notes

1   I am aware that some feminists would say that men can be feminists, as opposed to saying that men can only support feminism.
2   Nagda *et al.* (2003: 170) provide a useful table of three contributions made by: critical pedagogy, Friere, and Kolb's view of active learning.
3   I am indebted to Richard Ford at Goldsmiths College for this insight.

3 'Emotional literacy', 'emotional intelligence' and dialogue

In Chapters 1 and 2, I have argued that there is a need to improve pupils' emotional capabilities. In this chapter two widely used terms are introduced in connection with this development, namely 'emotional intelligence' and 'emotional literacy'. Through this I will explain some of the principles that will be related to the school curriculum in Chapter 4. Figure 3.1 provides a summary of this.

There are many issues about developing pupils' emotional stability in schools. A wide range of terms are used in this debate and Weare (2003; Weare and Gray 2003) discusses the pros and cons of these. Terms such as 'emotional literacy' (used mainly in Britain) and 'emotional intelligence', (used mainly in America) have marked out much of the debate. These terms can carry different connotations, as signalled by the words 'literacy' and 'intelligence', which in turn can influence our perceptions. I will consider the use of 'emotional intelligence' to gain a better understanding of the features required for positive emotional development in schools. In particular, my endeavour is to consider the extent to which 'intelligence' and 'literacy' are helpful in the educational context, and this will be the focus of Chapter 4.

The meaning of 'literacy'. The word 'literacy' is often associated with language. At one level, functional literacy is the teaching of language so that people can gain sufficient vocabulary and understanding of grammatical structures to help them function in society. However, in a another sense literacy is recognized as a dynamic process that is intimately connected with the culture in which the literature is generated (Lankshear 1997). Further, literacy can be seen as enabling people to extend their control over their lives and to deal with problems and uncertainties. If we can all agree on empowerment as an educational goal, then in turn we can 'proclaim the virtue of an empowering literacy' (Lankshear 1997: 79). To this extent, literacy is not an end; it is a process that involves decision making about choices in life, and in turn involves emotions and intellect within a social context.

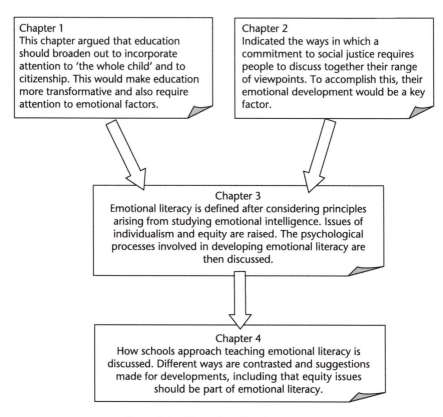

Chapter 1
This chapter argued that education should broaden out to incorporate attention to 'the whole child' and to citizenship. This would make education more transformative and also require attention to emotional factors.

Chapter 2
Indicated the ways in which a commitment to social justice requires people to discuss together their range of viewpoints. To accomplish this, their emotional development would be a key factor.

Chapter 3
Emotional literacy is defined after considering principles arising from studying emotional intelligence. Issues of individualism and equity are raised. The psychological processes involved in developing emotional literacy are then discussed.

Chapter 4
How schools approach teaching emotional literacy is discussed. Different ways are contrasted and suggestions made for developments, including that equity issues should be part of emotional literacy.

Figure 3.1   Chart of the first four chapters.

These are aspects that have a resonance with emotional development, as pupils need to operate emotionally at a level that enables them to control themselves and develop emotionally all their lives. Further, to deal with uncertainties and ambiguities is emotionally important. Also, emotions are experienced with others, and this automatically involves equity issues.

The meaning of 'intelligence'. Much of the debate on the notion of intelligence usually refers to rational abilities and excludes the emotions. Additionally, intelligence is commonly used in education where it is linked to paper tests designed to measure rational thinking. Intelligence is an individualistic concept within itself. The idea of a paper-based test being able to measure intelligence implies that what is being measured is independent of the social context. For example, two people of equal intelligence would be expected to get similar marks on a test irrespective of their country, upbringing or sexuality. Next, I will consider some writings on emotional intelligence so as to bring out some important principles.

Emotional intelligence

An individualistic or social term?

The way that 'emotional intelligence' is defined can make it appear as something that belongs to an individual. The term 'emotional intelligence' developed from the work of psychologists, and in particular Salovey and Mayer, who defined it as:

> the ability to perceive accurately, appraise and express emotion; the ability to access and/or generate feelings which facilitate thought; the ability to understand emotion and emotional knowledge; the ability to regulate emotions to promote emotional and intellectual growth.
>
> (Mayer and Salovey 1997: 10)

Salovey and Sluyter (1997: 5) define it as 'the ability to perceive emotions, to access and generate emotions so as to assist thought, to understand emotions and emotional knowledge, and to reflectively regulate emotions so as to promote emotional and intellectual growth'. These definitions are basically individualistic in that the words used can be read as if they apply just to the individual. There are no direct references to social interactions with others – this is only implied. For example, there is no mention of empathy incorporated into this definition. In a book on emotional intelligence in business, Weisinger (1998: xvi) defines emotional intelligence as when you 'intentionally make your emotions work for you by using them to help guide your behaviour and thinking in ways that enhance your results'. This could be called a capitalist definition that implies that the development of the emotions is for oneself and advancement at one's job. The book does cover more on communication, empathy and interpersonal expertise, but the original definition emerges throughout the writing. There is no mention of looking critically at the organization in terms of bullying, use of power, sexism or racism (and how these should be countered as an integral part of communication, empathy and interpersonal expertise). This could be because emotional intelligence is seen as an individualistic concept.

There are broader definitions of emotional intelligence. Goleman (1996) is the main popularizer of the term 'emotional intelligence' and his book has been influential and stimulated thinking in this area. Goleman argues that 'emotional intelligence' is integral to learning and involves five areas of development:

1   Emotional self-awareness
2   Managing emotions

3   Harnessing emotions productively
4   Empathy; reading emotions
5   Handling relationships

Goleman pointed out that people who did very well academically at school often did not go on to use their abilities in society:

> What factors are at play when people of high IQ flounder and those of modest IQ do surprisingly well? I would argue that the difference quite often lies on the abilities called here *emotional intelligence*, which include self-control, zeal and persistence, and the ability to motivate oneself. And these skills, as we shall see, can be taught to children, giving them a better chance to use whatever intellectual potential the genetic lottery may have given them.
>
> (Goleman 1996: xii)

It is interesting that in this list of what is included in emotional intelligence Goleman does not include empathy. He uses recent evidence from brain research to back up his ideas. There is an implied link with biology and emotional intelligence in the last sentence in the quote above, and in the quote below:

> ... the emotional lessons we learn shape the emotional circuits, making us more adept – or inept – at the basics of emotional intelligence. This means that childhood and adolescence are critical for setting down the essential emotional habits that will govern our lives.
>
> (Goleman 1996: xiii)

The links with biology strongly support the idea of emotional intelligence as being an individualistic concept. However, Goleman argues that 'IQ and emotional intelligence are not opposing competencies, but rather separate ones' (p. 44). Hence, emotional intelligence is defined in a comparatively individualistic way.

Emotional intelligence, social context and ideology

The individualistic nature of the term 'emotional intelligence' is reinforced as paper tests have been devised to measure a person's emotional quotient (EQ) (Bar-on 1997; Cooper and Sawaf 1997; Mayer *et al.* 1999) in a way that parallels tests for 'cognitive intelligence'. Tests for intelligence (IQ tests) have a long history and have been strongly criticized (Block and Dworkin 1977; Kamin *et al.* 1984). These tests measure a small range of attributes and infer that intelligence is a property of the individual. I would now like to deal with the features of the IQ debate, as it can illuminate some issues relevant to studying the extent that the same principles apply to EQ.

IQ (Intelligence Quotient) tests were seen as a practical way of separating out children by cognitive ability. Proponents of IQ tests see them as part of a rigorous branch of psychology that holds that tests can be objective and culturally neutral. It is based on a method of study called *positivism*, which holds that the scientific method can find out facts about people. So IQ tests were seen not only as individualistic, but culturally independent. Consequently, when IQ tests purported to show that people from different social classes and some ethnic groups did not do as well as others, this was taken to mean that they were less intelligent (Herrnstein and Murray 1996). The results have been used to argue that putting money into educational programmes to help low achievers is largely wasted, as IQ has a genetic component and so is not open to change. Further, Herrnstein and Murray (1996) argued in *The Bell Curve* that crime and dependence on social security was associated with low cognitive ability – and hence social class. An example of the political nature of this is that when they discuss crime it is ignored that the middle and upper classes probably steal more money through tax dodges than the working class ever steal! It is in this way that ideology enters. At first sight it may seem reasonable that if people do less well in a test designed to measure intelligence, then they are less able. However, the tests go through a process known as *standardization*. In this process, questions that show a bias, or do not fit with the rest of the results, are discarded. So, for example, questions that showed that girls scored higher than boys were not used, so that the tests gave on average the same results for both sexes. It was also possible to standardize the test questions for ethic background; that this was not done illustrates how ideology permeates what are presented as objective and neutral tests.

A series of books argued against the findings on IQ on a wide range of grounds (Heather 1976; Block and Dworkin 1977; Kamin *et al.* 1984; Fraser 1995; Jacoby and Glauberman 1995). Overall, it is argued, the assumption that intelligence can be measured objectively and neutrally has been used to legitimate racism and class discrimination. They argue that the idea of the bell curve 'gives a sophisticated voice to a repressed and illiberal sentiment: a belief that ruinous divisions in society are sanctioned by nature itself . . . [and] confirm a dark suspicion: the ills of welfare, poverty, and an underclass are less matters of justice than biology' (Jacoby and Glauberman 1995: ix). *Hence the concept of IQ encourages an analysis that locates the problems in the individual rather than society.*

A further criticism is that human qualities are capable of being reduced to numbers. This means, for example, that a person's happiness can be given a number that represents the strength of its presence. The process pretends that (a) all people experience happiness in the same way and (b) it is independent of the social and cultural context. To the extent that measures of cognitive ability are held to be individualistic and culture free, it allows the possibility of discrimination and the location of social problems in individuals rather than society. Clearly, if measures of emotional intelligence were to be based on the same assumptions of objectivity, neutrality and individualness, they would be likely to give rise to the same concerns. However, there is a further issue. While some people consider it possible that cognitive ability is the property of an individual, it is clear that even the emotional abilities defined by Goleman like empathy, and handling relationships do involve other people. As a result, it is difficult to see how emotional development can be considered first as only the property of an individual, and second, that it can be assessed using only paper tests.

A principle that emerges is that the introduction of emotional literacy into schools could avoid locating emotional and social problems solely in the individual.

The measurement of emotional intelligence

Some people believe that the emotions can be quantified through written tests which measure a person's emotional quotient (EQ) (Bar-on 1997; Cooper and Sawaf 1997; Mayer *et al.* 1999). Different forms of paper-based tests are being devised, but many of the tests for EQ are self-reporting in the sense that a person fills in how well they think that they are doing on a particular area. A common type of format is as follows (Cooper and Sawaf 1997: 330):

	This describes me Very well	This describes me Moderately well	This describes me A little	This describes me Not at all
I accept my feelings as my own				

The questions usually start with 'I', as a result explicitly reinforcing the individualist approach. It is possible that the same critiques discussed above that apply to the measurement of IQ could also apply to EQ. However, the situation is complicated because of the differing uses of the term. Mayer *et al.* (2000) argue that the term emotional intelligence is useful because it stresses the interconnection between emotions and cognition (i.e. intelligence). For example, Bar-On's test EQ-i is widely used and includes:

- Intrapersonal skills: emotional self-awareness, assertiveness, self-regard, self-actualization and independence
- Interpersonal skills: interpersonal relationships, social responsibility and empathy
- Adaptability scales: problem solving, reality testing, flexibility

- Stress-management scales: stress tolerance, impulse control
- General mood: happiness, optimism

It is clear, whatever approach is used, that EQ tests have to be seen as valid, reliable and norm referenced, as illustrated by the following quote. EQ-i has been translated into 23 languages and is cross-culturally normed and validated (Bar-on and Parker 2000: 367):

> Analysis of variance was employed to examine the effect of age and gender on EQ-i scores. Although the results indicated numerous significant differences among the age groups that were compared, these differences are relatively small . . .
> With respect to gender, no differences appeared between males and females regarding overall emotional and social competence . . . Based on the normative sample studied, females appear to have stronger interpersonal skills than males, but the latter have a higher intrapersonal capacity, are better at stress management, and are more adaptable. . . .
> Lastly, an examination of the North American sample did not reveal significant differences on emotional and social intelligence between the various ethnic groups that were compared. This is an interesting finding when compared with some of the controversial conclusions that have been presented over the years suggesting significant differences in cognitive intelligence between various ethnic groups.

Since these EQ tests are applied to people in different countries it is assumed that emotions are experienced and evidenced independently of the cultural context. However, it can be argued that emotions vary from culture to culture. Lynch (1990) argues that there is a real problem with trying to universalize emotions. For example, if you saw someone kill a seagull you would probably be horrified. However, if you were in a family living in icy waste and were constantly looking for food, such an act would be greeted with joy. In one social context the emotional response is horror, in another it is joy. That is, emotional responses are at least in part shaped and given meaning by social and cultural forces.

The integration of emotions and cognition is a theme of Harré's (1991) work and of research into the brain (LeDoux 1998). Whatever we do is guided by the emotions. For example, if you were asked if you wanted a cup of tea or coffee, you might try to make a 'rational' decision – 'Are you thirsty?', 'Which would give you more sustenance?', and so on. However, you could continue forever in this vein until you said, 'I feel like a cup of tea'. People who have had part of the brain that deals with emotions damaged have been unable to make decisions (Damasio 1996). Lynch (1990: 8) argues that all emotions are 'essentially appraisals, that is, they are judgements of situations based on cultural beliefs and values' and that emotions involve moral judgements about the social situation. Given this, it is difficult to see how paper tests that assume there is no social or cultural context can measure a person's emotional capabilities.

Another 'legitimacy' is given by reference to brain research, as illustrated by Goleman's approach and by Baron-Cohen (2003), who argues that the female brain is predominately hard-wired for empathy, and the male brain is predominately hard-wired for understanding and building systems. This supports the view that EQ tests are valid, because if such biological differences exist they must exist outside of the social context and hence can be measured.

Zeidner *et al.* (2002) indicate some of the difficulties of assessing EQ, but they are also in keeping with fears about the way EQ is seen. For example, they think EQ 'is most likely to have a heritable component' and quantitative models 'would tell us how correlations between parents' and children's EI scores . . . derived from common genes and the influence of the family environment' (p. 219). However, they move away from the IQ position when they add, 'heritability of EI does not imply that the individual's EI is fixed and insensitive to interventions' (p. 220). They are uncertain about the value of introducing emotional intelligence programmes into schools until there is more quantitative analysis and call for a tight definition of EQ so that it can be properly assessed and statistically validated. On this basis, the assumptions of IQ appear to be accepted. Certainly it is a long way from many views of the nature of learning where, for example, Barab and Plucker (2002: 178) argue 'that ability and talent should not be viewed as constructs possessed by individuals but, instead, as sets of relations that are actualised through dynamic transactions'.

Overview

There is a case for not using the term 'emotional intelligence' because the term shapes and influences the way that we think about the emotions.

However, there is a major way in which the assumptions surrounding emotional intelligence differ significantly from those surrounding IQ. The assumption is that by measuring a person's EQ or 'emotional intelligence', you can find ways to enable them to change it. That is, it is not fixed and anyone, no matter what their class, sexuality or ethnicity, can improve their social interactions. In education emotional intelligence is seen as contributing to improving classroom relationships, decreasing risk behaviours and increasing creativity and problem solving. The terms 'emotional literacy' and 'emotional intelligence' are not used consistently and there is an overlap in the application of the terms. Josh Freeman, in an e-mail letter from 6 Seconds, wrote that emotional intelligence was: 'To raise a strong, self-reliant generation: to develop social equity and tolerance'. In a way, what is crucial is the sense in which the term 'emotional intelligence' is used, rather than the term itself.

The key points to emerge from this discussion on the term 'intelligence' are that it can incorporate positivist views that run counter to the nature of the emotions. Emotions may be experienced individually, but they arise out of social interactions and this is a feature that can be built into any consideration of emotional development. With this in mind, I will now look at the term 'emotional literacy'.

What is emotional literacy?

We saw that the word 'literacy' carried connotations of being a dynamic process that involved culture and empowerment, as opposed to the more individualistic meaning attached to, and reflected in, emotional 'intelligence'. The term 'emotional literacy', defined in 1997 by Steiner, grew out of an interest in counselling and psychoanalysis. There are differing views on what constitutes emotional literacy, but they incorporate a view of emotions being experienced individually and arising out of social situations and interaction with others. Claude Steiner says:

> Emotional Literacy is made up of 'the ability to understand your emotions, the ability to listen to others and empathise with their emotions, and the ability to express emotions productively. To be emotionally literate is to be able to handle emotions in a way that improves your personal power and improves the quality of life around you. Emotional literacy improves relationships, creates loving possibilities between people, makes co-operative work possible, and facilitates the feeling of community.
>
> (Steiner 1997: 11)

He breaks emotional literacy into five parts:

1   Knowing your feelings
2   Having a sense of empathy
3   Learning to manage our emotions
4   Repairing emotional damage
5   Putting it all together: emotional interactivity

The emphasis is on using emotions in relationships, like taking responsibility for the mistakes one makes. To do this, according to Steiner, one has to focus on one's self and work to change psychologically. Emotional literacy involves being able to savour your own feeling, listen and respond to others' needs and fix your emotional damage, and so navigate the world of feelings. The importance of developing relationships is also stressed in Weare's (2003: 2) definition:

> The ability to understand ourselves and other people, and in particular to be aware of, understand, and use information about the emotional states of ourselves and others with competence. It includes the ability to understand, express and manage our own emotions, and respond to the emotions of others, in ways that are helpful to ourselves and others.

Similarly, the organization Antidote (2003a) states:

> Emotional Literacy is the practice of thinking individually and collectively about how emotions shape our actions, and of using emotional understanding to enrich our thinking.
> Emotional literacy is the practice of engaging with others in ways that facilitate understanding of our own and others' emotions, then using this understanding to inform our actions.

These definitions all have interpersonal relationships at their heart and entail the need for dialogue. This reflects the backdrop of psychoanalysis. Emotional literacy is a term used more in Britain than other parts of the world. For example, Sharp (2001) has taken a broad approach to emotional literacy in a local education authority (LEA) where he considers its development is important for teachers as well as pupils. I believe that the term 'emotional literacy' reflects well the types of activity and aims that are required in schools where the emphasis on interpersonal relationships means that pupil–pupil and pupil–teacher dialogue would be central to developing emotional literacy. However, it is worth noting that Goleman's (1996, 1999) definition of emotional intelligence has many similarities with Steiner's but with less emphasis on interactions.

Emotional literacy: group as well as individual

Personal interactions and dialogue are at the core of emotional literacy and place the individual within a cultural setting. But how might we judge the emotional literacy of a person in a group?

Suppose a group contained men and women, people from a range of ethnicities, classes and sexualities. The range of possibilities an observer could study as the group worked could include the extent to which these people communicated with each other, talked and listened, took on board constructively what each other said, reviewed and reflected on the process of working together, and brought about understandings. One would expect the extent to which these were accomplished would be irrespective of a person's sex, cultural background or sexuality. However, this is not to say that sex and politics would not enter into the group dynamics. Two people may find they are sexually attracted to each other and this could be expressed appropriately or inappropriately. If the group had been formed to devise a product for manufacture, some people may have greater regard for environmental factors than others and so a political dimension might emerge. The list of factors could be extended greatly, but what an observer would be looking for is that each person, in that social situation, could value the others for what they brought to the situation, and that the way they interacted showed empathy and recognition of 'self' and 'others'.

The group would also be trying to reach some agreements and this involves being able to understand each other across different understandings and viewpoints. Gadamer (1989) stresses that we all bring prejudices with us, and that those prejudices are constantly in the process of being formed and tested in encounters. Further, that one has to gain a *fusion of horizons* where, as individuals, we gain from what we bring to a situation and from the encounters. Within discussions, interpretations play a role and to gain understanding, both for ourselves and of others, we have to be open to questions so that 'the possibility of truth remains unsettled, this is the real and fundamental nature of a question: namely to make things indeterminate' (Gadamer 1989: 375). Hence, developing emotional literacy involves being able to handle indeterminacy and ambiguity, which in turn makes it more likely that people will learn to cope with being challenged and to use the experience to change. If they were accused of being dominant and not allowing others to speak, would they reflect on the extent to which this was true, or whether it was a way of the others avoiding an unpleasant viewpoint? Reflection is another key skill. Emotional literacy is a *social process* that takes place in a social setting and is not something that is ever achieved, unlike learning your 12×12 tables. You can judge it in action; for example, a person may think that they are not sexist, yet interact quite differently with men and women. Even assuming that people attempt to be honest in their replies on a test, they can still be self-deluding.

This brings me to a crucial point about emotional literacy: that a person's *emotional literacy has to be seen in conjunction with that of others*. People may be able to raise their self-esteem, express their ideas well and feel secure in themselves. However, if this is achieved through doing others down, and this includes being sexist, racist or classist, they have not really raised the level of their emotional literacy. To achieve an *individual-in-group* emotional literacy, one would have to increase, say, their self-esteem with others, and not at their expense by doing them down. Similarly, to just empathize with someone else is not enough; one can be racist such that one can empathize with another person's distress, but accept that the person is distressed and because one is racist do nothing to relieve it. Empathy must be combined with action. In this sense, emotional literacy is a group as well as an individual endeavour; it requires an inclusive environment, in so far as it is possible, as the presence of the complimentary sex, other ethic groups and social classes, offers the greatest opportunities for the interactions, reflection on feelings and behaviour, that can lead to emotional development. This is because different people's views of a discussion can be very different and reflection needs *other viewpoints and analysis* to be most effective. If, say, members of the other sex are not present, they cannot give their perspective; they are silenced. An acknowledgement of discriminations is one aspect of an improving emotional literacy. The aim is to develop an emotional responsiveness to others, which acknowledges the cultural context. For example, a girl may be working in an all-female group and display many of the attributes of emotional literacy, but this could change dramatically when the grouping includes pupils of different sexualities and religions. For the girl to change reflection would be essential.

Epstein (1998) indicates the importance of reflection. He argues for *constructive thinking*, which he sees as the interaction of the rational and the experiential (emotional) minds, which make for 'emotional intelligence'. He argues that it is not the actual events that we experience so much as the way we respond to them that matter. He says the reality you experience is largely of your own construction. He also states that people can wish to avoid responsibility for their actions and denying emotions and using rational arguments can achieve this. People tend to assume either that they have complete conscious understanding and control of what they do, or that their behaviour and understanding are influenced by a deep, dark, unconscious mind over which they have no control, with nothing in between. As a result, they fail to gain control of the thinking that produces their everyday emotions. It is easier to say, 'The way he acted made me angry' than, 'I am angry because of the way I interpreted his actions'. Hence it helps when something occurs to stop and think in quiet reflection to get in tune with why you acted/responded in such a way. *This indicates that key components of emotional literacy would include dialogue, acceptance of ambiguity and the ability to reflect.* Also, to judge people's *individual-in-group* emotional literacy would include watching them during group work and observing how well they interacted and helped the others in the group. This facet of evaluation will be returned to in Chapter 8.

Developmental precursors of emotional literacy

An understanding of psychological mechanisms, which underlie the development of emotional literacy, is often assumed rather than discussed in books. Child analysts signify the importance of school as a source of structure and guidance where pupils can develop emotional skills. Marans and Cohen (1999) argue for a psychoanalytically informed perspective that is attuned 'to how *unrecognised* thoughts and feelings colour and potentially shape behaviour and development' (p. 114). A psychoanalytical approach does not mean that the teacher has to be a psychoanalyst, but that the teacher will have a perspective that encourages them to question why the child acts in certain ways. This allows the teacher to have an integrative approach that will also enable a greater understanding and the role of the unconscious, which gives rise to unrecognized feelings and thoughts and affects our behaviour. The experiences and thoughts we encounter enable us to forge a sense of identity and 'self' through a personal narrative. A pupil may have built up a story that means that they consider themselves 'thick'. As Marans and Cohen point out, the conscious and unconscious meaning that he or she attaches to 'thick' need to be made conscious to facilitate modification. This requires opportunities to discover more about himself or herself. That is, healthy challenges that help him or her confront evasive behaviour.

Paul Greenhalgh (1994) argues that the human condition is never still, but always changes depending on our experiences (our outer world) and how they interact with our inner world. What makes an 'experience' is how we deal with these interactions. Greenhalgh argues that our capacity to learn depends on our ability to manage our inner and outer worlds. Psychoanalysis stresses the importance of how we build up from birth an 'inner psychic self' or 'inner child' that has an influence on how we see and interact with people and the world. The importance of psychological boundaries and such processes as splitting, projection and transference are inseparable from all aspects of learning, and I will now address these (Klein 1988; Greenhalgh 1994).

Splitting, projection and transference

Splitting and projection are unconscious psychological processes that occur all the time (Sandler 1987; Klein 1988; Greenhalgh 1994). We can have aspects of our personality, feelings or wishes that we do not like, or cannot face up to. These aspects can be denied and split off, and then projected onto others. These unacceptable aspects of ourselves are now located in others and so hostility can be expressed towards them as they 'hold' the unacceptable aspect. We can then attack this projection and feel that we have 'dealt with it'. For example, a macho man might not be in contact with his passive 'feminine' side, and so project it onto homosexuals. These he will attack, both as a defence against recognizing it in himself, and because by attacking it feels he has combated it. These processes contribute to people feeling that a situation is all bad or all good, rather than being able to see the good and bad in situations. Additionally, 'Transference is a particular form of projection which takes place when feelings from the past, or emotions one has about someone significant, are unconsciously transferred onto another person' (Greenhalgh 1994: 54). A pupil can transfer feelings about a parent onto the teacher, and the teacher gets the flack. This provides the pupil with a sense of security rather than having to confront the difficulty. It does, however, enable the teacher to make a guess as to what might be happening emotionally within the child. Greenhalgh argues that for people to develop emotionally, attention to these processes is important. If we are unable to manage our emotions, we are likely to lose our capacity for imagination and we become 'frozen, emotionally stuck, as if unavailable for [cognitive] learning' (p. 25). This emphasis integrates 'emotional literacy' with 'cognitive intelligence', and hence sees that in order for learning to take place emotional growth is essential.

What emerges from these theories is that the pupil needs to be in social interaction with other pupils and teachers within a safe environment so that they can learn to name, handle and respect feelings. People form their identity through the interactions that they undergo. The more that pupils are able to interact, discuss and enter into genuine dialogue with girls/boys, pupils of different ethnic origins and classes, the easier it will be for them to be able to empathize and gain a secure sense of 'other' and 'self'.

Kegan (1982), while not using the term 'emotional literacy', was interested in defining core facets of emotional development. He drew attention to the way that people have to, throughout their lives, in different ways, balance those aspects of the 'self' that favour *independence*, and those that favour *inclusion*. Independence includes differentiation, isolation and separateness, which help a person become autonomous, while inclusion recognizes attachment, connection with others, dependence and integration. Kegan is trying to integrate and use the tension between these two psychological aspects, without favouring one over the other, and recognizing the dignity of both. He wants to avoid the common dyad where differentiation and autonomy have often been associated with maleness, and integration and dependency associated with femaleness. There are connections between inclusion and equity; a person can feel included in one group (British) through accepting certainties about another group (e.g. African's are . . .). This foreclosure on what defines a group can lock identity development (Head 1997) and be the basis for discriminations. For this reason, pupils ought to be helped to develop some fluidity within inclusion.

Kegan points out that at every stage of life we experience tensions and difficulties with independence and inclusion, but how they are evident varies considerably with age. An adolescent who is comparatively integrated (inclusion) in the family might be trying to separate from his parents and to find himself as a distinct person with his own identity autonomous from adults (independence). A young person might be finding out how to relate to another in a sexual relationship that encourages exploration of inter-dependence and mutuality. These cases are very different but have the same underlying psychological processes involved; a person grapples with inclusion and separateness throughout their lives and it is an uneven process that never stops. Since adolescence involves forging new meaning about 'femaleness' and 'maleness', the processes of denial of parts of oneself (splitting) and locating this part in someone else (projection) can be increased (Kenway *et al.* 1998). Boys can deny their passive, emotional and nurturing sides and locate these in girls to confirm their 'masculinity'. Meanwhile girls project their aggressive, objective and hard sides onto boys to confirm their 'femininity'. In the co-educational environment, provided suitable communication takes place, these splitting and projection processes can be checked, worked on and challenged in constructive ways that can never be done in single-sex schools. In one's search for sexual identity, 'certainties' are very useful, hence the power of accepting stereotypes. To challenge such certainties requires a lot of psycho-logical and emotional energy, but it can be effectively confronted with, for example, the many passive boys and assertive girls, who refute the projection at the same time as it is being constructed.

The maturing processes that are important for emotional literacy can be stunted by relying on uninspected 'certainties' or foreclosing (Kegan 1982; Head 1997). Parts of the self can be projected onto others, which thereby impoverishes and curtails the development of self because the required exploration of differences is truncated. The maturational processes are weak-ened by oversimplification. The 'certainties' can also help see others as need-objects rather than maturing to seeing the relativization of different individuals' needs and that people are defined through the relationships between them.

The single-sex environment is important in that it provides group solidar-ity and enables cathartic talk. However, if unchecked it can be very negative. Male group solidarity and projection processes enable 'stereotypical females' to become the repository for society's ills. Female teachers who enter this environment soon become painfully aware of this, and some boys can confirm their 'masculinity' by displaying their aggressiveness and lack of emotion. As we can see, the argument that male teachers can tackle this problem in all-male schools is quite untenable, for the longer the separation the more strongly will be the internalizations of projection and splitting, and the attendant 'monocultural' responses. Exactly the same processes can go on in girls' schools, and it is just as important for them to explore differences and mature. The girls can confirm their 'femininity' when a male teacher enters the environment by displaying their passivity and emotional concern. As a result, some become 'unable' to do tasks – like replacing an electric plug – and expect the man to do it, and give more weight to male utterances. The suppression of attitudes has a negative effect. The female sees the man as 'taking over the situation' and not giving her credit for her ability. The male sees the woman as not being able, and expecting him to do the work. Attitudes can be confirmed with mutual resentment. In each case, self-esteem can be maintained and gender roles reinforced in a way that leaves them uninspected.

It is possible to challenge both of these mutually destructive situations, although the aggression of males is more visible and condemned. The point is that because 'femininity' and 'masculinity' are processes, and the definition of one is inseparable from the other, synchronous changes can occur. These changes have to be tackled in tandem, as the more that girls and boys go through the processes together the greater the likelihood of change. Feelings can be relativized by different contexts. Finally, if the person continues to mature, she or he 'Acknowledges and cultures capacity for interdependence, for self-surrender and intimacy, for interdependent self-definition' (Kegan 1982: 120). The way we interact is inseparable from both the social beliefs brought to any situation and the defence mechanisms, like splitting and projection, because what is projected, or denied, is influenced by social values.

Summary

We have seen that the term 'emotional intelligence' tends to focus on the individual aspects of emotional development, while 'emotional literacy' can incorporate a social and individual view. The latter connects with equity issues and places dialogue at its heart. The psychological processes of splitting, projection and transference underlie the development of a sense of 'self'. The struggle to develop a secure identity involves the recognition of 'self' and 'other', and the processes of *independence* and *inclusion*. These all underlie the development of emotional literacy and require dialogue involving reflective interactions and the acceptance of ambiguity. A great deal of inclusive pupil–pupil interaction is needed, with analysis of different viewpoints, so that pupils can engage with their emotions and so move forward. Pupils can then be empowered in their emotional lives.

4 Emotional literacy and education

In the previous chapter, I indicated that the terms 'intelligence' and 'literacy' could influence the interpretation of emotional development. In particular, it was argued that pupil dialogue was key to developing emotional literacy, which could be seen to have both individual and group dimensions, so incorporating equity issues. In this chapter, I reflect on two main pedagogic approaches, one that is mainly teacher-centred with fixed curricula and the other that is pupil-centred, to determine the effects of pedagogy on how emotional literacy is experienced in the classroom. Also, the extent to which present schemes address equity issues will be explored. However, before doing this I first need to outline what is done in schools.

Emotional literacy in schools

There are many courses and books on teaching emotional literacy. Some of these focus on teaching it in its own right (Antidote 2003b), while others set it within a social framework (Elias *et al.* 1997) and others within a behavioural framework (DfES 2003a). There are many similarities and overlaps in what is proposed for the classroom, and I will now focus on those similarities. In general, the areas covered match those identified by Steiner (1997) and Goleman (1996, 1999). For example, the emotional literacy intervention produced by Southampton Psychological Service (Faupel 2003a, 2003b) for primary (age 7–11) and secondary (age 11–16) schools covers: self-awareness, self-regulation, motivation, empathy and social skills. Hence social and emotional skills are integrated, and this is often called Social and Emotional Learning (SEL). The Department for Education and Skills (DfES 2003) in Britain stressed the need to improve pupil behaviour through Social, Emotional and Behavioural Skills (SEBS) in a project initially for 4–11 year olds but later extended to include secondary schools. It aimed to improve pupil behaviour and attendance and set emotional development within the whole-school curriculum. SEBS has been developed for primary schools into the Social and Emotional Aspects of Learning (SEAL) (DfES 2005: 6) which uses domains that are almost identical to the Southampton model: self-awareness, managing feelings, motivation, empathy and social skills.

Similarly, Weare (2003), in stressing the need for a whole-school approach, uses the headings: self-understanding; understanding, expressing and managing our emotions; understanding social situations and making relationships.

A variety of reasons are given for implementing emotional literacy projects. Weare and Gray (2003) list: greater educational and work success; improvements in behaviour; increased inclusion (referring to children with emotional and behavioural difficulties); improved learning; greater social cohesion, increase in social capital (meaning less violence and staying out of trouble); improvements in mental health (including less alcoholism and drug use). Other people use different terms, but cover very similar ground. For example, Elias *et al.* (1997) include sexual behaviour. Weare (2003) and the Collaborative for Social and Emotional Learning (Casel 2003) describe a range of taught courses, most of which argue for emotional literacy to be covered because of the expected improvements in pupil behaviour in schools and the prevention of drug use, delinquency and sexual activity. Some courses place an emphasis on links with the community, which Casel sees as a characteristic of effective SEL practice. In all, then, the courses aim to help pupils to get on better with peers and adults. The belief is that engagement with emotional literacy improves the health of students, helps them manage their own behaviour and helps learning. I will now consider two approaches to teaching emotional literacy – teacher-curriculum and pupil-centred – to uncover if different approaches affect what goes on.

Teacher-curriculum approach to emotional literacy

As Weare and Gray (2003) discovered, the teacher-curriculum approach is overwhelmingly used in Britain and the USA. A common context for these teacher-led programmes was to place them around behaviour support plans. SEL approaches (Elias *et al.* 1997) have a substantial research base to indicate they improve pupil behaviour, increase learning and reduce aggression and violence, and this is to be greatly welcomed. The following are the common features of the programmes using Faupel's categories, although there are a lot of overlapping interconnections.

- *Self-awareness*. Naming emotions through the use of pictures of faces and a 'feelings vocabulary'. Pupils are encouraged to articulate (circle time) how they are feeling, draw or fill in a worksheet. Games can also be used. The context of feelings is sometimes made explicit; the pupils can be asked to talk about the situations that lead up to the way they felt. Even so, this usually involves the universalizing of emotions.

- *Self-regulation* (learning to control emotions) means that pupils learn to modify their behaviour. They are seen to be responsible for their own behaviour and can receive rewards (or reward themselves). Often self-regulation focuses on negative, angry feelings. Pupils can be taught calming techniques, ways to control them. Behaviour (often pupil–teacher) is often targeted, with teacher told to use praise, to recognize the signs of anger arising. Procrastination can be a topic. Self-regulation overlaps a great deal with conflict resolution (see below in 'Social skills').
- *Motivation.* This is nearly always focused on schoolwork. Avoiding distractions (focus on work). Developing teacher–pupil relationships. Placing pupils in situations where they have to consider a goal and think if they have achieved it. Teachers can be encouraged to set problems for pupils.
- *Empathy* (with self-awareness) and naming how others feel. Using circle time (largely in teacher-controlled situations rather than group work). Using stories to get pupils to hear and see how others see the world. Pupils paired to help each other, sometimes called 'buddying'. There is often an emphasis on listening to the teacher.
- *Social skills.* Conflict resolutions, often with peer mentoring. This includes having school rules, effective supervision and close liaison with parents. Group work is used, often as a class group but including small groups, which can focus on particular emotions and then discussing them. Noticing when pupils are unhappy. Teaching about tolerance, etc.

There are many positive features to the courses. At a minimum, they encourage a re-focusing away from purely cognitive learning. Young children are at a crucial point in their emotional development and learning to forge relationships with others while away from their parents. These courses, in their use of story, circle work and other techniques, can make positive contributions to children's SEL development. For example, the Primary National Strategy for developing children's social and emotional skills (SEAL) has seven themes, which include materials on 'Getting on and falling out' and 'Relationships' (DfES 2005). Both SEAL and the New Haven scheme (Shriver *et al.* 1999) take a whole-school approach, rather than seeing SEL as a separate subject.

There is a wide range of good published schemes (Casel 2003; Zins *et al.* 2004), but a number of them lack an emphasis on pupil–pupil dialogue. If pupils are going to learn to empathize, become self-aware, listen and talk supportively, then peer-group interactions are valuable. Also peer–peer relationships are very important to school success (Asher and Rose 1997). An example of the lack of emphasis on pupil–pupil dialogue, in an otherwise very useful book, is provided by *Promoting Social and Emotional Learning* (Elias *et al.* 1997). In its index there are entries under 'self-awareness', 'self-concept', 'self-control', 'self-esteem', 'self-reflection' and 'self-regulation'. 'Empathy' only gets one reference, while 'sexism' gets none. There is also no entry for 'discrimination', although it is occasionally mentioned. These indicate the attention paid to individuals controlling themselves. It is also noticeable that cooperative learning has only about a column devoted to it. Group work has a greater importance but 'A didactic whole-class or small-group activity with the teacher imparting new information *may* be followed by discussion' (p. 50). Later it says, 'Other discussion *may* focus more on the feelings generated than on solving the problem' (my emphasis). Another example is provided by Faupel (2003a, 2003b) at both the primary and secondary levels. The section on 'enhancing empathy' does not mention pupil–pupil interactions, but instead focuses on the teacher modelling listening by allowing the pupils to speak to them. This is backed up with having clear rules about listening, combined with the teacher dealing with issues and showing sensitivity to pupils by acknowledging them. These approaches can be contrasted with that taken in the *Handbook for Emotional Literacy* (Antidote 2003b), which focuses on dialogue and pupils' interactions.

The lack of emphasis on pupil–pupil collaboration is due in part to the aims – that is, of improving classroom behaviour and reducing anti-social behaviour like taking drugs, which switch the focus away from pupil–pupil and towards teacher–pupil interactions (with the teacher as controller of behaviour and morals). There are no references to racism, sexism and classism, or how you help pupils to address power differences and address their particular prejudices and how they may come to accept multiple differences. Additionally, there is little opportunity in teacher-based curricula for the development of peer relationships and friendships, which are crucial factors in social-emotional adjustment (Asher and Rose 1997). Asher and Rose list ten social tasks of friendship. These include recognizing and respecting the 'spirit of equality' that is at the heart of friendship; being able to help when friends are in need; managing disagreements and conflicts; recognizing that friendships are embedded within the broader social network of school and home; and conceiving friendships as relationships that transcend a specific context. The lack of focus on pupil–pupil relationships in some curriculum teacher-led courses I characterize as an emotional literacy with a pedagogic 'emotional distance', as real problems of power, prejudice and difference in persons are not confronted. The self–other interaction is left relatively uninspected, as interpersonal relationships are often under-emphasized. I would, however, strongly support the above schemes, and in what follows I am not trying to undermine them, but rather to point out some of the problems with this approach so that they can be avoided.

Individual focus and control of pupils

Any educational development can be a two-edged sword. One has to ask the question, 'To what extent is the development of emotional literacy in the curriculum going to empower and enable pupils to lead happier and more reliant lives, and to what extent will it become an extension of social control so that the emotions are taught, assessed and graded in similar ways to the control of cognitive abilities? In other words, will pupils be pathologized for their behaviour? As Boler (1999: 86) puts it: 'It is cost-effective to teach students to take "responsibility" and learn "self-control". Thus the social, economic, and political forces that underlie these youth crises are masked, and the individuals are blamed for lack of self-control'. An example of this would be the 'Just say NO' campaign, which takes the line that adolescents should not engage in sexual activity. The line taken is that it is wrong for adolescents to make love and the campaign relies on denial rather than encouraging open discussion making (Kirby 2002; Alwyn 2004; Hessel-Mial 2004). If love making takes place, then the youths are blamed for having sex too early. This individualizes emotional actions and masks how anxiety can be created around sexual activity, which in turn promotes silence and misinformation (Lambert 2003; Phillips 2004). The anxiety and associated guilt act on the adolescent and can make open discussion with the prospective partner less likely. On the other hand, open discussion about many aspects of sexual activity can decrease it at the start, and make it more considered, especially if making love is recognized as a complex issue (NCPTP 2002; Apter 2004). This is because it helps the individual come to terms with their emotions and become more able to be positively self-regulating. The individually felt emotions are located within the social and emotional situation that the couple come together in, and so they are more able to take into account their moral and ethical values. This approach can be contrasted with one that sees emotions located in the individual alone, who can be blamed if they deviate from particular traditional teachings. As Bay-Cheng (2003) argues, this individualized conception of sexuality is what 'justifies' its approach of blaming individuals, and until changed 'will continue to propagate a narrow and unrealistic version of "normal" adolescent sexuality, failing to truly inform and empower teens to make healthy and responsible sexual choices' (p. 71). Hence, the expression of certain emotions in the 'Just say NO' campaign is praised (e.g. denial) or attacked (e.g. desire). As Megan Boler (1999) argues, emotions can be a site of social control.

Boler (1999) researched four of the emotional programmes in America. She points out that the programmes tend to view pupils as individuals who are in need of development through enabling them to control their impulses. Clearly, the more that emotions are seen as individual, the less any problems are seen as due to culture or community. For example, a pupil who is constantly disruptive has the problem located within them and they are seen as responsible for changing; a boring over-assessed curriculum would not be automatically entered into the mechanisms of analysis. Boler looked at conflict resolution programmes and found that these had a greater potential for including social factors, although emotions were categorized into 'healthy' and 'unhealthy' ones. In conflict resolution situations, pupils are encouraged to find creative solutions to their difficulties. This can involve locating the solutions in the social situation that led to the anger or bullying. In some cases, peer mediation is used where one pupil acts as a mediator. Boler (1999: 103) argues that in cases like these, the pupils are being encouraged to ask questions and self-reflect so that they engage in an analysis of the dynamics of pupil–pupil and teacher–pupil relationships. Consequently, rather than imposing a teaching programme from above, it has the potential to generate genuine dialogue. Pupils are more likely to encounter complexity and ambiguity, and use their own perceptions to generate analysis and their own solutions.

There is an inherent tension between seeing emotional literacy as only an individual property, and seeing it as a function of the social setting. Faupel (2003a: 6–7) says:

> Emotional literacy cannot just be discussed in relation to the individual. It is important to be wary of the within-child deficit model of emotional literacy. It is equally important to remember that our emotionally literate behaviour is profoundly influenced by the context or environment in which we function.
>
> The core activity of education is the building of community. Community is about how individuals develop and maintain their own sense of value and self-esteem while at the same time maintaining that of others.

This viewpoint reinforces that we are not individuals in isolation, but are our lived relationships with others. As Cohen (1999: 116) puts it, 'Life is fundamentally relational'. This emphasizes the requirement for the inclusion of pupil–pupil dialogue to enable pupils to develop emotionally, and changes the focus from the individual to the group. However, we have seen that a focus on teacher-centred SEL or emotional literacy courses can lead to an individualistic view of emotional development that undervalues dialogue. I will now turn to emotional literacy programmes that try to incorporate dialogic approaches.

Pupil-centred approaches to emotional literacy

Engaging in dialogue can help pupils' progress emotionally. Group work allows pupils to interact with others, and think and reflect on exchanges. The connections between emotion development, language and learning go back to Vygotsky, whose work indicates that collaborative group work with dialogue is the basis of one pedagogic approach. Vygotsky developed a cultural form of psychology and argued that 'Every function in the child's cultural development appears twice: . . . First *between* people (*interpsychological*), and then *inside* the child (*intrapsychological*) . . . All the higher functions originate as actual relations between human individuals' (Vygotsky 1978: 57; italics in the original). Others have built on Vygotsky to try to reintegrate psychology and sociology and, as Cole (1996: xii) put it, to see that the 'mind emerges in the joint activity of people and is in an important sense coconstructed'. Hence schools can play a significant role through enabling pupils of all backgrounds to interact in a safe environment while forming their identity. Cole argues that psychologists had falsely separated out the mind from culture through seeing culture as the stimulus and the mind as response, when culture can be seen as co-constitutive of the mind. Many educationalists have developed the implications of Vygotsky's work for the classroom where humans are seen as people who both actively engage in, and affect, the cultural setting in which they learn. Daniels (2001) draws out the importance of teachers having a mediating role in pupils' learning, but where learners are not passive recipients of knowledge. Rather they make meaning in a world that is influenced by previous experiences from their culture. Vygotsky linked, through his notion of activity, the psyche with society when he wrote:

> Pedogogics is never and was never politically indifferent, since, willingly or unwillingly, through its own work on the psyche, it has always adopted a particular social pattern, political line, in accordance with the dominant social class that has guided its interests.
>
> (Vygotsky 1997: 348, quoted in Daniels 2001: 5)

However, Daniels and other writers then tend to focus on cognitive development to the exclusion of how to advance emotional maturity and the psyche. This cognitive perspective tends to place an emphasis on the individual. It is clear though, that using Vygotsky's emphasis on activity and problem solving, that the community of learners, and their social and emotional interactions, can be placed at the heart of the learning process. As Traianou (2005: 15) puts it: 'understanding is constructed first on a social plane before it becomes internalised by the individual and is best described as an "evolving spiral" '.

One aspect of emotional development is the challenging by other pupils during exchanges so that individuals are engaged in emotional work. The pupil-centred approach to emotional literacy recognizes the importance of feelings being activated and worked through as they arise. Hence, emotional literacy is seen as developing in a social context through interactions. In *The Emotional Literacy Handbook* (Antidote 2003b), the importance of dialogue is stressed while accepting that internal and external experiences of emotions can lead to anxieties. A person can hold these anxieties internally, or opportunities provided to help him to verbalize tensions and work through them to help him feel more secure and empowered. To do this, pupils are helped by having 'relationships based on a spirit of mutuality, collaboration, negotiation of conflict and appreciation of difference' (p. 20). (One approach for use in schools will be outlined in detail in Chapters 7 and 8.)

This marks a significant change in focus from *how adults* want children to change (better behaviour, less drug use, increased self-esteem, etc.) to *what processes enable children* to be more likely to develop emotionally. Therefore, what matters more than the curriculum are the opportunities that pupils have to explore and be open to feelings, and the quality of pupil–pupil and teacher–pupil relationships. The pupils ought to be able to discuss with teachers how they feel about lessons and school life in general. When pupils can explore their feelings and relationships in a spirit of mutuality and feel appreciated, they are more likely to understand their emotions and so confront and work on their anxieties, rather than project them. Emotions are not 'good or bad', 'healthy' or 'unhealthy'; we need all of them, from anger to love. Conflict resolution programmes (see above) that use 'healthy and unhealthy' emotions can make people feel they are 'unhealthy' and feel guilty if they experience those emotions, and can feel they are a bad person for having those feelings. What is crucial is that we develop the ability to know when each feeling is appropriate, and can find ways to understand inappropriate feelings so that they can be transformed into more useful ones. 'Love' can be just as inappropriate a feeling as 'anger'. Rather, all emotions should be accepted and people learn how to deal with feelings constructively. Hence pupils might develop positive personal narratives of their emotional lives through dialogue.

As well as being encouraged to fit into the common-sense assumptions and values of the school and community, pupils could also be encouraged to challenge common assumptions and explore personal beliefs so that they can develop their personal capacities. These, according to Antidote (2003b: 85), are best promulgated through the core values of:

- safety (emotionally safe, including 'holding')
- openness (of emotions combined with honesty in all aspects of school life)
- compassion (taking a genuine interest in others)

- connection (genuine commitment to bring people together, personal and organizational)
- reflection (deepening understanding of each other and the organization)
- growth orientation (a commitment to encourage people to believe in and develop their own potential)

The emphasis on dialogue and interactions is also made clear when ten principles for shaping emotional literacy programmes are elicited (Antidote 2003b: 86). These include that emotional literacy is a process rather than something that is achieved, that 'Emotional literacy is generated through dialogue' which cannot happen without reflection. Also 'Dialogue enables us to develop new stories about ourselves as learners' and 'emotional literacy is sustained through our continuing curiosity'. This emphasis is crucial and is covered well, along with incorporating pupil dialogue within a school and community setting. However, issues of equity are not centrally addressed and it is to this I now turn.

Emotional literacy and discrimination

As I outlined in Chapter 3, there are two issues that I see as inseparable: developing emotional literacy and equity. However, as we have seen above, emotional literacy in schools may not address equity issues centrally. Indeed, most books on emotional literacy only pay lip-service to equity, while those on equity only play lip-service to emotional development. Emotional literacy and equity can be linked through a consideration of the power differences between groups and individuals within each group. An emphasis on emotional literacy can romanticize the power of dialogue, and so lack an analysis of power and a political perspective. However, the identities of individuals and their cultures are always changing and so pupils have to develop the emotional and psychological maturity to cope with ambiguity and uncertainty. Part of this is recognizing others in ourselves, and ourselves in others, despite the differences between us. We are more similar than different; there is a great overlap of attributes and attitudes. Each group, like 'women' or 'Asians', has more social variation within it than between the complementary groups of 'men' and 'non-Asians'. Recognition of the power differences that exist in non-uniform ways between these groups and individuals lies at the heart of equity and social justice. However, if definitions of emotional literacy stop at the borders of the individual's self-esteem, self-regulation and ability to empathize, then the political dimension is left out. McIntosh and Style (1999: 137) argue that schools are always involved in social, emotional and power relations, yet 'power relations are a taboo subject in K-12 schooling and in the majority culture of the United States. Power relations are therefore little understood systemically. Students, however, learn about power by watching, by imitating, by avoidance of what they fear'. School, with its tracking, target setting and grading, trains pupils to 'suppress most emotional responses to the stratified political and psychological structure within which their socialisation takes place'. The hidden message is that power relations are not the province of education, while power is always present.

Hence emotional literacy can involve connections, working with difference, similarity and the exercise of power. However, McIntosh and Style (1999) argue that 'Educational practice today rarely connects training of the *mind*, seen individualistically, with the *emotions* and with the *power* relations attending both'. Unless this changes, 'current attempts to promote SEL will be apolitical, ahistorical, and sentimental, despite good faith, preventing students and teachers from obtaining balanced self-knowledge, social fairness, and intellectual tenacity and depth' (McIntosh and Style 1999: 156–7). Alternatively, **through accepting emotional literacy as having individual and group elements, pupils can be helped to understand how the nature of 'race', poverty (social class) and gender (sexism and homophobia) impinge on people's social and emotional states in order that they can come to an understanding of how society could change.** If pupils can come to understand the complexities, changing nature and overlap of the categories, then their development of independence and inclusion is more likely to be based on a continuing maturity that can accept that categories change with time. Additionally, the power relationships between these groups can be seen to be both individual and relational, and not one or the other. Through these processes, pupils may then develop emotionally to enable them to question society. We can see why government and others might wish to limit emotional literacy in schools to an individualistic notion like EQ, which indicates the importance of not individualizing and reifying emotional attributes. Similarly, we know that constant comparisons of all sorts, from one's appearance to performances in school tests, decrease self-esteem (James 1998). There are people in the government who would be opposed to the following question being raised: 'Does the constant pressure on teachers and pupils to increase academic results and the attendant trend to stream pupils contribute to a lack of self-esteem and so decrease emotional literacy?'

Respecting our Differences (Duvall 1994) does address equity issues but is not explicitly part of the emotional literacy movement. Duvall (1994) points out that the world is changing culturally and that increasingly schools contain pupils from different ethnic backgrounds. She draws attention to the importance of helping pupils gain tolerance of differences, of confronting prejudice and learning to accept diversity. This also means being able to resolve conflict. Addressing these in the classroom could support initiatives to reduce discrimination and, along with emotional literacy programmes, encourage the

---

Box 4.1 'Race', ethnic and ethnicity

It is a commonly held belief that people can be grouped into races that are biologically different. This is untrue; there are on average more genetic differences within one so-called 'race' than between different 'races' (Lewontin 1987; Cole 2005). Genetically, groups that are supposedly from different 'races' are much more similar than they are different. As a result, race is written as 'race' to remind the reader that actually there is no such thing as biological 'race'. When 'race' is used, it is used as a social category, although it is usually paraded as if it were biological. Some people may think that because of the supposed biological differences, the groups can behave differently. This is one way that racism occurs.

The terms ethnic group and ethnicity are now being used. These are groups that contain certain cultural features in common. These words have the advantage that they are clearly social categorizations and do not have a biological basis. While these terms are better, they have similar problems to the use of the word 'race'. Take, for example, Asian-British as an ethnic group. The variation within this group is wide and so the use of the term can hide the fact that the people within it will overlap greatly with other groups. Also, there is a tendency for some people to label 'Muslims' as an ethnic group when this is a religious group. This also means that, for example, white Muslims can be overlooked and only Asian Muslims focused on.

We need to categorize and have a naming system, as there are important differences between groups, despite the greater similarities. People wish to self-identify with a certain set of views and to indicate similarity with others. Also, if one did not have a categorization one would not be able to identify, track or find out the effects of interventions made in an attempt to combat racism or discriminations on the basis of ethnicity. However, one has to be aware that the ways in which people are categorized are often related to why the information is needed, and the power relationships that exist between the groups.

The term 'race' draws attention to what is a problematic area more than the term 'ethnicity', and so in this book I will generally use the term 'race'.

---

pupils to be more self-aware and reflective. They should be enabled to see the effects that sexism, racism and classism have on each other's behaviour and identity.

Children build up an account that makes sense of their family, cultural and gender experiences to see themselves as a subject with a personal meaning, but with a recognition that they are also part of others' stories. Identity emerges from interactions with others, and all interactions are pervaded with power. Since discourses are central to forging identity, the constitution of the groups will have an effect. If the sexes are together, the discourses are different to those that could take place in the single-sex setting. In co-education, it is

possible to challenge gendered spaces – for example, through raising emotional literacy in science lessons (Matthews 2003a). In collaborative group
work, it is possible for femininities and masculinities to be continually acted
out, inspected and confronted. Gender power relations can be made visible
and when the teacher makes the expectation that boys and girls will work
together cooperatively, 'then working together becomes normalised within
this classroom culture because of specific techniques used by the teacher to
help children understand and achieve such co-operation . . . How power is
exercised in constructing classroom cultures plays a very important part in
bringing about more productive gender relations in the classroom' (Allard and
Cooper 2001: 167). This enables an opening-up for inspection of gender and
power and can help dispel the gender binary while assisting the establishment
of narratives of 'self' and 'other' that broaden conceptions of 'feminine' and
'masculine'.

It is easy, but a mistake, to assume that if everyone is emotionally literate a
situation emerges where everyone gets on well and all is 'hunky-dory'. However, this is not the case, as emotional development also includes passion and
argument. It is not just about being nice and responding cooperatively. Issues
like war and racism should evoke strong feelings. Hence engagement in emotions should not be about individual progress as if it could be separated out
from the social context. Emotional literacy and empathy inherently involve
an appreciation of what sexism, racism and heterosexism can feel like, and a
concern for action, which is a matter for the whole school.

Emotional literacy and the whole school environment

Weare (2003) and Antidote (2003b, 2005) have both stressed the importance of
whole-school approaches from a practical level, while Kegan (1982) uses a
more theoretical approach. There are many similarities in the approaches.
Kegan (1982) draws attention to the way in which children need to be psychologically 'held', so that they can feel secure despite internal struggles. Antidote's
heading for this is 'safety', while Weare combines it with 'Creating Warmth,
person centeredness and involvement'. Schools are at their best when they
form a good 'holding environment'. To do so, Kegan suggests schools should
provide a *role-recognizing culture* and should acknowledge and support the
child's search for self-sufficiency; and provide opportunities to speak and be
listened to in the public life of the schools, especially during decision making.
Pupils are helped by having the opportunity for personal responsibility while
succeeding in at least one large area of schooling. Secondary schools can recognize the adolescent's struggle to emerge from embeddedness (inclusion) and
permit – and not repudiate – the changes in relationships and self-definition.
For an adolescent to form a secure sense of 'self', they need to work through

their relationships with the complementary sex and accept male and female, masculinity and femininity, as mutually interdependent. They can also explore cultural and ethnic realities and fantasies of the 'other' and how this impinges on 'self'. The search for inclusion – Weare uses the expression 'autonomy and self-reliance' – can be balanced with embeddness – Antidote refers to this as 'compassion', 'connection' and 'reflection'. Kegan argues that the school should also provide a *culture of mutuality* that acknowledges and supports the person's capacity for collaborative, self-sacrificing, idealized interpersonal relationships. Kegan argues that teachers should ask themselves if they have a *culture of self-authorship* that supports the person's exploration of self-definition (autonomy). Does it confirm the person rather than negate them? Does the school recognize him or her as a player in the public arena in which he or she can exercise personal powers? Does it allow them to have influence and assume responsibility?

Finally, Kegan asserts that the school should provide a *culture of intimacy* that enables interdependence as well as self-surrender through mutually reciprocal relationships. These include intimate associations with work and possibly significant other(s). It appears that the average age for adolescents to engage in love making is about 16 years (Kirby 2001; Wellings 2001; FPA 2003; HDA 2004). This means that up to half of pupils in secondary schools are having intimate relationships, a reason why schools adopt the Ostrich Position (Lee 1983).

These facts speak to the nature of the community as a whole, including teachers and parents, a point covered well by Antidote and Weare. The community of a school can commit to developing the person, not to encasing them in the mould of cognitive achievement. We can see how the emphasis on individualist cognitive attainment measured through exams would encourage a culture for both boys and girls to focus on themselves as individuals, rather than to move on emotionally to explore connection through social intimacy and mutual interdependence. For schools to encourage pupils to join in activities from local schemes to international ones like Oxfam, would encourage a move to a more inclusive balance.

Assessment of emotional literacy in schools

There is a need to assess emotional literacy – indeed, consciously and unconsciously teachers do it all the time. The advent of EQ tests has reinforced the individualist aspect. Some schools, especially in America, use commercially available tests. These include the EQ-i Youth Version by Bar-On. The EQ type of question is used by Faupel (2003a, 2003b), but interestingly it is combined with checklists for both teachers and parents, thus allowing different perspectives to be raised in discussion. The recommended use of the pupil checklists is in small group or individual counselling environments. The teacher's checklist is for intervention identification, since shy and quiet pupils can be overlooked. The parents' checklist can be used as part of an auditing or screening procedure, but is mainly for parents of pupils who are causing concern. The emphasis can thus be on those pupils at risk while neglecting the development of all pupils. Faupel (2003a: 27) states that:

> It is not the purpose of these checklists to label students. Since labelling can act against inclusion, it can only be justified when it leads to positive and empowering action . . . these checklists are not concerned with individual students as such but much more with classroom and school averages or distributions.

This statement reflects the real concern that many teachers have with the assessment of emotional development. These are issues that Weare (2003) covers comprehensively. Weare reports that many teachers are concerned about labelling pupils and recognize the complexity of assessing emotional states. In general, teachers recognize that a range of techniques is required, and that teachers are actually good at making informal assessments of their pupils. Indeed, it is impossible for teachers not to form opinions on the emotional and social stability of their pupils!

One main use of assessments is to evaluate innovations and to determine how to improve interventions. These are targeted either at individual pupils, or at classes or school as a group. In addition to the EQ type checklist questionnaire, other forms are being tried, including the range of approaches used by Mayer, Salovey and Caruso (Mayer *et al.* 2003). Short writing frames or 'bubbles' of thought can also be used. Weare's research using these methods indicated that children had good ideas on how to deal with their own worries. However, many teachers were concerned with how long multiple-method assessments could take and wanted checklists that were easy to administer and reliable. Weare (2003) identifies EQ type questionnaires and reports on others that are being developed to incorporate a range of assessment methods.

There are, however, a set of general issues that apply to assessment, and in particular assessment of emotional development. Emotional change is a journey that does not have set end points. Pupils, in developing emotional openness, have no fixed route, or even fixed order. It is crucial that the child is enabled to be a critical questioner who is also analytical so they can reflect on their feelings as well as how others have felt about the social interactions. It is through these processes that progress is possible, but these processes always occur in a contextualized learning context. Hence, because of the varied nature of emotional development, the teacher and pupil can be involved in constructing good practice to help the pupil, as there is no set pathway. As a result, the effective teacher will try to find ways of responding to the pupil's needs. So how is the teacher to assess if the pupil is making progress? With difficulty! But we can see that ideally the teacher, in collaboration with the pupil, would discuss what is to be assessed and have to justify the criteria used in the varied situations. In doing this, the pupil would have some ownership, within his or her own way of working, of the learning/evaluation cycle. This sense of ownership will help the pupil to engage with his or her own personal development and to see the worth of this approach in school. Furedi (2004), although arguing from the strange position that emotional literacy should not be part of the curriculum, makes some important points. He says that while the aim of helping pupils to deal positively with feelings may seem good, it raises the questions of who decides what is 'positive' in any situation. The child, parent, teacher or psychologist? 'Sometimes children have very good reasons for dealing "negatively" with emotional issues. Indeed, not expressing feelings may be an appropriate way of dealing with individual circumstances' (Furedi 2004: 19). Training a child how to feel can be very intrusive. These are valuable points to bear in mind and are precisely why pupils have to feel a sense of ownership in their own personal maturity, and that to a degree their definitions of what is happening in their lives are accepted. Assessment is more likely to be authentic with different modalities of reporting as it moves away from responding to the demands of an imposed external system of assessment control and places responsibility back on teachers' professionalism.

When assessments are focused on the individual separately from a social context, they ignore the group dynamic, as covered in Chapter 3, and conceal equity issues, prejudices and power. For these to be assessed, pupils would have to interact with others so teachers can observe how their interactions change with pupils of different sexes, sexualities, classes, and ethnic and religious backgrounds.

These are contradictions in emotional evaluation and the debate will run and run. Assessment is a thorny issue, still to be resolved, but we can see some approaches are better than others and I will return to this topic in Chapter 7.

Teacher and pupil-centred programmes for emotional literacy

Clearly there are compatibilities between aims and methods of emotional literacy. Chart 4.1 contrasts the teacher- and pupil-centred approaches, although it should be remembered that there is a substantial overlap between them, and they are not always incompatible with each other.

Even though I have concerns about the aims of the first column in Chart 4.1 I support them, as it is essential to help pupils to be in class and learning. Emotional literacy is at least in part a property of the individual, and all points in the first column are essential. The second column also reinforces

Chart 4.1. Compatibilities between aims and pedagogy of emotional literacy

Teacher-centred pedagogy Primary aims could include: to improve classroom behaviour, anti-social behaviour and school attendance through emotional literacy programmes.	Pupil-centred pedagogy Primary aim could be for emotional literacy to improve relationships within a social and political context.
The teacher–pupil interaction takes precedence over pupil–pupil interactions. Increases teacher control. Whole-class work.	Pupil–pupil interactions with dialogue vital. Cooperative group work, with relevant strategies, is at the centre of the development of emotional literacy, along with an overall teacher-led curriculum.
Pupil as individual (as want them to be 'good', attend lessons, motivated, and this requires self-control. This is a good subsidiary aim in its own right). Teacher-led/-controlled curriculum.	Pupil and identity set in self–other relationships and the political context of emotions. Emotional curriculum will include opportunities to reflect on the relationship of 'self' and 'other', as well as more individually defined aspects of emotional literacy (like self-awareness). Space for pupil input into the curriculum, especially emotional components.
Focus on individual pupils who are in need due to poor behaviour, etc.	Focus on *all* pupils maturing, with extra time available for some pupils.
Self-awareness. Self-regulation. Motivation. Empathy (defined as the property of an individual). Social skills.	Self-awareness; self-regulation; motivation important, but the main aim is to develop emotional responsiveness, which is not a given set of responses. Viewpoint of others essential for analysis and reflection. Requires an analytical critical person, and a total curriculum that will help to develop this. Ambiguity, analysis, self-awareness, all developed with others so a different perspective is provided. Emotional literacy bound up with society/relational groups and power: sex, 'race' and class. Opportunities for inner anxieties to be verbalized and worked through.

Assessment of the individual pupil. Tendency to believe that emotions can be analysed at an individual level alone and can be objectively measured.	Assessment by teacher with pupil. Pupil has some ownership of the criteria and process.
Comparisons between pupils made (e.g. through tests and gradings). Hence autonomy valued over interconnectedness.	Belief that emotions cannot be measured in an objective sense as they always have a cultural as well as an individual context. Emotional literacy has both individual and group components, as it is dependent on others. Components of emotional literacy can only be assessed in group-equity settings.
	Interconnectedness and interdependence stressed while autonomy valued.
Pupils develop emotionally to enable them to be more self-controlled and fit into society.	Pupils develop emotionally to enable them to challenge society as well as engage positively with it.
Separates emotional literacy from issues about the development of the whole child and social justice.	Integrates emotional literacy, whole-child development and social justice.

the importance of integrating social justice for a transformative education. In this sense, emotional development is individual and personal experience is key.

Clearly, efforts to achieve the above are greatly hampered when education is controlled to a large extent by centralization by government and teachers have taken away from them, or abrogate, their responsibilities for curriculum development.

Emotional literacy and academic achievement

Teachers may be concerned how the academic achievement of pupils would be affected if there were an emphasis on emotional literacy. There are good reasons why an integration of social, emotional and academic learning could lead to greater achievement. Put briefly, many of the skills necessary for good learning are also integral to social and emotional development. Schools are social places and there are social dimensions to learning. The use of language is important to learning and much learning is done through communication in collaboration with peers and teachers. Yet the abilities to communicate, listen, talk and collaborate are all key to emotional development as well. Similarly, pupils learn well in a safe, secure and caring environment where they have good relationships with their teachers and peers, yet this is precisely the type of environment that emotional literacy programmes wish to develop (Elias *et al*. 2003; Weare 2003; Antidote 2005). Greenhalgh (1994) studied how a pupil's emotional development was part of the engagement with learning. He argued that pupils, especially those with emotional and behavioural difficulties, needed to feel emotionally secure and able to handle their emotions to be able to learn most productively. Otherwise, the emotions block learning to some degree: 'Effective learning is dependent upon emotional growth. If we are to facilitate better learning ... then we need to understand better the relationship between affect and learning' (Greenhalgh 1994: 21).

Greenhaulgh, like Vygotsky (1978), draws attention to connections between our internal world of feeling, the external social world and learning. Hence, there are sound theoretical reasons for there to be a positive connection between emotional development and learning, and there is research evidence that supports this view. For example, Malecki and Elliott (2002) found a positive relationship between pupils' social and emotional skills and their academic test scores. Similarly, Wentzel (1991a, 1991b, 1993) found that factors like pupils' ability to empathize and manage their anger and impulses, were related to their grades and achievement test scores. Zsolnai (2002) also found a positive correlation between achievement and SEL factors that included dynamism, politeness and scrupulousness.

SEL programmes vary in their approaches, emphasis and content. Haynes *et al*. (2003) looked at improving mathematics and science grades, while Zins *et al*. (2004) assessed different programmes and found evidence that they lead to greater achievement:

> 83% of such programs [that promoted the integration of social and emotional learning with academic curricula] produced academic gains. In addition, 12% of the programs that did not specifically target academic performance documented an impact on academic achievement.
>
> (Zins *et al*. 2004: 14)

Other research has studied how a wide range of social and emotional factors link with academic achievement. For example, the Search Institute researched achievement and developmental assets – defined to include factors such as social competences, commitment to positive values and identity, as well as family support and community links (Scales and Roehlkepartain 2003). It was concluded that schools that sought to promote such assets showed an increase in grade scores that were probably greater than traditional school strategies for boosting achievement. Similarly, WestEd (Hanson and Austin 2002), in a large-scale Californian study, found a relationship between assets and academic performance.

Much of the research indicates positive links between SEL and achievement, but because of the complex factors involved it is difficult for definitive research to be completed. As Weare explains:

> The evidence is that holistic approaches to the development of emotional literacy are more effective, but they are a nightmare to evaluate, and comparing the evaluations of different holistic interventions is even more difficult. Holistic approaches by definition look at a vast number of aspects of the situation: in the case of schools this can include the organisation, its climate, its ethos and all its personnel, relations with parents, and with the community . . . If we look across a range of interventions we find a distinct lack of any standardised measures or agreed indicators to assess all of this. What we have is a plethora of programmes and approaches, all with slightly different but overlapping goals, a vast array of tools for assessing individuals' attitudes, beliefs, behaviours, various checklists and inventories to assess a wide range of features of organisations, and almost as many ways of assessing the impact of interventions as there are interventions.
>
> (Weare 2003: 12)

Weare concludes that there is much evidence to show that emotional literacy interventions have a beneficial effect in many areas. People interested in academic achievement and emotional literacy could keep their knowledge up-to-date through the Collaborative for Academic, Social and Emotional Learning, which has a very good website with a section devoted to the research evidence on the connection between these areas (Casel 2005), while the Centre for Social and Educational Education (CSEE 2005) lists research publications under a wide range of headings.

Why have emotional literacy in schools?

Earlier I quoted Steiner (1997: 11): 'To be emotionally literate is to be able to handle emotions in a way that improves your personal power and improves the quality of life around you. Emotional literacy improves relationships, creates loving possibilities between people, makes co-operative work possible, and facilitates the feeling of community'. This reflects that *emotional literacy in schools can be justified for and in itself*. It ought not primarily be to improve behaviour, attendance, academic achievement or reduce conflicts. Hopefully it will do all of these, but in making these the aims it can distort what and how it is done. Developing emotional literacy is important for all pupils, and if, for example, improving behaviour is targeted, it makes it more probable that only some pupils will be focused on. It is likely to make a curriculum that is more teacher-centred and has the potential to increase control and surveillance over pupils. While teachers cannot be psychotherapists, schools can engender an atmosphere where pupils are able to engage in helpful activities. However, this is less likely in a formal teacher-led situation and much more likely in informal, pupil-centred schools and classrooms. However, this approach must involve helping *all* pupils to mature emotionally, not focus primarily on those who have emotional and behavioural difficulties (although of course they will always require special help). All pupils need help in the early years and adolescent years.

Emotional literacy can be an essential area in its own right and returns to an aim of care – for both pupils and teachers – that can be a central feature of schools. Any definition of emotional literacy, and I will define it in the last chapter, should include the raising of issues of discrimination so that the pupils can understand the negative impact of stereotypes, while accepting the possibility of celebrating difference. However, to do this, one has to be non-judgemental.

There are no easy answers for how to introduce emotional literacy programmes, just a complex of issues. Indeed, a central feature of emotional literacy is to be able to deal with ambiguity and contradiction. I would like to stress at this point how much I support the introduction of schemes such as SEAL (DfES 2005) but also to raise critical questions in order to see how they may be improved. The next chapter looks deeper into issues of individuals, groups and power.

5 Groups and power

In the first four chapters, I have argued that the development of pupils' emotional literacy should be a central part of education, and that dialogue between pupils is a vital classroom strategy. This chapter will begin by considering more evidence that equity can be approached through group work and dialogue before raising issues about power between individuals and groups. Finally, I will consider the implications for education.

Allport's contact hypothesis

There is research that indicates that direct communication between people can improve their attitudes to each other, and so could contribute to social justice. In this section, I focus on Allport's contact hypothesis (Allport 1979), which concerns the conditions for reducing prejudice among people. His original work concerned racial rather than gender prejudice but can be applied to both. Allport (1979) argued that for groups to come together to reduce prejudice and discrimination, the following conditions are required:

1   The groups meet in a situation where they are aware that the authorities support a reduction in prejudice.
2   When the groups meet they are given equal status (in the tasks required).
3   The groups must participate with each other with cooperative independence.
4   The contact of the individuals holds the potential for friendships.

In addition to these four criteria, Cook (1985) has suggested that when the groups work together the activities must include aspects that will challenge stereotypes. So, for example, if boys and girls do a practical together in a science lesson, but the boys take the notes and the girls do the majority of the hands-on work, it may counter stereotypes.

If boys and girls were to meet and work where all five of the above conditions were satisfied, say in a collaborative learning setting, they could see that the other sex behaved and acted in ways that countered the stereotypical views they have of them. This can, according to dissonance theory, lead to a change in behaviour and attitudes (Festinger 1962, 1964). Dissonance theory says you work in such a way that you reduce internal conflict. According to Festinger, if a person holds two contradictory psychological beliefs, she will wish to decrease the anxiety produced. Because the experience of dissonance is unpleasant, the person will usually find a way to make them more consonant with each other. One of the applications of dissonance theory is called *induced (or forced) compliance*, where people are placed in a situation where they are likely to have to behave in some ways that go against their attitudes (Perlman and Cozby 2000). They may then, in order to reduce their dissonance, change their attitudes. Dissonance theorists argued that de-segregation in America was a valid way of challenging stereotypes and changing behaviour at a time when accepted wisdom said the reverse – namely, that attitudes had to be changed before bringing people together. Indeed, the *Jigsaw Classroom*, which was pioneering work on tackling racism, was based on dissonance theory (Aronson *et al.* 1978; Aronson and Yates 1983; Aronson 1997). In Allport's work, individuals have to work together in positive social interactions with people about whom they may hold negative or stereotypical views. Recent research using Allport's hypothesis and dissonance theory has shown that they can be used to reduce prejudice in terms of racism and sexism (Oskamp 2000; Sharma 2000; Stangor 2000). One of the strengths of dissonance theory is that it offers a model for tackling many forms of prejudice and discrimination, especially since these can be interactive (e.g. gender and 'race') (Sidanius and Veniegas 2000). Scarberry *et al.* (1997) found that greater changes were forthcoming if the person was seen as a representative of a group rather than just an individual. It is worth reiterating that intergroup contact requires a structure and that cooperative group learning is an important setting for tackling stereotyping (Aronson *et al.* 1978; Johnson and Johnson 2000). Indeed, Oskamp (2000) lists cooperative learning as one of the six accepted techniques for reducing discrimination. Clearly, this indicates that co-education could have an important role in increasing equity.

Hence, Allport's hypothesis and dissonance theory provide support for multi-racial, co-education schools provided they involve thought-through strategies for the classroom.

Power

The implications of power have not been raised directly in Allport's contact hypothesis and in this section I will look at how power can impact on personal and group communications. Human interactions are pervaded with power in complex ways. We may say that a man has more power than a woman, but the power is fluid in different contexts. The same is also true when discussing ethnicity. Bound up with power are ideas of identity and how identity incorporates difference. There are alternative ways of explaining differentiation of power and roles within both gender and ethnicity. Some writers use what they see as biological differences to give reasons for unequal power relationships (Dawkins 1976; Wilson 1978; Bly 1990; Hoff Sommers 1996; Tooley 2002). The argument is often that men and women have different genes that have fitted them for different roles. These different roles are invariably associated with justifying power differentials. Head (1999: 10) covers the ground of these arguments well and shows that they are false, while indicating that 'We may wish to challenge the ideas of biological *causes* of behaviour, but that does not deny biological *influences*'.

Role theory has been a common way of explaining gender and ethnic differences. This derives, in part, from the work of Erikson (1950, 1985), who thought that identity is influenced by the meanings one makes of life's conflicts and friendships. One's interactions are dependent on community, its history and mythologies (Head 1997). Hence, children can grow up accepting as true certain sex-roles and a set of beliefs about their and others' cultures. Skelton (2001) provides evidence that feminists saw education as a way of changing sex-power inequalities through showing children how they could act differently to the societal script of being masculine or feminine. There are many masculinities and femininities that boys and girls can draw on. Boys and girls are able to draw on multiple and contradictory subject positions that do not conform to any simple analysis, and are constantly undergoing interpretation and re-interpretation of their experiences and interactions. The conscious and unconscious emotions experienced matter as much as what the boys and girls know cognitively when they interact (Haywood and Mac an Ghaill 1995).

Linking power and individuals: Dalal

Psychologists such as Allport have put forward theories that concentrate on the individual rather than being concerned centrally with political issues. So, for example, psychologists can say that racism is due to internal psychological difficulties experienced in childhood. Drawing on the work of Foulkes (1948,

1990) and Elias (1978, 1991, 1994), Dalal (1998, 2002) argues that our internal psyche is a function of the group (family and society) into which we are born. Further, that the structures of society are reflected in the structure of the psyche. Dalal argues that power, and the wish to preserve power, is the cause of people *generating* difference between groups. I will summarize Dalal's argument as it has much to contribute to our understanding of personal and group interactions, and their connection with power. Dalal (2002) is concerned with racism, which is one of the pathologies we need to tackle to move towards a healthy society.

Dalal considers the work of Foulkes, who argues that an individual only exists in a social setting:

> Everybody wants to belong, so the family, group and community are central to the formulation of the individual. The mechanism of belonging is communication. Foulkes is continually inviting us to focus on interpersonal space, rather than the internals of persons. He is putting forward the idea that things only exist as emergent processes, and that they have no independent existence of and by themselves.
>
> (Dalal 2002: 112)

Foulkes (1990) argues that what we call the internal processes of the individual are actually the individual responding to social pressures. Hence the individual and society are intimately connected and it does not make sense to see the two as separate.

However, we live in a complex world in which we can only make sense of all the visual, kinaesthetic, cognitive and spiritual information through categorization. We have to categorize in order to make sense of the world. Additionally, categories are often dependent upon one another, so, for example, the term 'pond' only exists if one also understands 'land'. In many cases, the categories are not binary, but rely on multiple understandings, for example to understand 'liquid' also requires 'solid' and 'gas' to be understood.

To make clear the importance of category forming (a major aspect being of 'self' and 'other'; 'us' and 'them'), I will go over Dalal's (2002: 176–7) example of red and brown shoes. In what follows, 'conscious' and 'unconscious' are used to illustrate the principles of psychological processes, and are not being used with their specific psychological meaning. When we talk about red and brown shoes, we are emphasizing similarity over difference [what Matte-Blanco (1988) calls *symmetric logic*, which makes things appear the same rather than different]. Our acceptance of 'red' shoes makes conscious 'red' and unconscious whether they are men's or women's, stiletto or flat, brogues or platform. Other complexities are ignored, such as if a 'trainer' is a shoe, or when 'red' becomes 'brown'. Dalal argues that all identity formation is based on this sort of process. Our identity is based on stressing similarity (white/female/Spanish) rather than difference.

We form a view of 'us' and 'them', of 'self' and 'other', through splitting, repression and projection. However, to form this view of 'other', we have to suppress the similarities between 'us' and 'them' that exist and relocate the similarities into our unconscious. This is called *asymmetric logic*, where difference is stressed by denying similarity (as if red shoes had little in common with brown shoes). Hence our identity is under psychological/social strain because denial leads to anxiety, and we cannot get rid of our anxieties, they are never destroyed, only relocated into the unconscious.

> If we replaced the language of the instincts with notions of similarity and difference, then we would be able to say that these social structures are threatened from within by 'asymmetry and difference' and from without by 'symmetry and similarity'.
>
> (Dalal 2002: 179)

Consequently, our identity, which is formed in relation to the 'other', is threatened by the unconscious bursting out. The following example should make this clearer. People can grow up in a society where there are strong strictures on sexual activity and so suppress their sexual desires into their unconscious. This is an unwanted part that is split off and projected onto 'others'. This can be a racial 'other' and is why, as Dalal points out, that racism is often also infused with a view of the 'them' being sexually overactive or good in bed. Our racial sense of security comes from symmetric logic (the similarity of the 'whites' being faithful and trustworthy is stressed, and the variation of sexual voraciousness within the group 'white' denied). It also comes from asymmetric logic ('they' are different to 'us', which suppresses the similarities of the range of sexual activity and faithlessness within each group). Consequently, a racist identity can be threatened from *without* – interpersonally – by meeting people from a different 'race' and being able to psychologically accept that they are sexually similar, and from *within* through recognizing psychologically that the two groups have similarities. The sexualized unconscious also can emerge because there is part of us that recognizes that sexual uninhibitedness and passion also belongs to us, and we want to explore it. So envy for what we have lost (relocated to the unconscious) resides somewhere. Hence racism is not due only to hate, but also to envy. This develops the point made in Chapter 2, that it can be argued that since we 'see' part of us projected into the other, it is similarity that is interpreted as difference that leads to hate (Moore 2005). Aggression towards others, therefore, may arise because difference is focused on, which is really 'an experience of conflict and aggression within the "self" ' (Samuels 2005: 5–7).

Because any group – say 'women' or 'Asian' – is a construct, we have to do psychological work to maintain any suppressions, and this is why we can be so violent outwards rather than focus inwards so as to not recognize parts of our self that we have suppressed. The less we are able to accept ambiguity, the more we could feel that our 'self' would unravel if we recognized those parts of ourselves. Therefore, a man can believe that all women are bad drivers, just one good woman driver could possibly undo his sense of 'maleness' and 'femaleness', and so any good female drivers become an 'exception to the rule' (or the exception that proves the rule!). The same processes are in operation when a pupil in class who makes a racist statement realizes his friend is from the ethnic group, and so says, 'Not you of course, you're one of us'. Similarly, a woman can say that 'all men are potential rapists' to categorize 'maleness' as violent and 'femaleness' as non-violent.

Dalal (2002) points out that this reverses our normal explanation of why difference (racial) exists. The commonly accepted explanation is that we project into the different racialized group. Dalal argues that projection is a way of *generating* difference. 'In other words, rather than the "other" being used as a container to carry evacuated aspects of the "us", what is being said is that the impression of "otherness" is *created* by the projection of these elements' (p. 54). However, even as we project aggression, our libido[1] wishes to extend and include, so internally love is undermining the process, and so remarkable amounts of anxiety are generated.

> This formulation goes some way to explaining the phenomenon in which the racialised object is simultaneously sexualised as well as hated. It also sheds light on the mythology that says that 'they' are the oversexed ones, and it is 'they' who want to have sex with 'us'. The theory suggests that this imputation of sexuality in the 'them' is a projection of something (libido) that belongs to the 'us'.
>
> (Dalal 2002: 54)

This can also be seen as part of the explanation of why the forbidden is also often desired/erotic and people are drawn to transgressive acts.

Evidence of links between anxieties over difference can be found in studies on authoritarianism. It can be argued that there is a link between a person's beliefs – in part generated through the psychic work to maintain symmetric and asymmetric logic – and power. To take an extreme example, psychological studies have shown that:

> The *Authoritarian* personality is . . . said to arise out of extreme parental rejection or domination in childhood, leading to repressed hostility. This hostility finds expression in adult life in attacks on minority groups, as in anti-Semitism. The authoritarian personality

pattern includes highly conventional behaviour, superstition, destructiveness and cynicism, desire for power, and concern over sex.
(Hilgard 1953: 480)

Clearly, there is a continuum of personality types, with complexities and contradictions within them. Adorno *et al.* (1982) and Kreml (1977) have undertaken studies on personality and attitudes. They have found that, as a general conclusion, authoritarian individuals are often concerned with categorizing people into two groups, the weak and the strong. Authoritarians also tend to believe in 'natural' dominances of the 'strong over the weak, smart over the dull, the able over the incapable' (Kreml 1977: 52). Contact with those perceived as powerless can lead authoritarians to the wish to dominate or humiliate them. When combined with a generalized hostility towards people who are different, it is easy to see that racism and sexism (and other -isms) are likely to be common outcomes. Similarly, women are often seen as either 'good' or 'bad' (Adorno *et al.* 1982: 397). There can be an anxiety over sex, which can make relationships with the other sex pervaded with rigidity. In terms of broader relationships, Adorno *et al.* (1982: 415) found that those people with authoritarian attitudes could form friendships based on what they could get from people, rather than on making relationships based on mutuality. Hence, for the authoritarian personality, many forms of relationships tend to be based on emotional distance, because of accepted rigid differences, rather than grappling with the complexities and ambiguities of close emotional relationships. Clearly, for such discriminations to be justified, people would have to fit into the categories believed in, like smart and dull, so it is no surprise that people with authoritarian attitudes tend to rigidity and intolerance of ambiguity. As a result, they can believe in power based on inequality.

Kreml (1977) found that the type of institutionalization of power people wanted was related to personality type and to general political categories. Thus there can be a relationship between personality and a belief in how people should be controlled by others. Once the rationalizations enter the unconscious at the meta-mythical level, control and power based on inequality are unquestioned. The basis for the inequality can be based on 'race', sex, class, academic ability, sexuality or any other perceived difference. Adorno *et al.* found that people can have broad groupings in their thinking, and that this has a connection with feeling unloved. Both of these indicate in their different ways that the issues of 'race', sex and class are intermingled, albeit from different perspectives. One linking theme is that of the need for certainty as opposed to acceptance of ambiguity. The extent to which we respond negatively with aggression depends in part upon our ability to deal with ambiguity; the more we can accept ambiguity, the less likely we are to be prone to such strong reactions. Similarly, the more we can accept our own aggression, the more able we are to deal with, and not displace, it. One aspect of being able to deal with aggression towards groups is to be open to uncertainty and that social categories change. If people can psychologically accept that a category like 'Indian' or 'asylum seeker' is not closed, and that with more information and experiences their view of that category may change, then they are holding a 'moratorium' on it and so do not undergo foreclosure (Head 1997). Foreclosure is when a person psychologically seizes on a 'solution' or 'view' and no longer scrutinizes it. If they foreclose, they are not open to exploration of the ideas. Hence pupils should be encouraged to hold open views.

It is worth stressing at this point that in human relationships we have to categorize. One reason is simply to deal with the complexity of nature and relationships. Another is that we need to feel part of a community, to be wanted and valued by others. Nitsun (1998), from a more Freudian perspective, argues that it is a fear of hunger, and a scarcity of love and resources, that drives us to categorize. He also says that much of our aggression – and self-destructiveness – can be due to an absence rather than the presence of an identified enemy (which in Elias's and Dalal's terms, we create through projection).

Individuals, groups and power

Elias (1978) draws together the individual psyche (psychology) with relationships between people (sociology) with history. Elias argues not only that the psyche is generated in a social situation, but also that the historical context in which people are born has an effect on the processes involved. Also, that all interactions are infused with power. Here are two examples that Elias (1994) uses to establish the links. As the 'might = right' system in medieval Europe gradually changed to a less violent one, the powerful used different means to generate the 'us' (with power) and the 'them'. One was the development of a language (King's English in Britain) that would differentiate between social classes. The development of this dialect was not to do with increasing communication, but rather to decrease it and to mark out a power difference as only one group had access to it. Another example is the use of cutlery and the etiquette. In medieval times, people used their fingers to eat from communal bowls. This practice changed and cutlery was introduced, with rules about how it should be used. According to Elias, this had little to do with hygiene. What it did was to distinguish the powerful from the poor, as the poor could not afford the cutlery and so were much less likely to learn the etiquette. Difference was generated to maintain power. Hence Elias establishes a link between power, history and group separation. Now we need to see how these can be linked to the psyche.

Dalal provides as an example of people growing up today in Western society. For them, it is common for the word 'rose' to signify a flower. This is at the level of linguistics. However, there is also a mythical level, namely that the 'rose' is often imbued with romance and passion. For the person growing up and being part of a group, these two levels of meanings can enter the psyche. Dalal, building on Elias's work, uses this analogy to show how the terms 'white' and 'black' have evolved historically to enter our psyche. Dalal traces how, starting with the bible, 'black' was used to signify dirt, death, evil and the emotions of depression, sorrow and anger. Similarly, 'white' became was used to signify moral purity, cleanliness and honesty, while being associated with the emotions of endearment. The terms 'black' and 'white' did not initially refer to skin colour, but became so and, at a conscious level, linked with racism. 'Black' and 'white', then, have a meta-mythical level and enter the unconscious, and racism entered the psyche. The intrapersonal and interpersonal are linked (Vygotsky 1978).

Once the process of meta-level meanings is established, and people are born into a family, community or society that has it embedded into the unconscious, it can become seen as 'natural' and people argue that racism – and sexism – is just part of the natural order of things (Dawkins 1976; Barash 1978; Wilson 1978; Barker 1982; Sayers 1982; Kitcher 1985). In contrast, rather than being seen as natural, the differences between groups, which are created through projection and symmetric and asymmetric logic, are generated to ensure power differences.

> difference is not the cause of hatred, rather, particular differences are called forth by the vicissitudes of power relations in order to organise hatreds (and other emotions) in order to achieve particular ends. These mechanisms work by lending the differences and the required hatreds an air of naturalness and so legitimates them. One such difference is that of race, which because of its fragility relies on the notion of colour. And finally, it is shown that the structures of society are reflected in the structures of the psyche, and if the first is colour coded, then so will the second.
>
> (Dalal 2002: 7)

So, according to Dalal, racism can enter the psyche and be used, consciously and unconsciously, to 'justify' certain ways of interacting with people and expressing power. Elias argues everyone exists within a society and so is connected in a web of power (Elias uses the term 'figuration') where each person is connected, like each strand in a spider's web, and where each person affects the other, as they are interdependent. Power is embedded in every social relationship. Elias is proposing that the emotions of aversion and attraction that build into behaviours have been *socially* generated for socio-political reasons. This means that emotions are relational because they are always about something, but are not just an individual response. They are a product of a socio-political setting. A football match provides an illustration. Each team is interdependent with the other team, although they do not have the same power (to win). Similarly, within each team, individuals are all interrelating, but they do not have the same power (skill and influence). Each time a person moves or passes the ball, he or she affects all the individuals in both teams. They bring power to bear because they are interdependent, and at the same time constrain the others as each move affects what everyone else can do.

At this point, a brief recap of the main points is worthwhile. We categorize because we have to, and desire to be part of a community, need to feel wanted, and to preserve or gain power. Aspects of these categorizations can lead to defining 'others' in negative ways, leading to discrimination. An acceptance of ambiguity and contingency can help counter negative categorizations. This gives us an understanding to reflect on the educational setting so we can consider ways of uncovering unconscious stereotypes and flesh out key features of general classroom practice that would help counter prejudice.

Education and symmetric logic

Equity involves being able to appreciate the common humanity in everyone, while celebrating difference. However, both teachers and researchers can focus on difference without celebrating it, or placing it within a common humanity. I will now carry my argument through the use of an example using gender and aggression, although the principles derived will apply to 'race' and class as well. I will first show how some procedures might help explore similarity and difference, and then show the additional complexities of relational groups and why this matters on changing power differentials.

Exploring similarity and difference

Suppose some people said that they want to research how good female drivers are. They could do this research and come to a set of conclusions. One conclusion could be that women are poor at parking cars. In formulating a piece of research in this way strikes me as problematic because it focuses only on one sex. The conclusion that female drivers find it difficult to park can easily become: female driver can't park; and this then becomes a characteristic of femininity. That is, asymmetric logic and difference have been focused on and there is no explicit mechanism to check a person's acceptance of stereotypes, prejudices or cultural and psychic beliefs. Even if female drivers do find it difficult to park, this tells us little about women drivers as the focus on one sex only means you cannot tell if poor parking is an attribute of one sex, or humanity in general. You can only tell this is if both men and women drivers are studied. Men may find it difficult to park as well, and so this is a characteristic of humanity, even if one sex finds it easier to park than the other. Additionally, the variation *within* each sex would very probably be much greater than any average difference, and there could be a diversity of ways of parking. Hence, through a consideration of similarities and differences across and within sex, it would become clear that the overlap and variation would help prevent any simplistic categorization of 'feminine = can't park'. Ambiguity and indistinctness over categorizations would surface. That is, both symmetric and asymmetric logic could be used to check conscious and unconscious beliefs. The first principle I want to draw from this example is that we need to study both sexes at the same time; otherwise, conclusions are likely to promote discriminations. Second, those comparisons of variations should help ambiguities to be brought to the surface. Further, suppose that the research report spent 90 per cent of the time on why women weren't good drivers. I think one would conclude that the report was biased. What percentage would be acceptable if one were to think it wasn't biased? I leave it to the reader to decide. The educational situation is more complex than driving. To be able to park is something that can be simply described. Yet for many aspects of human behaviour, the lack or presence of one attribute is then subscribed (partly through projection) to the 'other' – for example, 'girls cry' implies 'boys don't'. That is, the aspect can be relational, which adds a further complexity I will return to at the end of this chapter.

The focus on one sex only occurs when, for example, only masculinity is studied in schools, or it is studied without a similar focus on girls. This focus on one sex is problematic, because as illustrated above it can increase the likelihood that aspects of boys' behaviour will be taken to be part of masculinity when in fact they are a feature of humanity. Researching just boys makes it more likely that, say, their aggression will be focused on and reported in ways that reinforce the stereotype of aggressive males and, by implication, passive females. As many commentators have found, the overlap between the sexes in all aspects of human behaviour is much greater than any average difference (Nicholson 1984; Epstein 1988; Kirsta 1994; Lewis 1998; Gaine and George 1999; MacGeorge *et al.* 2004). Now I take it as axiomatic that boys and girls have similar potential for aggression, otherwise we have to resort to essentialist explanations of behaviour. However, aspects of community are entered into the psyche, and so the way that this aggression is acted out can be different. There is evidence to show that women are as aggressive as men, but they tend to turn it inward rather than outward (Miller 1987, 1990; Kirsta 1994). For this reason, it is more visible in men, but this is not to say that it isn't present in women. Therefore, it becomes important to review aggression as a feature of humanity (symmetric logic), which may be expressed in different ways (asymmetric logic). Through doing this, both similarity and difference can be expressed.

The statement 'boys are aggressive' (and by implication this is part of masculinity) could become 'boys and girls are aggressive, but in boys it is more overt and easy to see, and in girls it is expressed in more psychological ways and turned inwards more'. This alerts teachers to look at aggression in all its forms. The friendships girls have with other girls are often difficult relationships that involve aggression and feelings of being rejected (Hey 1997; George and Browne 2000). George's (2004) research on girls' friendships shows how complex girls' relationships are, including aggressive elements. When other authors do not discuss the latter aspects of female–female relationships, it raises the possibility that there could be unconscious myth-supporting psychic work going on. Also, boys' (and girls') aggressiveness can be positive. They can also be very similar, especially when the context is similar – this struck me when the captain of the Charlton women's football team was interviewed after losing to Arsenal in the 2004 Cup Final. She said, in effect, they lost because the Charlton defence had not 'made their presence felt' on the main Arsenal striker.

To take fully into account aspects of many human behaviours across ethnicity, sex and class, one would have to explore and question interrelationships, and not try to extract just one. Hence in the classroom or in research, all of the complexities listed in Table 5.1 could be considered.

A consideration and comparison between the results both horizontally and vertically enable similarity and difference to be explored. If any boxes are left out, then difference is likely to be accentuated. Further, exploration of the variation within any box, in comparison with variation within another, will show an overlap and help make any tight distinct categorization less likely. Fluidity and uncertainty in categorization, and as a result less stereotyping, could be an outcome. Therefore, it seems to me, much can be gained from inspecting the male/female dichotomies around all areas that support gender differences. However, those aspects that reveal differences (e.g. what girls think of boys) should be considered alongside questions to reveal similarities (e.g. what girls think of girls). Then it is possible to challenge symmetric/

Table 5.1 Elements to explore gender similarity and difference

Male–male Consider how boys interact and think about their relationships with the same sex, and how they display their attributes (like aggression or creativity)	**Female–female** Consider how girls interact and think about their relationships with the same sex, and how they display their attributes (like aggression or creativity)
Male–female Consider how boys interact/display and think about their relationships/attributes with girls	**Female–male** Consider how girls interact/display and think about their relationships/ attributes with boys

asymmetric logic and so help teachers and researchers inspect their psychic and power assumptions: A male researcher can project his passivity onto females, and female researchers their aggression onto males. Nothing can stop projections taking place, and we are all prejudiced, but through considering similarities and difference *and considering how any faculty in one sex manifests itself in the other*, we are more likely to reduce the effect of them.

Power differentials and aggression

To change power differentials not only similarity and difference need to be explored, but also the relationship between them in order to make it more probable that conscious and unconscious beliefs will be made known. It is problematic if as teachers we idealize females for being 'passive' and 'compli-ant', as it does not help boys/men acknowledge their passivity, and girls/ women acknowledge their aggression. This also underplays the intricacy and contradictions of gender relations, which are essential to make best use of any analysis of gender issues. There is a great deal of ambiguity in gender relation-ships, which has to be uncovered to challenge power relationships. Samuels (2001: 41) says: 'We know, too, that men are scared of women. Never the mind the fear of "the feminine", what scares men is *women*. How can a man be said to be powerful if he is scared of women?'

To some extent, this is a rhetorical question to make a point. The point is that both men and women are ambivalent towards each other. In psycho-logical terms, ambivalence is defined as being able to hold feelings of love and hate at the same time, and psychologically it is a sign of maturity. While loving their children, which parent hasn't also felt like strangling them at some point! The ability to recognize and live with ambivalence is an aspect of becoming emotionally literate and it is not helped by denial of the complex-ities of gender, sexualities and relationships. Rather than facing up to ambigu-ity, we can reinforce gender rigidity by projecting parts of ourselves onto the other sex. Females can project their aggression onto males so making aggres-sion a more 'certain' masculine trait, rather than accepting it can belong to femininities as well as masculinities – and vice versa with males projecting passivity onto females. To a degree, some books link boys' violence and aggres-siveness with power. But this is a problematic link that at a mythic psychic level helps maintain male power. We know that the strongest and most aggres-sive men do *not* control society (if they did, then boxers and weightlifters would be near the top of the pile). The ability to be in control in society is dependent on many things. In most countries, wealth and the family you were born into are important. This is not to deny that the threat of violence is a tool to obtain one's way and silence opposition and in certain social situ-ations may be the main one. But it is usually only one aspect of control. How-ever, the acceptance of the equation 'violence = control' makes it easier to accept male control, as males are seen to be more aggressive. The more so if women's aggression remains hidden. This is the point that Kirsta (1994: 381) makes, in her study of female aggression and violence, when she states:

> It [female aggression] signals the approach of a less inequitable, unjust world in which the subordination of women was taken for granted, where women at last are becoming equipped to overcome male domination and aggression. We might do worst than accept the aggressive female as the most powerful symbol of women's liberation.

If it is accepted that girls are aggressive (even if in different ways to boys), then aggression will be less of a valid psychological reason for boys to be more powerful than girls. Similarly, more research into boys' 'passivity' and how it emerges or is hidden is required. I do not believe that boys are less passive than girls – or we are back to essentialist arguments – but would speculate that the reason boys appear less passive is a mixture of their passiveness not being 'seen' and it appearing in different ways. I would speculate that since passiveness can be associated with not engaging the emotions, that it is possible that the passiveness is expressed in some boys by emotional distance. Hence it is unrecognized as passiveness, but this is just speculation.

Changing power relationships are helped if the complexities of relationships, and the way psychic meanings help support them, are uncovered. We have to find ways of challenging our assumptions, prejudices and projections. One way of undermining power is to inspect the way that traits surface in different sexes through looking at similarity and difference together. This means finding ways to make the attributes or qualities visible, even when they are hidden, or take a different form that is hidden under assumptions and projections. The same principles, that the complexity of interactions needs to be inspected, apply not only to gender but also to ethnicity and class. I have focused on aggression because the issues are clear, but the same principles, of seeing different constructions of any attribute, apply in most areas of human life. Certain pedagogic practices can help traits and assumptions to be made visible during pupil interactions, and it is to this I now turn.

Classroom practices and equity

A common approach to equity in schools is to give pupils materials for raising and discussing issues around 'race', sex or class explicitly. The implications of this chapter, along with those on emotional literacy, are that equity can be enhanced through certain classroom processes, which would contribute to the psychodynamic development of pupils to enable them to accept and celebrate difference without feeling threatened. The principle is that the anxieties the students experience through being in the presence of members of the other sex or 'race' can be confronted face-to-face, but only if the possibility is seized. The issue is about giving people the opportunity to see what anxieties they are dumping in the 'other'. If that doesn't happen, then it doesn't make that much difference whether the other 'race' or sex is present or absent. The following strategies would *permeate all lessons*. The processes would, to varying degrees, include group work with Allport's and Cook's criteria, namely:

1 The groups meet in a situation where they are aware that the teachers support a reduction in prejudice.
2 When the pupils meet they are given equal status (in the tasks required).
3 The pupils must participate with each other with cooperative independence.
4 The contact between the pupils holds the potential for friendships.
5 The activities must include aspects that will challenge stereotypes.

To these I would also add that it is essential to have strategies that enable pupils to verbalize and analyse what happened during the group's interactions. I will cover one of these strategies in detail in Chapter 6. As well as these aspects, classroom practice should enable pupils to:

- collaborate through dialogue, with mutuality, negotiation of conflict and enjoyment of difference;
- empathize with one another;
- examine the variation of behaviours and attitudes within each sex, and then see how much they overlap;
- realize that behaviours and attitudes are not distinctly different between the sexes – or 'races', social classes or cultural beliefs;
- deal with uncertainty and ambiguity;
- celebrate difference while recognizing communality;
- be open to the fact that social categories change, and accept the ambiguity and uncertainty without foreclosure;
- make explicit power differences and exchanges in their group work and relate these to society.

Clearly, multi-ethnic co-educational comprehensive schools would be ideal places for promoting such equality. However, it would still be possible to make a significant contribution to challenging discrimination and stereotyping in all forms of schooling provided that classroom experiences were designed to promote specific parts of emotional literacy. The purpose of the pupil–pupil and pupil–teacher interactions is to enable pupils to become tolerant. However, to the list above can be added aspects developed in other chapters. For example, in Chapter 1, this would include *learning-in-relationship*, and that education should be concerned with developing *integrated* and *coherent* pupils who are emotional and cognitively able to contribute to a changing society. Chapter 2 on social justice raised the importance of developing sound ideas of 'self' and 'other', which combines with the need to develop an emotional responsiveness. I would emphasize the point again, that the whole-school approach that eschews the fetish with difference in cognitive performance is more likely to contribute to equity and social justice. The latter is more likely to be propagated in schools that have a concern for all facets of development, and that promote social cohesion and focus on the communality of all, irrespective of 'race', sex or class. As Chapters 3 and 4 indicated, pupil dialogue that promotes an individual and group emotional literacy based on relationships with mutuality, negotiation of conflict and appreciation of difference, would be a promising classroom strategy.

Complexities of relational groups

Further complexities emerge when one wants to effect changes in equity issues because of the interdependence of behaviours. This is a theme to which I will return, but to give one small example, Skelton (2001: 172) says that 'laddish' boys are popular. Clearly, if girls admire and like 'laddish boys', this is a big disincentive for boys to change their behaviour! Over the past few years I have been asking primary and secondary teachers what type of boys it is that girls are attracted to. I have used the following question sheet with about 40 primary and secondary teachers:

Girls: and the boys they are attracted to

Imagine a class of boys/girls you have taught in a school. In very broad terms the boys can be seen as having traditional attitudes through to very modern; the emerging non-macho or 'new man'. On average, and this can only be very rough, which type of boys are the girls most attractive to/who the girls would go out with/are the most popular? Here is a chart of this continuum: Please draw a line that indicates the range you would guess at.

Name: Sex: Age range of pupils taught:

Boys with macho/ traditional attitudes			Boys with 'new man' attitudes

---

In general, teachers debated their answers with me after drawing in their line answer. The discussions have brought out the complexities of desire, and that there is no simple answer. However, despite this, there is general agreement with Skelton's findings and most teachers, both male and female, put their line as:

Boys with macho/ traditional attitudes			Boys with 'new man' attitudes
■■■■■■■■■■			

No teachers said that the girls were attracted to, or found the most popular, the more non-macho boys. To elaborate on this result, I asked some secondary-aged girls what they meant by 'macho' to check its meaning to them, and also what type of boys were found attractive. Again, there were a variety of answers, but nearly all conformed to the stereotype. One perceptive girl of 15 years answered that the boys most girls wanted to go out with were those that were most popular with boys as well. She also said that these boys tended to be emotionally distant. After a bit more discussion another relevant point emerged, that boys who talked about their emotions were 'gay'. This supports the first finding that girls find macho boys attractive.

My point is that tackling boys for being macho and trying to get them to change in isolation to girls is unlikely to have much effect. All the time girls are fond of macho boys, and machoness is valued by boys, boys have a disincentive to change. Again, the lived-out masculinities and femininities are mutually interdependent and both will have to change together. Each has to face up to their anxieties. Therefore, there is a need for boys and girls to work together with a sense of agency. The setting in which they work should also raise questions about sexual identity and so enable them to form a reflective 'self'.

I recognize that in the latter part of this chapter I have over-emphasized similarity because I have focused on showing ways of reducing the use of difference to discriminate. I emphasize again that acceptance of difference is the key to equity. Differences, both within and between categories, make life interesting and joyous.

Summary

- There is a complex interrelationship between the individual psyche, social contexts and history. Power is a part of all human intercourses, at least in part because meta-mythical meanings from culture enter the psyche. This level of analysis adds to that gained from economic and political analyses.
- 'Racism', sexism and class discriminations are generated to a degree by projection.
- Consider similarity and difference, but explore variation *within* each group as well to make visible the overlap of categories and their indistinctness.

- Acceptance of ambiguity (in both psychological and everyday terms) is central to reducing discriminations and challenging power differentials.
- People bring unconscious logics to their investigations and deliberations. This may be exacerbated if only either masculinity or femininity is focused on.

Note

1   Libido was used by Freud to mean a positive energy of sexual desire, although a satisfactory definition has not been arrived at. Jung and others have used libido to mean a general psychic energy that wishes to bring together psychological objects. Hence we can say that psychologically what is happening is that in order to achieve an internal 'wholeness' (i.e. the parts are joined by the libido), aggression has to be projected outwards.

PART 2

Emotional Literacy and Equity in the Classroom: Communication Between the Sexes

6 Approaching emotional literacy and equity in the classroom

In previous chapters I have argued that emotional literacy has both individual and group dimensions, and that equity issues are part of the latter. There is, however, a lack of research into the relationship between emotional literacy and equity issues. This chapter describes strategies for integrating emotional literacy and equity that teachers can use in their classroom, and the next chapter discusses the results of using them (Matthews 2003a, 2004). These chapters mark a change in emphasis through focusing on classroom practice and start with considering learning in groups, as this technique showed potential for allowing the development of emotional literacy and equity to be embedded within the classroom.

Group learning and pupils enjoying lessons

One of the many factors that affect how much pupils enjoy lessons is the inclusion of group work; others include being involved in the lessons and being challenged and stimulated (Kutnick and Rogers 1994; Kutnick *et al.* 2002). Pupils like to be able to discuss their work, and to have a measure of control over what they are doing (Hodson 1998). Vygotsky (1997) and Daniels (2001) emphasize that language and problem solving are key to learning, and so the inclusion of group work can be a crucial strategy (see Figures 6.1–6.3).

A social atmosphere in the classroom is important because of messages implicit within the pedagogy (Figure 6.1). One key element in developing emotional literacy is to acknowledge that both cognitive achievement and identity are fluid and influenced by the social situation. However, it is not uncommon for teachers to give messages, often hidden, which imply these factors are fixed and not open to much change. As indicated in Chapter 2, Dweck (2000) found that children can hold two self-theories. The first is called the 'entity' theory, in which factors are seen primarily as fixed traits that dwell within us and are unlikely to change. In contrast, other children see

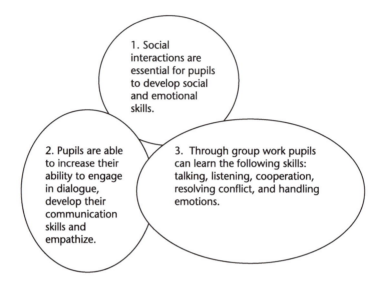

Figure 6.1 Aspects of learning in groups.

'intelligence' as something that is not fixed, but that can be cultivated and is open to change, and Dweck calls this the 'incremental theory'. Incrementalists are, in comparison to entity theorists, more likely to believe that achievement is affected by social factors. Hence, if they fail at a task, they are more likely to work harder as they can feel that the failure was due to social factors, such as how they were taught, rather than that they are not intelligent enough, and so their self-image is less likely to be affected by failure. They are less quick to stereotype and more likely to believe that people are open to change, and so reflect on a range of social experiences. Dweck (2000) also studied views on relationships. She found that people who tended to hold an entity theory were liable to have a fixed or *destiny* view of relationships. On the other hand, those with an incremental view of relationships were more likely to believe that relationships were open to change with effort to resolve conflicts, and so provided opportunities for growth. This was called the *growth* belief of relationships. Dweck does not mention gender specifically, but we can see that for boys and girls growing up, the more they hold incrementalist and growth views, the more likely they are to see the complexity of the other sex, to work harder, to learn from failure and to have a less vulnerable self-esteem. These views are in accord with the idea of transformability: pupils can have the self-belief that they can change their learning patterns (Hart *et al.* 2004). Dweck also gives clear hints about classroom practice and praise. Teachers can offer praise for attainment, which can reinforce the entity theory of learning as the pupil can interpret this as meaning it is good if you are 'bright'. However, praise for effort and the way learning is being tackled results in pupils not seeing success and failure as fixed, but that they can learn through their own efforts, and this can help self-esteem.

This research reinforces the idea that boys and girls will benefit if educated in ways that enable them to learn, through experience, the social and emotional nature of (a) learning, (b) establishing relationships and (c) overcoming difficulties. That is, they develop their emotional literacy. This approach can be contrasted with the emphasis in many countries on teaching in non-social ways, where the teacher is nearly always the centre of learning and the font of knowledge. Whole-class teaching exemplifies this approach and is typically driven by the need to measure how well pupils are doing and then using the test and exam results for streaming or banding pupils. Teachers are driven into labelling pupils as 'bright' and 'achievers' or 'thick' and 'non-achievers'. This emphasis implicitly accepts 'intelligence' as being a property of the individual (that is, implicitly supports the entity theory). Similarly, an emphasis on cognitive learning can support the entity theory if it focuses on the individual at the expense of the social and emotional aspects of learning. The idea that achievement can be related to whom you work with, that peers can help learning, and individuals are responsible for learning can get lost. Hence, Dweck's work gives support to the view that pupils would benefit if a major part of their learning were social and ways of improving their emotional literacy found. Group work provides a framework for those aspects of learning identified above, and Figure 6.2 shows the overlapping nature of different aspects of collaborative learning.

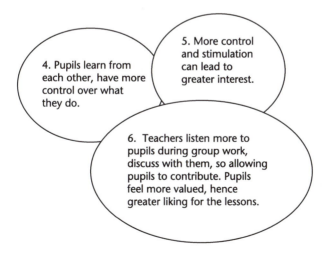

Figure 6.2 Advantages of learning in groups.

With a suitable classroom structure, the processes outlined in Figures 6.1 and 6.2 can help to develop a greater understanding and empathy between pupils with different life experiences (see Figure 6.3) (Duvall 1994; Singh 2001).

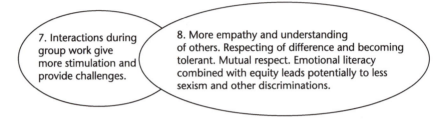

7. Interactions during group work give more stimulation and provide challenges.

8. More empathy and understanding of others. Respecting of difference and becoming tolerant. Mutual respect. Emotional literacy combined with equity leads potentially to less sexism and other discriminations.

Figure 6.3 Group work and understanding.

I have argued that promoting 'difference-as-normal' as a positive to be celebrated could potentially help pupils respect all people in a community, rather than believing that their own way of doing things is the 'right' way. Structures are needed that will encourage genuine dialogue, engagement of feelings and the resolution of conflict. One key element is to raise issues of sexism and other discriminations as part of developing emotional literacy. Our understandings of 'masculinity' and 'femininity' arise from the family but are forged through males and females socializing together. They only have meaning in tandem and are processes. By this I mean that we only learn what it means to be masculine or feminine through the ways that we interact with people of the same and other sex. In a sense, we are our interactions, and these are often comparative. It is through these interactions and experiences that we come to have a sense of identity, which can change with time. Hence, masculinity and femininity are processes that are learnt, negotiated, changed and forged. It follows from this that what are seen as 'boy' or 'girl' problems are often better solved in tandem. Hence the problem becomes, 'How can we change boys and girls together so that they understand and empathize with each other?' Then there can be understanding, acceptance and a celebration of difference. The communication and interconnectivity between all people is such that each other's attitudes can be understood and open to change.

Another aspect is to teach in ways that emphasize communality rather than gender. I was teaching a lesson that involved the use of a computer. I was concerned that boys did not dominate the computers and keyboards. I had a range of options. One was to accept boys' groups and girls' groups, and another was to say, 'I want the girls to have the first go on the computers'. What I did say was: 'Hands up all those who have computers at home, or feel that they are very familiar with them'. Significantly more boys than girls put their hands up, but all I said was, 'When you are in your groups I want those who have *not* got their hands up to use the computers first and start on the keyboard, and the other person to help them'. By taking this approach sex was not the issue, but experience (that is, social factors) was; nor was I implicitly reinforcing gender stereotypes as I would have done if I had organized the class along the lines of the first two options. By doing it the third way, attention was drawn to the students' experience on computers, and both sexes had this. The boys and girls were treated as potentially the same. The strategy that separated the boys and girls could reinforce biological definitions of gender as biology was placed first as the determining factor. Hence, the idea is reinforced that gender roles are set in biology.

Background to the research

I have always been interested in trying to enable pupils to understand each other. I taught science to pupils aged 11 to 18 years in multi-ethnic, inner-city single-sex and co-educational schools. During this time I wanted to make science lessons more interesting and find ways of enabling the pupils to relate better with each other, if for no other reason than it would make life easier! When I moved into Initial Teacher Education, I carried these interests with me and researched ways of developing pupils' emotional literacy. The methods and strategies developed in the project can be used in all subject areas even though they were developed in science lessons. The strategies were devised for both primary and secondary pupils, although the research project focused on secondary pupils aged 11 and 12 years. One interesting aspect of the research is that it was developed in science lessons. Science is often seen as 'rational and remote' and not involving the emotions. Hence, if pupils' emotional literacy can be improved in science lessons, then clearly it can be done in all other lessons as well!

In particular, I was interested to find out if strategies to engage pupils with their emotions during learning in a group context would:

- enable boys and girls to understand each other more
- help each other learn
- engage with their emotions
- learn to handle conflict

Also, I wished to examine what boys' and girls' attitudes to each other were when they worked in groups.

The strategies in the project were designed to be completed within the normal teaching context. One reason for this was that the cognitive, physical, social and emotional are all intertwined. It was felt important that all teachers accept responsibility for developing the whole person (Chapter 1) and the pupils' emotional abilities. For this reason, integration was preferable to separating off these aims so that they were to be achieved in a distinct subject (social and emotional learning, SEL), or tackling them in personal and health education. With the present emphasis on academic development a focus on the social and emotional, as an important contributory backdrop, within subject teaching becomes more vital. Another reason is that engaging pupils' emotions can help them enjoy subjects more.

Emotional literacy in lessons

The Improving Science and Emotional Development (ISED) project – funded by the Gulbenkian Foundation – was set up to explore the possibility of improving pupils' emotional literacy in subject lessons. Rather than just engaging the pupils' emotions, the idea was to devise ways of enabling pupils to handle their emotions. One way of engaging pupils' emotions is to get them to feel happy, sad, angry or concerned about aspects of science. Another is to engage their emotions about each other and science to improve their social and emotional skills in general and to explore how that affects their attitudes to science. The project set out to test the hypothesis that pupils in co-educational schools could be helped to develop their communication, social and emotional skills within the normal curriculum. Co-educational schools were selected because, for pupils to progress emotionally, they need to gain an understanding of each other and to do so across gender divides (Matthews 1998). Collaborative group work was chosen as a way of ensuring dialogue between pupils and holds the possibility that equity issues would surface during the interactions. Additionally, feedback mechanisms were introduced where pupils were observed and then had to discuss social aspects of their learning. The aim was to engage pupils with their emotions, rather than just telling them how they should change. Hence dialogue and the interactions were seen as central to helping pupils develop their sense of 'self' and 'other' within an incrementalist framework.

Principles for developing emotional literacy

For pupils to develop emotionally, they need to have time to be involved in collaborative group work so that they are able to:

1   Communicate with each other in a safe environment.
2   Think and reflect on social processes and feelings.
3   Verbalize (through writing and talking) what the interactions meant to them.
4   Compare this with what other people thought had gone on (understand that there are different perceptions of the same discourse). Hence

they have some evidence about different feelings. [*This stage can contribute, along with those below, with countering splitting and projection processes that may have occurred: those parts of 'self' projected may be refuted by the others in the groups, or be shown that the projection was not valid, e.g. girls in the group were not passive.*]

5   Have time to think, reflect and analyse. Discuss their perceptions so that they come to understand their own and each other's viewpoints; emotional and cognitive. [*This stage, along with the next two stages, can contribute to developing a mature open sense of inclusion. Also, ambiguity and fluidity, sameness and difference, will be evident as different pupils in the same group (e.g. boys or Asians) will act differently.*]

6   Learn about each other and empathize with each other, both individually and across groups like sex or 'race'. Become aware of power differences across and within groups. [*This stage can help pupils develop a sense of equity and to experience that emotional literacy is connected to equity issues. Through taking on different roles and responsibilities at different times, there can be an exchange of power. The overlap and diversity of abilities and attitudes within each group (e.g. sex) can be seen to be large and so counter any simplistic certainties in categorizations.*]

7   Learn to understand the subject (science in this case) and become aware that it involves social interactions.

A key point is that the strategies will bring these stages into conscious deliberation through the discussion based on different viewpoints. For pupils to encounter a wide range of social and emotional viewpoints, it is preferable that there are mixed-ability, multi-ethnic and mixed-sex groups, although this is not always possible.

Developing emotional literacy in the classroom

In what follows I will outline the strategies developed in the research so that readers will be able to apply the principles and materials used to their classrooms. The materials were used with pupils who were performing below the national average in standardized tests. The details of the research, together with the methodology and analysis, are given in Appendix 1. I will now explain the different materials and how they were used with younger primary (7 to 11 years) and older secondary (11 to 18 years) pupils.

Initially, it was necessary to decide how to orientate the pupils so that they were aware that it was legitimate for them to discuss how they felt about the work and each other. The teacher explained that they were to work in mixed-sex, multi-ethnic and mixed-ability groups. The pupils then had to produce a poster that showed what they thought could be the benefits. The teacher collated these and extended the results as necessary, and then explained it was so that the pupils could develop their:

(a) **Learning**, including:
   (i)   discussing techniques that enhance learning
   (ii) talking and listening skills
   (iii) cooperative skills
   (iv) learning from each other
   (v)   taking responsibility for their own learning
(b) **Relationships**, including:
   (i)   communication skills
   (ii) being able to express feelings
   (iii) get on better with friends, parents and others
   (iv) learn to understand another's point of view
   (v)   be more aware of sexism and racism
(c) **Developing ourselves**, including:
   (i)   to sense and understand our emotions
   (ii) to apply the power of our emotions to learning and relationships with others
   (iii) to empathize with others
   (iv) to make ourselves understood by others

The pupils were told that it was important to develop listening and talking skills. The overall theme was for pupils to work in mixed-sex groups, monitor their interactions and to make written comments on their cognitive and emotional interactions. The pupils were then able to engage their emotions and, through discussion, to develop some additional maturity of approach. A problem was how to provide a framework for these discussions. Initially, it was important for pupils to have an observer to monitor the pupil-groups as they worked together so as to provide some data on how the groups worked and cooperated with each other. The teacher formed groups of five so that there were two girls and two boys in each group, with another pupil who acted as an observer. The observer was only used while the class got used to the procedures; the pupils then worked in groups of four. Where there were uneven numbers, single-sex groups were used to avoid a ratio of three to one. Usually, the teachers decided beforehand who they wanted in each group and either organized them as they came into the classroom, or simply told them at the required time. Alternatively, they handed out cards with four As, four Bs etc., written on them to the pupils and then told them to get into groups with the same letter. In one class, the boys and girls were seated alternately in lessons, and so the nearest pairs were put together. Initially, the pupils were quite resistant to working together, but it became easier as time went on. The group members were changed regularly so that the whole class had the opportunity to work with each other.

In the classes, pupil-observers monitored a group of two boys and two girls who were working on a collaborative learning task (see Box 6.1 at the end of the chapter). To provide some data, the observer filled in a Discussion assessment sheet (Figures 6.4 and 6.5).

The monitoring criteria were: (a) the amount of talking, (b) the extent of listening, (c) interrupting, (d) being supportive and (e) how much they learnt. At the end of the collaborative learning activity, the four members of each secondary group were required to fill in a Guesses sheet (Figure 6.6) and estimate, without consulting anyone else, how well they and the other three in the group had performed. *This stage is intended to make visible any gap between what one thinks happened, and what others think happened, so that consciousness might be raised.* It also relates to the first four *principles for developing emotional literacy.* The primary pupils sometimes used the Guesses sheet, but were often just asked to write down or think how well they had talked and listened to each other. The secondary pupils estimated how well they had done, using the same categories in the Discussion assessment sheet (*principle 3 for developing emotional literacy*).

For the pupils to compare with each other and discuss how the group had functioned, the next step was for all the sheets or notes to be given to the

Figure 6.4 Discussion assessment sheet used in primary schools. The observer puts in the names of the two boys and two girls in the group, and then puts a tick in a square each time a pupil says something. Responses like 'Yes' or 'Uhm' are ignored. Any other comments about how well the group collaborated and worked can be written at the bottom or on the back of the paper.

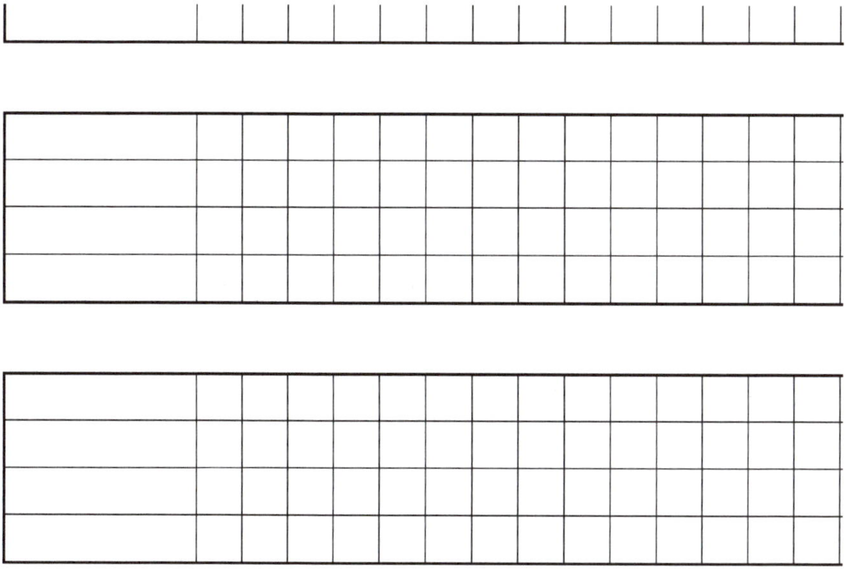

Figure 6.5 This is the Discussion assessment sheet used with older pupils. While the group of two boys and two girls are engaged in discussion, the observer only fills in the top half and makes notes in the **Other comments** section.

DISCUSSION ASSESSMENT   DA1

Observer: _____   Class: _____   Date: _____

Name	Each time a person talks, put in a ✓.

Main comments   When you fill in the chart below, do **not** use ticks or numbers. Make a comment like: The most; a lot; the least; frequently; well; not at all.

Name	talking	listening	interrupted others	helped others	how much did they learn?

Other comments

PLEASE CONTINUE ON BACK

Figure 6.6 Guesses sheet. This Guesses sheet was only used with the older pupils. Each pupil filled this in without looking at what others were writing. While this was being done, the observer filled in the lower half of their Discussion assessment sheet and made any other relevant comments.

GUESSES

Class: _____ Date: _____

Fill in the chart below, **without looking at anyone else's.** Do **not** use ticks or numbers but make a comment like: The most; a lot; the least; frequently; well; not at all.

Name	talking	listening	interrupted others	helped others	how much did they learn?
Yours:					

Other comments (Use the back of the paper as well)

---

pupil-observer who would then use the data to compare the differing viewpoints and run a debate so pupils would be engaged in a feedback process on their social and cognitive performance. These sheets, with their different pupil-perceptions, were designed to encourage a dialogue between the pupils. This stage is essential as it makes evident any gap between what each group member thought had transpired and what the observer had found. *The purpose here was to promote a discussion on how people felt about the social and emotional aspects of learning, and to have some evidence on which to base the debate.* It starts the process of legitimating discussion, both formally and informally, of the emotional and cognitive aspects of learning. The pupil-observer then discusses the results with the group to bring attention to the different ways the pupils had interpreted the talk, and to raise questions about the patterns of talk. In general, it is useful for the observer to get the members of the group to go over their estimates and to see the extent to which they correlated. This relates to *principles 4–6 for developing emotional literacy.*

Teachers would use the Discussion assessment and Guesses sheets until the pupils were familiar with the orientation of this part of the procedures; this took about six weeks. When the pupils were familiar with the procedures, and understood that social aspects of their learning were seen as important, the observer was removed so that *all* the pupils were engaged in learning. The above sheets were replaced with Opinion sheets, which were given to pupils after they had completed a collaborative task and were filled in individually. The pupils could then look at each other's sheets and discuss the results. The Opinion sheets were pro-formas with between eight and ten open and closed short-answer questions on which to elicit responses to: (i) how well they perceived themselves to be learning science; (ii) attitudes to each other; and (iii) feelings about group work. Appendix 1 contains details of how often the sheets were used and how they were analysed. Each sheet focused on a different area. Figures 6.7 and 6.8 are sample sheets used in primary and secondary schools, respectively.

The Opinion sheets were used in classroom about every three weeks. Samples of three different sheets are given in Appendices 2, 3 and 4. Filling in these sheets and discussing them enabled pupils' meta-cognitive, and what I call their 'meta-social' or 'meta-emotional' skills, to be developed. These procedures were designed to legitimate pupil–pupil and pupil–teacher discussions around social and emotional issues as well as cognitive ones. In essence, the aim was to enable pupils to develop social coherence based on mutual acceptance of each other and their differences. Since the pupils had to write down their feelings on questions, this provided a way of getting them to think about the relevant issues. The original idea was that the pupils would always discuss how well they collaborated and learnt using the Opinion sheets as a basis. However, pressure of time due to curriculum coverage meant that this could not be done all the time. As it turned out, this had a silver lining; it emerged from the interviews with the pupils that because the others in the group may not see them, they felt that they could be honest about what they wrote. Also, especially if they were unhappy, they would discuss how much they had collaborated after the lesson had finished.

These procedures were designed to legitimate pupil–pupil and pupil–teacher discussions around social and emotional issues as well as cognitive ones. In essence, we were trying to encourage pupils to develop a social coherence based on accepting (a) each other and (b) differences. They needed to value each other for those differences. The purpose of the sheets was to generate discussion and for the pupils to see that other people may hold quite different views on the way the group worked and got on.

This classroom practice was seen as only a start to legitimate some practices that incorporate essential elements in enabling pupils to reflect on themselves as people and as learners. It will not solve the problems in schools, but over years will enable pupils to develop emotionally and move towards greater understanding of each other through covering all the *principles for developing emotional literacy*.

Other ways of getting pupils to think about each other

To encourage the pupils to reflect on how they felt about working with pupils of the same and the other sex, they were asked to fill in a 'Learning with other

Figure 6.7 Sample Opinion sheet used with younger pupils.

Discussing sheet   (groups)
P2

Name: **Class:**   **Date:**

Write down how each pupil did using words like: very good, good, OK, poor, did not do it all, all the time, they were helpful.
OR put a tick in each time they do the things below.

Names of pupils in group:	**Me:**			
Talking clearly blah, blah				
Listening				
Smiling or not ☺ or ☹				
Looking at you				
Nodding when you spoke				
Helped people learn ✓				
We argued (ring one statement)	I argued a lot I argued a bit I argued hardly at all I didn't argue at all None of us argued	I argued a lot I argued a bit I argued hardly at all I didn't argue at all None of us argued	I argued a lot I argued a bit I argued hardly at all I didn't argue at all None of us argued	I argued a lot I argued a bit I argued hardly at all I didn't argue at all None of us argued

Figure 6.8 Sample Opinion sheet was used with older pupils.

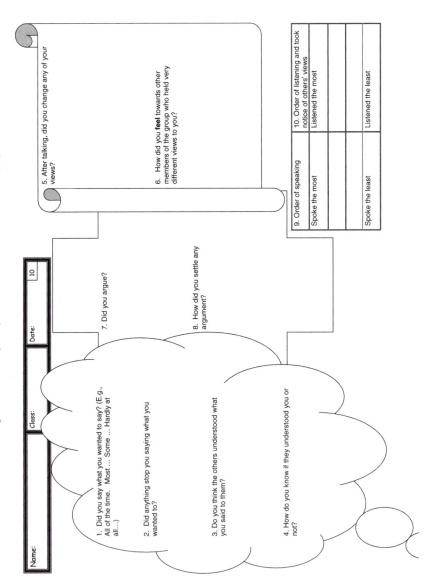

Name:

Class: Date: 10

1. Did you say what you wanted to say? (E.g., All of the time.   Most … Some … Hardly at all…)

2. Did anything stop you saying what you wanted to?

3. Do you think the others understood what you said to them?

4. How do you know if they understood you or not?

5. After talking, did you change any of your views?

6. How did you **feel** towards other members of the group who held very different views to you?

7. Did you argue?

8. How did you settle any argument?

9. Order of speaking	10. Order of listening and took notice of others' views
Spoke the most	Listened the most
Spoke the least	Listened the least

pupils' questionnaire. They were also asked how they were *Getting on with pupils* of both sexes.

The pupils completed a ranking exercise, 'Why do mixed-sex collaborative work?', on why they thought doing group work in mixed-sex groups might be valuable. This was to ascertain whether the pupils felt that the development of (a) learning science, (b) inter-gender social skills or (c) life social skills was the most important. The results of this exercise have been reported in detail in Matthews *et al.* (2002), but the girls reported that they thought the 'inter-gender social skills' were the most important, while the boys placed 'learning science' first.

Box 6.1 Examples of collaborative classroom materials

Typical activities for the group work were on some aspect of science, but where the pupils had to agree their answers. For example: (a) The pupils were given a series of questions, requiring short answers, on radiation. They were only given one copy of the sheet so they had to agree their answers. (b) The pupils had to decide jointly how they were going to do a practical and fill in details on a sheet. (c) A directed activity related to text activity on electricity. The control groups covered the same scientific content, but without the intervention techniques. Here are some specific examples:

1   The pupils had been taught some lessons on heat transfer. They were given a series of questions requiring short answers. They were only given one copy of the sheet so they had to agree their answers.
2   The pupils had finished some lessons on forces. They had to write some questions for the rest of the class, and also have the answers available. The questions were then given to another group who had jointly to write down the answers.
3   A collaborative learning task, involving underlining some text in different colours on how the heart worked.
4   After a section on acid rain, the pupils had to prepare a poster giving their solutions to the problem of how to cut down acid rain.
5   The pupils had to decide jointly how they were going to do a practical and fill in details on a sheet. Only one sheet was given to them initially. When the teacher had checked it, they were given more blanks so that everyone could have a copy.
6   A practical, using circuits, was done with four pupils in a group.

Henderson and Wellington (1998) give a good range of ideas of activities that could be adapted to generate discussion in lessons.

Summary

There is a lack of research into the integration of ways of teaching emotional literacy and equity issues in subject lessons. I have outlined an approach used to develop emotional literacy in the classroom and outlined strategies that teachers could use generally in the classroom. In the next chapter, I will indicate how successful the strategies were.

7   Emotional literacy and equity: some possible outcomes

In the previous chapter, I drew attention to the lack of research into links between equity and emotional literacy, and then set out a possible classroom approach. This chapter outlines the extent to which the findings of the Improving Science and Emotional Development (ISED) project indicate that pupils can develop their emotional literacy while also learning to remove the veil of stereotyping. In the first section, I look at the ways in which the boys and girls interacted, together with evidence that indicates they understood each other more and helped each other learn. Further evidence will be provided to show how they engaged with their emotions and learnt to handle conflict. Then I examine the boys' and girls' attitudes to each other when they were working in groups, while also returning to the theme of similarity and difference raised in Chapter 5.

Gender relationships

In the previous chapter, it was explained that during the course of the year the pupils had to work with everyone in the class. This made it more challenging for them and they reported that although they found it difficult, they thought that it was very important to learn to get on with each other. The teachers reported that they found listening to the pupils as they worked in groups very interesting, and that they learnt a great deal about the pupils, partly because they had more time to listen, but also because the boys and girls were grouped with pupils they did not necessarily know.

In general, the boys and girls reported that they learnt to understand each other more. I will provide some evidence to support this contention, first with quotes from the pupils and then from questionnaires administered at the beginning and end of the year. Here are some quotes taken from the Opinion sheets:

> Sometimes it [group work in science] makes you get on better with people but sometimes they disagree, but I think that is good for girls to work with boys and boys to work with girls because it will probably help you to understand the other sex and race.
>
> (girl)
>
> I think that in life it is very important because as we grow we will come across many different people and it's good to get along with them at an early age.
>
> (boy)
>
> You get to understand each other and respect other people's views.
>
> (girl)
>
> Yes because you get to meet different people and get to know them and sometimes people have a lot more in common but they don't know it.
>
> (boy)
>
> At first they were really annoying, but now there [sic] fine.
>
> (girl)
>
> You get more confident talking to boys.
>
> (girl)
>
> I get on better with the girls as we do more.
>
> (boy)
>
> I think people don't like other people because of what they see. Doing group work can make them see what the other person can do.
>
> (boy)

The last four statements indicate that pupils were beginning, probably because of the reflective analysis during feedback discussions, to consciously recognize the indeterminacy of gender categories. The interviews completed with pupils at the end of the year also indicate they were learning to deal with the gender divide. Here is a sequence – pseudonyms have been used throughout this book – after the interviewer had asked how they felt working in a group with boys and girls in it:

> Susan: Sometimes I feel comfortable, most of the time I talk to girls about my problems, and if it's just normal issues then I can talk to boys about it too.
>
> Dan: It feels quite normal to work in mixed groups. It's better. It feels like you're working in a group.
>
> Jessie: Yeah it does make you more confident with other people working, and so when you're in big groups you don't feel nervous about what people are going to say about you.

Barry: Well sometimes you get to know someone and you speak to them, and then your group gets too loud and they get moved, so you have start off with another person. I don't really mind that because I know everyone in the class now.

Jessie: If I sit next to someone I didn't know, they might think I was stupid, but now the boys know if I get a question wrong, they don't laugh but help me.

These quotes illustrate and confirm that the pupils were developing better inter-gender relationships. They appear to be developing an emotional responsiveness to each other that incorporates a degree of fluidity. Details of more results and questions, including with older pupils and across ethnic backgrounds, can be found in Matthews and Sweeney (1997). These replies also indicate that the pupils helped each other learn. In the quotes that follow, the pupils are in mixed-sex groups so that when a boy or girl says the others helped, it includes those of the other sex:

> Group work is good, because if you don't understand the others will explain it and make it easier. Sometimes there are disagreements, but most of the time it is interesting.
>
> (girl)

> Because you can compare answers and if you are right it will make you feel good.
>
> (girl)

The following quotes are from one lesson:

> Yes, we all helped each other learn.
>
> (girl)

> Funnily enough, Liam taught me about solar power.
>
> (girl)

> Tasleem told me about lime powder.
>
> (boy)

> Yes, people helped me in my group and I learnt some more about pollution.
>
> (girl)

> Yes, all of my group helped me learn.
>
> (boy)

> [You learn science] because you get to know their [sic] people's views.
>
> (boy)

These comments are all positive, but a minority of boys and girls did not get on with each other and preferred to learn alone. Also, there were disagreements, and I will return to this later. Overall, though, the research indicated that the boys and girls were getting on with each other, understanding each other more and helping each other in their learning. This indicates that, with proper strategies in co-educational schools, gender relationships can be improved. It also holds out the hope that a change will occur in how boys and girls view each other and the power between them will alter. The culture of the classroom was changed and the gender relations underwent a negotiation because of the interactions. Teachers reported that the classroom atmosphere improved as the year passed and that the pupils enjoyed the group work.

The self-monitoring process was used about every three weeks, which enabled femininities and masculinities to be continually acted out, inspected and confronted. Here are some extracts from Year 7 pupils (aged 11 to 12 years) engaged in learning and discussing about how to address the problems of acid rain:

> Robert: We're trying to stop acid rain. Well what are the effects of acid rain? What makes it?
> Cheryl: All the gases and carbon fumes out of cars that makes it.
> Robert: Deodorant sprays.
> Patrick: Right, stop stop I'll write (INAUDIBLE).
> Stephanie: Yeah we'll tell you in a minute. Are you making a list of it?
> Patrick: Yes.

In this extract, we see that the boy willingly takes on the role of scribe, so countering the stereotype that girls usually do this. Later, a girl takes on the role of bringing in a boy to talk:

> Cheryl: Right, so everyone else be quiet while Robert says what he thinks. Go on.
> Stephanie: Don't be so shy.
> Robert: I think rockets use fuel.

This can be seen as both a girl confirming stereotypes by being considerate, and also that the boy is being quiet, so countering the research findings that boys dominate classroom conversations. About five minutes later, the following occurred:

> Cheryl: So I thought that we could try and stop the trucks spraying lime powder into the river cos . . .
> Stephanie: If we do . . . why do we spray the lime into the river?

Robert: Okay (INAUDIBLE) who wants to say something? Right Patrick, go on. Okay, Stephanie.

In this case, the reverse has occurred, and Robert has entered more into the group and now gives space for Stephanie. Both sexes have taken on the caretaker role. I am sure that conversations like these take place in many classrooms, but are hidden by the strength of stereotypes and so not made as conscious as they could be. However, by having the strategies for reflecting and analysing different pupils' opinions about group work, these actions are more likely to enter consciousness. These quotes illustrate how the pupils are, through dialogue, shown different versions of masculinity and femininity. The experiences could help counter simple projective stereotypes. In the following discussion, both a boy and a girl took the role of teaching the others:

> David: Nitrogen gas.
> Kerryanne: No, it's sulphur isn't it? Sulphur dioxide. And where does sulphur dioxide come from? Mr Kenny said it.
> Lucy: Fossil fuels.
> Liam: Burning the fossil fuels right. And then Mr Kenny said there's a big illustration of somewhere that fossil fuels are burnt, and that's outside.
> Lucy: Cars.
> Kerryanne: Cars right, cos they burn petrol don't they? And petrol comes from a fossil fuel. And you've got to be discussing ways you can stop sulphur dioxide going up into the atmosphere and making acid rain.

These types of interactions, when combined with the feedback discussions that were held at the end of an activity, enabled an opening-up for inspection of gender interactions and a possible undermining of power differentials as both sexes took on equivalent roles and responsibilities. Hence each sex was involved in a power exchange as, for example, each took on the role of teacher; this was not exclusively the province of one sex. This helps to dispel the gender binary.

These quotes provide an idea of how the pupils were interacting, but to gain an overall view of how the pupils were changing we need to study their answers to the questionnaire given at the beginning and end of the year (see Appendix 1). Since these questionnaires were given to parallel control groups of pupils, it is possible to make comparisons. The results indicate that the pupils learnt to work and understand each other. An overall impression of how the boys and girls changed over the year comes from the Survey (see Appendix 1 for details), carried out at the beginning and end of the year (Table 7.1). It was

Table 7.1 Sample question from the Survey questionnaire

	Research groups			Control groups		
	Score at start of year, mean out of 8	*Score at end of year, mean out of 8*	*Change over the year*	*Score at start of year, mean out of 8*	*Score at end of year, mean out of 8*	*Change over the year*
I prefer to work in a mixed-sex group rather than single-sex	5.8	6.0	0.2 boys: 0.2 girls: 0.2	5.8	5.6	−0.2 boys: −0.1 girls: −0.3

Statistical significance: $*p < 0.05$; $0.1 > p > 0.05$.

found that the techniques of getting the boys and girls to discuss their social interactions helped them to like working together. This is pleasing because the research pupils were moved around and made to work with all pupils, including those that they did not like. The pupils reported that they found working in this way difficult, but overwhelmingly said that they felt it was very important that they developed the necessary skills. The control groups only worked with pupils they wanted to. An indication that the change was due to the reflection and discussion the research groups engaged in during their social and emotional interactions is supported by the results from other questions (Table 7.2). The indications are that the pupils learnt to understand each other and helped each other to learn.

The research groups indicated that they underwent greater change than the control groups, and the only main difference in the classroom was the strategies that made visible the pupils' interactions in the collaborative group work [see Matthews (2003a) for a report on a wider range of questions]. The results from the questionnaires concur with the evidence from the pupils quoted above. In particular, the last result confirms that the pupils helped each other learn. This sets the scene for pupils to improve their academic learning; other research has indicated that this is a possibility (see Chapter 4).

Clearly, more research is needed, but the results are consistent with support for co-education schools. They show that boys and girls can, and should, learn together and from each other. Keeping pupils in single-sex groupings does not help them to face up to 'unconscious' and 'conscious' stereotypes. Past experiences that have led to a particular way of viewing the world are more likely to remain uninspected. However, we know that emotions are a central factor of interactions and are woven into the fabric of identities and stereotypes. By being in groups, with the feedback and discussion that opens

Table 7.2   Questions to research and control groups

	Research groups			Control groups		
	Score at start of year, mean out of 8	Score at end of year, mean out of 8	Change over the year	Score at start of year, mean out of 8	Score at end of year, mean out of 8	Change over the year
I understand the other sex very well	5.2	5.9	0.7* boys: 0.7 girls: 0.7	5.1	5.4	0.4# boys: 0.3 girls: 0.4
I understand the same sex very well	7.2	7.4	0.2 boys: 0.3 girls: −0.1	7.6	7.6	0.0 boys: 0.0 girls: 0.0
The other sex will like you	4.7	5.0	0.3# boys: 0.2 girls: 0.5#	4.9	5.1	0.2 boys: 0.0 girls: 0.4
The other sex will help you learn	4.3	4.9	0.6* boys: 0.6# girls: 0.4	4.4	4.4	0.0 boys: −0.2 girls: 0.2

Statistical significance: *$p < 0.05$; #$0.1 > p > 0.05$.

up feelings as well as academic learning, pupils experience both difference-as-normal, as well as it becoming normal for boys and girls to learn together, to help each other and to appreciate each other for the different things they can bring to the learning situation. The sharing of subjectivity helps interweave the psychological, social and cultural aspects of learning and community (McGregor 2004) and enables gender identification to surface (Creese et al. 2004).

The boys were generally more disruptive than girls, but there were instances where both sexes were equally disruptive and in some cases girls more so: 'One boy and one girl kept on arguing' (boy); 'There was some problems with Clodagh, everyone else was fine' (girl). Such events counter simple stereotypes that imply only boys are disruptive. Now at one level this is an obvious statement; boys and girls know both sexes can be disruptive. What the strategies developed here do is to raise the issues to a conscious level, and it is legitimated for social and emotional issues to be confronted in classroom in ways that make no assumptions about which sex is causing problems or is a source of support. Indeed, it is assumed that either sex can be supportive or compassionate. Teachers reported that as time went on, the classroom atmosphere became more supportive and there were less disciplinary problems.

Emotional literacy: feelings

When the pupils interacted, their emotions were often engaged and the processes involved in the classroom helped them to verbalize their emotions and so make them conscious. This is part of the process of developing emotional literacy, which includes the ability to access one's feelings.

Evidence for them engaging with their feelings comes from the pupils and their teachers. The following are some quotes from the pupils obtained during interviews at the end of the year:

[Group work] means that you can work with your feelings.

(boy)

When I first came I was really shy, but when you're working in groups in science it helps you to talk to other people and builds up your confidence.

(girl)

It's more interesting, you can talk about your feelings.

(girl)

When you work in groups that you don't know, you sort of feel a bit nervous at first, but when you get to know them you do feel a lot more confident and you start to show how you really are.

(girl)

You just stop to think and you do understand what the others are saying, so you feel that in whatever you think that it helps you think about how you feel about girls.

(boy)

When I work with boys I begin to understand how they feel.

(girl)

During the feedback discussions, pupils' feelings would be engaged. For example, in the feedback discussion it became clear that Laura had talked the most. She was annoyed and said to the observer, who was a girl: 'You just wrote that because you hate me'. The observer replied, 'That's true, but you did talk more than anyone else, look [at the record]'. 'Rubbish', said Laura. Another member of the group said 'But look Laura, we all put down the same [shows Laura the 'Guesses' sheets filled in by the group]'. But Laura said, 'Still don't believe it'.

In general, the discussions raised issues that were addressed to varying degrees as time went on. The pupils gradually developed the skills required to deal with the emotional situations. The teachers were very clear that the group work, with feedback and the changing of the pupils in the groups, had helped pupils with their emotional development:

> The more predominant one at the moment for Year 7s is the social side of it I think . . . Where they are actually learning to talk to the people that they don't normally talk to and think about what, what they've got to offer. They tend to be getting on better I think. They find it easier to work with anybody I put them with, doing this sort of research.
>
> (male teacher)

> It really helped having the children working in groups and changing them around, moving them out of friendship groups. So they got to know the other pupils and it really helped right across the board, right across school because they were a group that would talk to me as well as talking to each other. And so they tended to try to sort out their own problems, or they would come to me and discuss it as a group with me, and then because they had this open communication and because they were used to talking to each other we could sort things out much more quickly.
>
> (female teacher)

> Certainly, from what I've seen pastorally, they emotionally support each other. When someone's having a bad day, others rally round, they are extremely caring, very concerned about the well-being even of people they don't normally go to or get on with. When one of the boys is upset a lot of the boys are concerned not just the girls, so it *crosses* gender. It's also the same with showing emotions to each other and getting support from each other . . . So I think the programme overall has helped them recognize what was good and sensible behaviour. It gave them a framework [for discussing] a situation where they weren't readily going to do it, but once they got into the habit of doing it [in the research lessons], they realized how useful it was and integrated it into their mode of operation.
>
> (male teacher)

These teacher observations provide some evidence that the pupils were acting in ways that would counter simple stereotypes (e.g. that boys would not be emotional) and therefore any projection based on that (e.g. from a girl who was projecting her lack of emotion onto boys) would be countered to a degree. It also appears that the pupils were learning the skills necessary for open communication and implicit within this is that they accept relationships are open to change and transformability (Dweck 2000; Hart *et al.* 2004). One of the key indicators of whether or not the pupils had progressed with their emotional literacy was the extent to which they improved their social and emotional relationships across gender divides.

Evidence from the questionnaires administered at the beginning and end of the year supported the above findings. The questionnaire 'How are you feeling?' provided an indication of how the groups stated they changed over the year (Appendix 1 indicates how the questionnaire was scored). Table 7.3 gives examples of the questions, but note that the scores have been analysed so that for *all* results a positive score means a constructive change. For example, for the question 'I get angry . . .', the change of 0.3 indicates they got *less* angry than they did at the beginning of the year.

The questions are *not* used to track an individual but are a general guide to how the groups changed. Table 7.4 gives the overall results of the 25 items on intrapersonal feelings. These results are statistically significant and indicate that the scores for the pupils in the research group remained steady, while those for the control group declined. This result reflects that pupils find the transition from primary to secondary school difficult, can lose self-esteem, feel less good about themselves and take time to develop new friends (Wigfield *et al.* 1991; Galton *et al.* 2000). The control group results reflect these findings, so it is pleasing that the scores of the research group were not decreased.

Table 7.3 Questions relating to 'How are you feeling?'

	Score at start of year, mean out of 6	Score at end of year, mean out of 6	Average change over the year	Change in boys' and girls' scores
Research group: I can name my feelings	3.9	4.0	0.1	boys: 0.2 girls: 0.0
Control group: I can name my feelings	4.3	4.2	−0.1	boys: −0.1 girls: −0.1
Research group: I get angry when someone criticizes me	2.3	2.6	0.3#	boys: 0.5* girls: 0.2
Control group: I get angry when someone criticizes me	2.4	2.2	0.2	boys: −0.2 girls: −0.1
Research group: I have trouble asking for help	3.4	3.8	0.4*	boys: 0.1 girls: 0.7*
Control group: I have trouble asking for help	3.1	3.0	−0.1	boys: 0.0 girls: −0.1

Statistical significance (matched t-test): *$p < 0.05$; #$0.1 > p > 0.05$.

Table 7.4 Questions relating to the intrapersonal

	Average change per question over the year	Number of pupils answering
Research groups	0.02	75 pupils
Control groups	−0.21	80 pupils

Independent-sample *t*-test: $p < 0.001$.

Conflict and standing up to each other

Clearly, there was conflict in the groups, but there were indications that the pupils were learning to deal with it. In one group of two boys and two girls, the teacher noted that a boy, Paul, had dominated the group during the lesson, but that when the pupils filled in their sheets and discussed how they had worked together, they reported that they had all worked together well! The teacher passed no comment but watched the group with a great deal of interest the next time they worked together. A boy and a girl started to complain that Paul was talking too much, and this second time it was written on the Opinion sheets and so discussed. In the third group session, there was an argument and the group fell apart as the other boy and two girls stood up to Paul. After this the group members gradually began to communicate better with each other, and although Paul still spoke more than the others, they ended up working well together with a much more even spread of talking. Whether or not this group would have developed in this way if they had not been engaged in the research strategies is unknown. What is certain though is that the strategy of putting pupils together in groups gave them an opportunity to develop the necessary skills, and that the feedback discussions ensured that the uneven pattern of talking would surface, be considered and so enable the pupils to progress in handling their social emotions. As pupils get to know each other and to deal with different situations it contributes, over time, to a better classroom atmosphere, as indicated above.

Conflict arises in many situations. One area of interest is when it arises through sexism or other discriminations. One questionnaire that was given to the groups near the end of the project asked if they had been made more aware of sexism, and if they were able to stand up for themselves. The results (Table 7.5) indicate that girls and boys are learning the social skills and emotional development to deal with conflict. That the girls' results are higher at 95 per cent may in part be because the boys are more often the cause of disruption. Written comments indicated that most pupils were engaging with the difficulties of working together:

> I do enjoy working with boys as they are not all bad.
>
> (girl)

> It makes me get more understanding of girls.
>
> (boy)

> If you do group work often with girls you will find out their capabilities and work with them more and better.
>
> (boy)

> When I work with boys no-one thinks their [sic] better than each other. We just work together.
>
> (girl)

> Everyone has different opinions about people.
>
> (boy)

> I have noticed that some boys only share ideas with boys, and girls share ideas with girls.
>
> (boy)

> I'm only sexist when I'm in a bad mood. When I'm in a mood I hate all boys.
>
> (girl)

> Boys and girls are the same, so you can't be sexist.
>
> (girl)

> I think it [group work] has helped because you learn how to respond to boys' or girls' behaviour.
>
> (boy)

> It don't make any difference, why can't we work alone?
>
> (boy)

The ambiguities of finding the other (and same) sex both difficult and pleasurable to work with was evident in the classroom and is summed up by a girl who wrote: 'Well our group got along but Michael was all being sexus [sic] to me. But I enjoyed working with them all . . . I like working in mixed groups better and it does help me learn'. Pupils reported that they enjoyed working together, even if at times it was difficult. Some pupils, both boys and girls, said that they would rather work alone. Others reported that they learnt to ignore comments. 'In the end, students are deeply conscious of their own pedagogical foothold in the contested space that is the classroom, where issues of power and hopes for inclusion are ever present' (Gallagher and Rivière 2004: 140). Most preferred to work with friends, although they appreciated the import-ance of developing the skills of having to work with pupils they did not get on

Table 7.5 Conflict and sexism

	Boys		Girls	
	Yes	No	Yes	No
Has the group work [with feedback and discussion] made you more aware of sexism?	71%	29%	83%	17%
Are you able to deal with annoying situations from the other sex that arise in group work?	79%	21%	83%	17%
Has doing the group work helped in learning to deal with the annoying situations, or not?	71%	29%	95%	5%

with. It was a constant problem for teachers in trying to decide how to form the groups. Some pupils had poor social skills and nobody wanted to work with them, yet these are the pupils in most need of development. Teachers had to make such decisions on a day-to-day basis taking into account which pupils were present that day.

The overall patterns of the boy–girl interactions in the groups were fairly even and are another indication that they were learning the skills of dialogue and conflict resolution. The Discussion and Opinion sheets contained evidence of the speaking patterns. If a boy spoke the most, then another boy, and the two girls spoke the least it was coded as MMFF. If both girls dominated the discussion, then the code was FFMM. The distribution of speech among boys and girls, over the period of a year, when monitoring and feedback was used is shown in Table 7.6. There was a wide variation within groups, but overall the average contribution of boys and girls was similar.

Working independently of the teacher

One aspect of the approach was for pupils to learn the strategies for developing socially and emotionally, independently of the teacher. The quotes from the teachers near the beginning of the chapter are an indication that they did so. This finding was backed up by observations in the classroom. However, another effect was that pupils also felt more valued and independent, as evidenced in interviews:

> Jessie: And he [the teacher] says, 'I know that you're capable to do it yourself and I know that you're not going to, like, muck around', so we get to do it ourself and he makes you feel like older and worthy to be in science.

Table 7.6 Number of times this pattern was obtained in the classes over the research period

MMFF	12 (male dominated)
MFMF	20
MFFM	15 (even distribution of talking)
FMMF	8 (even distribution of talking)
FMFM	22
FFMM	23 (female dominated)

> Jamal: Gradually you start to feel more mature because he [the teacher] does let you do science like by yourself, he doesn't always come and say 'No, no, no' and watch you.
>
> Sara: You learn by your mistakes.
>
> Max: When I first entered this school it was like straight away you would do some experiments, he wouldn't sort of judge us and see if we were capable of doing it, he'd say 'right here it is, go and do it' and that was like a big step from primary school, you got treated like adults.

For pupils to learn both the strategies to enable them to engage with each other and to learn in an *independent* way is very important. It was not an aim of the research, but the extent that it occurred, however small, was valuable. Even if it was just a case of: 'They help me when I'm scared to ask [the teacher]' (girl). It is possible that the techniques of the research encouraged pupils to see that they could transform and enjoy their own patterns of learning (Hart *et al.* 2004). The above quotes also confirm the teacher observations (p. 115) that the boys and girls were developing confidence and is probably part of why they were able to integrate the strategies into their mode of operation.

Attitudes to the same and opposite sex

The pupils were asked what they liked and disliked about working with the same and opposite sex. Table 7.7 gives a flavour of their feelings. The girls in particular seem to have learnt to value the difference (e.g. they aren't the same and have different opinions/boys have different feelings about science). Learning to relate is about accepting difference. Also, the boy who says that he likes working with boys because you learn to understand girls has either just put it in the wrong column, or intuitively realizes that to understand the 'other' helps you to understand the 'self'. Some of the comments appeared more

Table 7.7   Boys' and girls' views of each other

Boys' comments

Like working with girls (other sex)	Dislike working with girls	Like working with boys (same sex)	Dislike working with boys
nice/smart/can say things to them/you learn to get on with girls/fun/they express their feelings/don't mess around/make work easier/sometimes they talk to you/learn more/you learn what girls talk about/can concentrate/don't interrupt the teacher/ more knowledge, know the answer/they are sexy and kind/they don't whine	giggle/muck about and do dumb things/ moan/annoying/ leave you out/ keep saying you fancy someone/ they are so bossy/I hate girls when they take charge of the group/girls get uptight and it's hard to learn how to get on with them/talk too much	fun/talk about football/easy to talk/help you talk about girls/have fun/cheer you up/ want to learn/ work with friends/ understand them more as same sex/ like working with you/they like what I like/talk about boys stuff/get to know them better/helps me understand girls	take the mickey/ get into trouble/ don't work as hard/you may get in trouble/muck about/drone out the teacher/can't keep still/will switch over and work with someone else/ silly/some really get on my nerves/ should get on with the work

Girls' comments

Like working with boys (other sex)	Dislike working with boys	Like working with girls (same sex)	Dislike working with girls
different opinions from other sex/sometimes smart and useful/ understand you/ cooperate/they aren't the same and have different opinions/give you ideas/learn about boys/sometimes not selfish/funny/help, understand things more/they understand you and get on with the work/know what they like and dislike/know how to speak to them/ sometimes boys can take more notice of what you say/boys have different feelings about science	go over the top/ too immature/ jokes that aren't funny/not sensible/annoying and stupid/mess about/call you names/talk to each other and mess about/make something you don't agree with into an issue/ rough/silly/ignore you/make sure answers are right before going on/ can be personal/ when they are with their friends they muck about	understand you/ cooperate well/ share ideas/fun/ know them/get on with our work/ talk better/learn better/communi- cate better/ friends so fun/ don't embarrass you/have same opinions/under- stand them better than boys/ sensible and responsible	can be bitchy/ think they're the boss/sometimes play with their nails/chat to boys and start to mess about/be annoying/get bossy and then you don't get to say anything/not work and chat all the way through/ moan at you/talk about boys/make you feel low

regularly than others. The main complaints made by boys were that girls were 'bossy' and 'moaned a lot', but they liked working with girls because girls worked well and helped. The boys felt that they were becoming better at relating to girls, at listening, explaining things and expressing their opinions/feelings. The main complaints of girls were that boys did not get on with the work and were 'annoying', but they liked the humour that boys brought and that boys would help them learn. The girls reported that they were learning to relate to the boys and speaking out even if they felt they might be wrong.

The ratio of comments on liking and disliking was examined, as this would provide some idea of whether or not the two sexes did get on. If there was a strong gender bias and, for the sake of argument, boys did not like girls, the boys would write few positive comments about girls and more negative ones: the ratio of positive comments to 1 negative comment would be low. For example, if 1 positive comment about girls is matched with 2 negative ones, the ratio is ½:1. If the boys liked working with boys, there would be more positive comments and so one would expect a higher ratio. The difference between the ratios would indicate the degree of gender bias. Interestingly, in the research groups, the boys and girls generated a *similar* ratio of comments for liking and disliking *each* sex. The boys made 2.4 comments on why they liked girls for each one disliking them, and for each comment they made about disliking working with boys, they made 2.1 positive comments. The girls wrote more than the boys, but the ratios were even more similar; they wrote 1.6 positive comments on boys for every negative one, and 1.7 positive comments on girls for each negative one. I had expected a more marked difference, which would have indicated a stronger gender bias in relationships. The similarity indicates that, even though the reasons were different, the relationships had less of a gender bias than one might expect.

The control groups made a slightly proportionally greater number of negative comments about disliking the other sex. The same-sex ratios were similar to those for the research groups. The main difference between the research and control groups was that the girls in the control groups made over four times as many comments about other girls being bitchy than in the research groups. These results provide possible evidence that the girl–girl relationships developed in the research groups. This is not unexpected, as the strategies for enabling boys and girls to relate should also help same-sex relationships. And, of course, one thing that could increase same-sex solidarity is having the other sex around!

In Chapter 5, the issue of symmetry and difference was raised. One point worth making here is that the research questions to the pupils were symmetrical in that each pupil was asked the same question about both sexes. If this had not been the case and only questions were asked about the other sex, then the interpretation of the results could have been different and the comparative lack of gender bias not be noted. I will now turn to another result to underline the importance of asking symmetrical questions in gender research. One of the items missed out in the original research was to see how much the two sexes trusted each other. I decided to ask the groups about trust a few years later using a scale of 1 ('not trusting at all') to 8 ('trusting completely'). The mean results are shown under *Other sex* in Table 7.8.

Table 7.8   Trust of the other and same sex

	Mean score out of 8
Other sex Boys would trust the **girls** in their class Girls would trust the **boys** in their class	 5.5 4.3
Same sex Boys would trust the **boys** in their class Girls would trust the **girls** in their class	 5.6 4.4

One interpretation is that the girls trusted the boys an acceptable amount, and the boys trusted the girls a reasonable amount. However, the pupils were also asked how much they trusted the *same* sex as well, see *Same sex* results in Table 7.8, which indicates that the trust was less gender specific than it might have appeared – for example, the boys' trust was almost the same (4.4 and 4.3) for both girls and boys. If a pupil trusted one sex, they were very likely to trust the other sex, and vice versa; the correlation here was very high for both sexes ($p < 0.001$). These results emphasize the importance in gender research of asking reciprocal questions of each sex. The girls' score of 4.3 by itself could have been used to reinforce the common stereotype that girls do not see boys as trustworthy. However, a consideration of all the results undermines this simplistic interpretation. It is common in much research on gender, for example, to ask girls what they think about boys *without* asking an equivalent question about girls. What this does is to focus on difference using asymmetric logic. Asking both sexes balances the situation and provides an opportunity to study both difference and similarity – this is not always possible because of constraints on the number of questions that can be asked (but see Appendix 4 for an example from the research). In the questions on trust (Table 7.8), the similarity of responses is evident, but it would be essential to explore the differences in how the trust was evidenced. There would be significant difference and variation in reasons, but also an overlap across the sexes. This point is easier to see in the example on liking and disliking each other (Table 7.7). The boys and girls had similar ratios in liking and disliking each sex, yet the reasons were different. Similarity and difference exist at the same time, but this is more likely to be exposed if symmetrical questions are asked of each sex about each sex.

Evaluation of individual-in-group emotional literacy

In Chapters 3 and 4, the issue was raised of how it might be possible to evaluate the group dimension of emotional literacy. My research has focused on finding a way of improving pupils' emotional literacy and has not been concerned with developing a system of assessment that could be used with pupils. This would require an altogether different research project. However, because ISED was interested in improving whole-group emotional literacy, we can see some pointers as to what might be included in an *individual-in-group* emotional literacy evaluation. These would include the extent to which an individual pupil:

1   Supports others in their learning. This has at least two components:
    • teaching;
    • listening and observing carefully so they can judge if the others have learnt.
2   Accepts challenges without getting defensive or angry; for example, when they have disagreements or another pupil does not understand what they are trying to explain.
3   Listens positively to what group members are saying.
4   Asks questions in a way that shows interest in others' thoughts and feelings.
5   Gets on with different sexes and sexualities.
6   Gets on with different ethnic and religious groups.
7   Supports others in their learning and emotional development.
8   Helps resolve conflict situations.
9   Empathizes with group members; is able to read their feelings accurately and respond appropriately.

These dimensions could be judged in a range of group situations. Additionally, judgements about emotional literacy development may be integrated with attitudes to learning and be incorporated into whole-school policies (Antidote 2005).

However, assessment in emotional literacy is an issue that will have to be grappled with.

Conclusion

This research has developed a set of strategies for engaging pupils with their emotions at both an individual and group (equity) level and more details of the research results have been written up with specific reference to science teaching (see Box 7.1). Clearly, one does not know the extent to which the expression of pupils' views produced lasting changes in attitudes and behaviour, but it appears that the approach has some potential in developing emotional responsiveness and enjoyment of working and learning together. This lays the foundation for an increase in academic achievement, although this was not an aspect of this piece of research. The work of Wegerif *et al.* (2004) similarly found that exploratory talk in the classroom improved social skills and inclusion, arguing that socialized speech has an interpersonal and intrapersonal function. I do not wish to make any great claims for my research other than that the strategies used – although only a start – indicate possible approaches to how individual and equity levels can be integrated within

---

Box 7.1 Science education and emotional development

The pupils engaged in the research were also more interested in science lessons and reported that they were more likely to want to continue with it as a subject. The effect was slightly greater with the girls than boys. Interested readers can consult the following sources where this has been reported:

Matthews, B. (2004) Promoting emotional literacy, equity and interest in KS3 science lessons for 11–14 year olds: the 'Improving Science and Emotional Development' project, *International Journal of Science Education*, 26(3): 281–308.

Matthews, B. (2005) Emotional development, science education and co-education, in S. Alsop (ed.) *The Affective Dimensions of Cognition: Studies from Education in the Sciences*. Dordrecht: Kluwer Academic.

Matthews, B., Kilbey, T., Doneghan, C. and Harrison, S. (2002) Improving attitudes to science and citizenship through developing emotional literacy, *School Science Review*, 84(307): 103–14.

Matthews, B. (2002) Why is emotional literacy important to science teachers?, *School Science Review*, 84(306): 97–103.

Matthews, B. (2003a) *Improving Science and Emotional Development (The ISED Project): Emotional Literacy, Citizenship, Science and Equity*, 2nd edn. London: Goldsmiths.

Matthews, B. (2003b) Making science more popular through group work and emotional literacy: a possible contribution to internationalism?, *Science Education International*, 14(2): 12–20.

---

emotional literacy. One can surmise – for it would take a much deeper project to establish – that the types of splitting and projection that reinforce stereotypes may have been countered. The processes of analysis based on evidence from others helped self-reflection and a realization of sameness, difference and the ambiguity of group categories. To the extent to which it has been effective shows that such approaches are important, although I am sure that many more effective strategies can be devised and would have an important impact if used throughout schooling. The use of collaborative learning with self-monitoring and discussion is an attempt to make visible the social-emotional interactions within classroom dialogue. Teachers can use this to raise issues of power imbalances, especially in terms of dialogic domination or disruption of the learning process, and to move towards changing them. Furthermore, through experiencing power exchanges, both boys and girls would see it benefited them – as each learnt more from the other – and so could learn the importance of equity. This is an important aspect for teachers to bring into consciousness and discuss with pupils. It helps pupils to understand and empathize with the other sex, an important part of the formulation of 'self' and the improvement in emotional literacy.

8 A new saying for old

This chapter is an interlude but continues the focus on the classroom by suggesting that a pedagogic saying that focuses on emotional development is required. I also hope that any poets among the readers will produce a saying to replace mine at the end of the chapter.

There is an old Chinese saying:

> *I hear and I forget,*
> *I see and I remember,*
> *I do and I understand.*
> (Confucius)

This saying is so accepted that it is easy to forget that it only really applies to cognitive learning. Hence we can ask 'What would a saying look like if it referred to developing the emotional aspects of ourselves?' The purpose of this chapter is to attempt to transform the above saying. This will be done by discussing the various possible elements and then distilling them into a short saying.

The first lines could be:

> *I see, and it usually means little emotionally*
> *I write, and it helps me gain meaning.*

How would I justify the above two lines? Here is an example to carry my argument: Pupils can visit Parliament or Congress, hear a talk, write about the visit and the Constitution, and still have not engaged their emotions in the processes of what democracy means in practice. However, if they take part in a democratic forum, for example a School Council, they can experience what democracy is like. The understanding they gain will be qualitatively different. Even so, this is not necessarily sufficient. The School Council may be restricted in that the pupils are not allowed to debate with teachers those issues that the pupils themselves are interested in. They may recognize it as a sham. The more the pupils have a real say and can take part in an authentic decision-making process, the more they will come to a better understanding of democracy and be more likely to have an emotional commitment to it. Democracy should not only be 'taught about', but experienced emotionally. However, in gaining these experiences the pupils will also undergo a range of social and emotional experiences that can contribute to their own social and emotional development. For example, they may have to learn to talk and listen more to people who hold different viewpoints. People can be helped to develop emotionally and socially if they are placed in situations where they can become open to challenge and change, rather than being prescribed actions. So, rather than teaching about the emotions, pupils can be put in situations to enable them to experience their emotions and so mature.

We could write:

> *I write about experiences personal to me and they may have meaning.*

Or better:

> *I have experiences that are personal to me and they have meaning.*

However, even this is not sufficient. To develop emotionally and socially is helped by reflecting on experiences. Some of this reflection is done by oneself, but the majority is done in conjunction with others. Social interactions are essential, and with as wide a range of groups as possible. One learns about oneself through understanding 'the other'. Understanding of one underpins and affects the other. Similarly, discussions with people of a variety of classes, 'races', religions and sexualities can bring together different perspectives that challenge one's viewpoints. These challenges help the interested person to gain a greater understanding of their own emotional make up, and what assumptions they hold. They are confronted, realize different meanings can be ascribed to same events by different people, and see the emotional and social gaps. In other words, people can learn to empathize. In the school context, it is easy to see how group work can provide a context to promote understanding.

Hence, I can now write some more lines, but in what follows I am laying out a pattern on a page that is necessarily sequential. However, I do *not* believe that emotions develop in stages, one after another, so progression is not as linear as laid out.

> *I have experiences; they can affect me.*
> *I have experiences and discuss them with other people.*
> *I can realize that others experience the same event in different ways.*

I can understand that my perceptions are different from those of others, and can think about that.
I can empathize with others.
I discuss with 'others', confrontation occurs.
I can begin to understand why they act as they do.
Through these interactions and thoughts I can learn a greater understanding of myself.
I can begin to reflect on my actions, and why I act as I do.
I can develop my emotional self.
I can understand that each person has individual rights that are different to mine.

It may appear from the above lines that it is possible to mature smoothly and with almost no pain, just a happy smooth progress. As we all know, internal conflict is an essential part of the process, and this can arise where there is a gap between where you are emotionally and where you want to be emotionally. This helps enforce an emotional dialogue with oneself and others. Unless one is prepared to do this and face up to conflict, change is likely to be slow.

I can undergo experiences, and reflect on them in ways that enable me to move forward.
I am confronted with how my actions feel and affect other people.
I feel conflict and pain, internally and externally.
I can mature.

Is maturity necessary?

Social and emotional development is essential for a caring democratic society that values freedoms – political, personal and sexual – accepts difference, and increases the happiness of its individuals. Maturity is important for the individual in his or her life as well as family living. However, maturity is not *ipso facto* necessary; if we were to live in an uncaring, selfish society, then the social and emotional development of its citizens would not really matter. People could remain self-centred and selfish in a hierarchical and authoritarian society. My illustration at the beginning on democracy was not random, for within it the connections between democracy, personal value and esteem for self and others were *implicitly* linked inexorably with social and emotional development. Now I want to make these links explicit through a discussion of social justice.

Social Justice, the 'I' and the 'we'

As outlined in Chapter 2, emotional development is required by people to achieve democratic participation, and this is reflected in the debates on social justice. To achieve a level of democratic participation would involve people working together cooperatively as members of a community. But in addition to this, the participants will have to be reflexive about their lives and conscious about the decisions they make in conjunction, and perhaps at odds, with others. Giddens (1993) calls this being socially reflexive. Trust, social capital (the building up of trust and working together for common goals) and social reflexivity can be seen as being central to a democracy. These ideals link well with arguments on equity and social justice.

Young (1990) argues that there are different forms of oppression (e.g. sexual and racial), that these experiences give rise to different concepts of justice, and that their viewpoints need to be expressed. Similarly, Anne Phillips (1995) argues for a politics of presence, where all people's voices can be heard. This also means that people have to listen.

Clearly, for people to participate in this form of democracy, they are required to be empathetic, reflexive and critical thinkers who are not psychologically threatened by such debates. This raises the question of how the emotions of people can be developed to enable the emotional, psychological and social groundings so that the voices of representation can be heard, debated and reflected upon. These require a level of individual self-esteem, ability to deal with ambiguity and uncertainty, and a sexual self-confidence. Or, to put it another way, the development of emotional literacy in all people becomes essential to the development of a democracy with a concern for social justice. Hence, while throughout this discussion I have talked about the 'I', we can see that the 'I' develops in a community and can only form through dialogue with others. The 'we' is central to the 'I'. Ideally we need a way to make this visible.

> *I develop only with others in a social and political world.*
> *My 'I' is also 'we'.*

Now the task is to reduce the above down to a brief saying:

> *I hear and write, and stay the same.*
> *I experience life, it has meaning.*
> *Confronted by others; I progress.*
> *Through dialogue, I empathize and reflect.*
> *We feel conflict; and I change.*
> *I develop my emotional self.*

Anyone can add their own line or lines, and although it breaks a pattern, I would add one extra:

> *Together we can enhance democracy, social justice and happiness.*

But, if we go back to basics:

> *I experience life, and I change.*
> *I examine life, and I mature.*
> *I encounter conflict, and find desire.*
> *I understand others, and know myself.*

Please add your own version:

PART 3
Moving Forward

9 Single-sex and co-educational schools

The previous chapters have shown how a concern for social justice and democracy places importance on people being given voices of representation. This means that boys and girls (of all sexualities, religions and cultural and class backgrounds) could be educated together so they are brought up understanding and taking part in the processes involved from as young an age as possible. One key consideration is that pupils might be able to form a secure sense of 'self' and 'other' while accepting ambiguity, similarity and difference. These are part of the development of emotional literacy, which requires communication, dialogue, reflection and the development of empathy. As such, it would appear that there is a case for co-education, but we need to consider other arguments about the organization of schooling. In this chapter, I first consider the argument that girls' greater academic success in single-sex schools constitutes a justification for segregation. I will also discuss whether it is valid to use differences in exam results or learning styles to separate pupils. Then, I will open up the arguments that focus on the social interactions that exist in co-educational schools.

Debates about single-sex and co-educational schools have a long history (Grant and Hodgson 1913; Dale 1974; Deem 1984; Mahony 1985). The disputes over co-educational schooling continue today and are similar around the world (Arnot *et al.* 1998; Kenway *et al.* 1998; Datnow and Hubbard 2002; Salomone 2003). In America, millions of dollars have been authorized for the creation of single-sex schools and classes as part of wanting to raise academic standards in Bush's 'No Child Left Behind' education plan (CBS 2002; Zittleman and Sadker 2003). Although there are many factors involved, the arguments can be placed into two broad categories. In one, the main emphasis is on the cognitive aspects of schooling. This debate has centred mainly around how academically successful the two types of school groupings have been, with writers focusing to differing degrees on social factors (Dale 1971; Kenway and Willis 1990; Smithers and Robinson 1995; O'Leary 1999). In the second category, the main emphasis is on equity issues. These two are not mutually exclusive, and both can be seen as important. Supporters of both single-sex and co-educational schooling have used both emphases to advance their case.

Academic achievement and the argument for single-sex schools

It has been claimed that the single-sex environment helps girls achieve more academically (Smith 1984; Lee and Bryk 1986; Riordan 1990, 2002; Kelly 1996; Maslen 2001; Jackson 2002; Rowe *et al.* 2002; Spielhofer *et al.* 2002; Salomone 2003) and that subject choices are less divided along gender lines, with girls tending to take so-called 'masculine' subjects like mathematics and science more readily than in a mixed environment (Deem 1984; Stables 1990; Colley 1994; Cornwell 1997; Haag 1999), although this appears to be less marked as time goes by (Arnot *et al.* 1998: 31). Others have argued that the type of subject teaching, and what counts as knowledge, may be affecting subject choices (Kelly 1985; Harding 1986). Some of the explanations for the patterns are that pupils work harder when they are not distracted by the other sex, feel more comfortable in the single-sex situation, subjects are associated with particular gender identities, and that boys and girls have brain differences and different learning styles (Davidson and Edwards 1998; Noble and Bradford 2000; Tooley 2002; Baron-Cohen 2003; Salomone 2003; Sax 2005). As a result, it is argued that it is possible to adapt the classroom to meet the different perceived needs of boys and girls (Kruse 1996; Bray *et al.* 1997; Bleach 1998).

Others argue that it is not clear if single-sex schools do produce better academic results for girls. Reviews of the research have shown that it produces contradictory results, at least in part because of the samples that have been used (Bone 1983; Willis and Kenway 1986; Hannan *et al.* 1996; AAUW 1998; Shmurak 1998). For example, in Britain there is a debate that focuses on how one takes into account the varied social class backgrounds of the pupils (Smithers and Robinson 1995; Robinson and Smithers 1999). Indeed, it has been shown that differences in academic achievement based on social class are greater than those due to sex (Murphy and Gipps 1996; Gaine and George 1999).

More recently, there has been a change in concern regarding academic achievement, as girls' exam performance has reached or overtaken that of boys (Wheatley 1996; Epstein *et al.* 1998; Head 1999; Duffy 2002; BBC 2003; Freeman 2004). With the concern that girls outperform boys, there has been a focus on ways to increase boys' achievements in examinations. One of the main methods suggested has been to separate the sexes on the basis that boys and girls have different learning needs (Kruse 1996; Bray *et al.* 1997; Bleach 1998; Swan 1998; Noble and Bradford 2000). It is now no more correct to say that single-sex classes for boys will help boys catch up with girls, than it used to be to say that single-sex classes for girls would help girls catch up with boys!

As far as boys' and girls' academic achievement can be measured, it has been found that the similarities in their performance far outweigh any overall differences (Murphy and Elwood 1998). Therefore, it seems that there is not a strong case for using academic achievement as a basis for separating boys and girls into separate schools. The case is further weakened as 'achievement' in schools is defined to include a very narrow range of human mental activities (Epstein *et al.* 1998; Sternberg 2000).

Difference and separation

The reasons given for separating pupils on the grounds of academic success include that boys and girls have different learning styles, or that boys distract girls and hence will learn more apart. In principle, the argument is that if boys and girls achieve differently academically, then this is a valid reason for their separation. This is a principle that deserves discussion and incorporates ideas on difference, sameness and equality. To draw out some of the issues, I will focus on Rosemary Salomone's (2003) arguments in support of single-sex schooling. Salomone argues that single-sex education tends (in America) to be aligned to the political right and that at core the arguments are about freedom of choice, freedom from government impositions, and that 'social and religious conservatives . . . view single-sex schooling as a means to accommodate what they consider the inherently different capabilities, tendencies, and preferences of the women and men' (Salomone 2003: 39). On the other hand, Salomone argues that liberal men and women are inconsistent, and that feminists in particular have been split, arguing for two different views of equality. One is that 'equality' means 'different' – that is, single-sex schools are valid because any differences can be accommodated differently. The other is that 'equality' means 'the same', and that separation inevitably means that one provision will be worse than the other. Some feminists take a slightly different line in that it is not the separation that is the problem, but unequal treatment. Salomone argues that underlying much of the debates are beliefs about the extent to which men and women are different or the same, and the extent to which any differences are biologically determined or socially constructed.

My position is that I regard men and women as both the same and different. There is a large overlap of any attributes and abilities that females and males have and this is much greater than their average differences (Nicholson 1984; Epstein 1988; Gaine and George 1999). Hence, when applied to humans 'same' and 'different' are not dichotomies, but ambiguities. Therefore, because of the overlap, it is difficult to see how any perceived differences could be used to justify different treatment. But another ambiguity is that all people, irrespective of sex, social class or 'race', have different aptitudes and abilities, and so should be treated differently. As the chapter on social justice pointed out, what is required for equal treatment is that people can voice their differing needs. This contrasts with single-sex schools, which are essentialist, as they are based entirely on biological sex and remove the other sex from being able to represent their views and values.

Because the overlap of the sexes is great, they ought be exposed to the same (equal) range of cognitive and emotional experiences. This is just one aspect of gaining equality. This is not to say that there wouldn't be differences. For example, a pupil from another culture will need help to integrate into school, but this is not a reason for keeping them separate. Teachers can differentiate materials to enable everyone to learn. Therefore, there is difference within sameness.

Now although it appears boys and girls tend to have different learning styles, none of these are the province of only one sex and it seems that everyone uses all of them. However, suppose pupils do differ significantly in their learning styles. One argument is that they should be separated into groups depending on their learning styles. A stronger argument would be to say that it is important all pupils meet a range of styles so they can develop their strengths and also become skilled at other ways of learning. For this reason, they can benefit from experiencing a range of learning styles. In principle, difference does not imply separation. Indeed, it can be seen as a reason for inclusion, as Noble and Bradford (2000: 158–9) point out:

> Many teachers feel that boys and girls bring separate elements of learning to a lesson, which the other gender needs to understand and use. Girls need to be more prepared to speculate, to volunteer answers, to take risks and to challenge the teacher and one another. Boys need to be more careful about their presentations, to reflect more on their work and to listen more carefully. Where are they going to learn this if they are surrounded by like-minded students? . . . Although girls do complain about boys' behaviour at times, the statistics suggest that they have not been held back from raising their achievement in recent years.

Difference is a resource and, as Belbin (1993) discovered, a mix of personal characteristics in members of a team is a major factor in a team's success. Hence, difference can be a reason for integration rather than separation.

Another example is provided by attitudes to science lessons. It is generally accepted that girls are more social and see science as remote and about facts, and so are not so drawn to the subject as boys. Also, girls are more likely to take up science in single-sex schools and pass the exams. Some people would use this as a justification for having single-sex schools, even though the extra percentage is not high. It seems to me that the main reason for taking science in schools is not just to pass exams. It is to have an understanding of science and how pupils will be affected by it. It is also about understanding, enjoying and being able to take a part in debates in society when scientific developments affect people. If girls do bring more social attitudes than boys to science, then this is a good reason for them to be together so that both boys and girls can debate different viewpoints. However, in saying this, as always, I do not want in any way to imply that boys think one way and girls another. There is a large overlap and both boys and girls appreciate the supposed 'objectivity' of science, and also like to debate social issues. There is a good reason to change the science curriculum and pedagogy, rather than use it as a reason to separate boys and girls when they have an overlapping set of views. A focus on the number of pupils passing exams emphasizes the academic side of the curriculum and encourages a neglect of wider issues. This focus moves away from curriculum and pedagogy being seen as a social process and reinforces the idea of schooling as the transmission of facts. It implicitly accepts a set curriculum. The problem with the current emphasis on exams and testing is that one purpose of education is lost. There is an additional problem. The focus on testing and exams influences the pedagogy used in the classroom. Hall *et al.* (2004: 814) found this focus promoted exclusion rather than inclusion and that 'The equity and social justice agenda is clearly subjugated to the imperative of . . . documenting "high standards" in narrow curriculum areas'. They go on to point out that celebrating diversity and difference is deeply contradictory with an emphasis on 'standards' in academic curriculum areas.

I wish to raise another issue about difference being used as an argument to support separation by switching from sex for a moment. Suppose an employer said that 'Men produce 10 per cent more goods than women, so I will pay the men 10 per cent extra'. There could be no grounds for this decision unless every single man produced 10 per cent more than every single woman. That there is an overlap in their output indicates that sexism (usually stemming from anxiety over sexual difference) is the problem, not the output. The principle here is that separation by sex is invalid if there is an overlap in production. If production was really the problem, one would argue to pay by output. That the employer chose to use sex as a basis is discriminatory and sexist. With this example in mind, suppose the achievement in mathematics by boys of an African background was low. How big a differential between them and other groups would there have to be before one would argue that they should be separated from the rest of the school population? Would the answer to this question change if both African boys *and* girls were included? Would one be loath to separate them out because it would be difficult to see how it would help, and also because of the racism it may engender?

Additionally, it seems to me that all the time there is an overlap with pupils of other backgrounds, the grounds for separation is undermined, as in the illustration with the employer above. Why pick on 'race', when the problem is exam achievement? If one were going to argue for separation rather than mixed-ability teaching, why not make it on the grounds of achievement in mathematics? That is, all pupils – irrespective of 'race', gender and so on – who did not achieve at mathematics could be separated. To select 'race' (or sex) as the issue rather than achievement in mathematics implies an anxiety over 'race' (or sex). This is a key point.

Here is another example to indicate that sexism is the key. The argument that women can achieve equity in society by getting the same exam results is fatally flawed. For example, there are more female biologists and with higher grades than boys, yet men hold key positions, and in other sciences the difference in exam results does not explain the career patterns of scientists (Greenfield et al. 2002; Rubsamen-Waigmann et al. 2003). Equity is about combating sexism, rather than academic achievement. The problem is sexism in society, and this is what needs to be focused on. There are many factors at work, as Paechter (1998) points out. She argues that while the academic success of girls has risen above that of boys in many areas, girls and women have not achieved equality. Clearly, examination results are not the major factor, so should not be the main focus. Rather, sexism ought to be the focus and therefore more engagement is required so that through interactions pupils can develop emotionally in ways that will enable them to handle the complexity of human diversity.

So far, then, I have argued that academic achievement cannot be used as a valid reason to separate out boys and girls, as their results are more similar than different. To focus on the small difference is inconsistent because if one were to separate pupils it would be on the grounds of achievement or behaviour, if one were to separate at all. In principle, difference is not of and in itself a reason for separation. Difference can be incorporated into 'sameness' and can be used as a resource. Also, the very act of separation has effects, to which I now turn.

Problems with separation

There are three problems associated with the act of separation I wish to discuss.

1 *Separation emphasizes difference.* When people are separated into groups, there is always a justification for separation; therefore, there has to be an emphasis on difference that is great enough to 'justify' separation. An example of this is provided by the National Association for Single Sex Public Education (NASSPE), which was formed in 2002. They state (NASSPE 2004):

We start with some very basic, but often overlooked, facts about girls and boys:

- The brains of girls and boys differ in important ways. These differences are genetically programmed and are present at birth.
- Girls and boys have different learning styles in part because of those innate, biologically-programmed differences in the way the brain works.
- As a result: single-sex schools offer unique educational opportunities for girls and for boys.

This exaggerates the biological variations between girls and boys and ignores the extent of overlap between and variation within the sexes. Also, childhood experiences are incorporated into the structures of the brain due to neural pathways being built up, which in turn can influence behaviour (Head 1999; Johnson 2005). Hence, what are claimed to be innate brain differences between boys and girls could be due to dissimilar experiences in childhood and may, therefore, be cultural in origin. Additionally, there are disputes over brain differences and whether they affect performance.[1] The concept of learning styles is also open to criticism, including that its application to education has little impact on learning and that some of the best-known and used tests are not reliable (Coffield *et al.* 2004). Further, it is disputed that any learner preference – if it can be identified – indicates a particular way of teaching (Curry 1990; Coffield *et al.* 2004). That is, even *if* boys and girls did have different learning styles, it is not possible to justify different pedagogic approaches. Coffield *et al.* (2004) are very critical of research on learning styles and argue that it represents an individualized, de-contextualized view of learning that is also depoliticized, and quote Reynolds (1997: 122): 'the very concept of learning style obscures the social bases of difference'. Another example of the exaggeration of difference is provided by Swan (1998: 163), who wrote about the reasons for establishing separate classes for boys and girls. These included that boys were less motivated, worked less and behaved more badly than girls. Where does this leave the motivated, well-behaved boys? One can see how the very existence of single-sex grouping will support the belief that boys and girls are very different, an essential ingredient in 'justifying' sexism! Also, there is a real inconsistency here; if the real reason for separation was motivation and behaviour, then you would expect this to be the basis for splitting the groups, so that the well-motivated and behaved – boys *and* girls – were in one group. That this was not the case makes one wonder if the decision to split up boys and girls was made first (unconsciously?) *and then* the reasons for separation made. To argue that 'But boys and girls are separated so that they will learn more' rests on the erroneous assumptions, like those of swans, that all boys are different from all girls and ignores the overlaps in behaviour, motivation and so on. The exaggeration of difference is exposed if one person says 'Boys' and girls' results differ by 10 per cent so I will separate them', while another says 'Boys' and girls' exam results have a 90 per cent overlap, therefore I am going to separate them'. The justification is clearly very weak. Also, the biological difference argument, even to the extent to which it is correct, does not determine behaviour, and focuses on academic achievement, not on whether or not boys and girls should learn to get on together. Indeed, it could be argued that the more biological differences are found, the more we need co-educational schools so that boys and girls can learn and empathize across difference, as indicated in Chapters 6 and 7.

2 *Separation reinforces power differentials.* As we saw in Chapter 5, separation encourages the psychological process of projection such that difference is emphasized over similarity. Separation can preserve difference and ensure power differences. For example, religious schools are set up to preserve and generate different religious views. Fee-paying schools separate pupils based on class and ensure the privilege of the rich. It is no accident that these are also more commonly single-sex than state schools, as the wealthy can also be concerned to preserve male power. Similarly, schools can be segregated by 'race' and class, often due to hidden admission policies, thus maintaining difference and hence control. The need that some people feel to separate and divide can often have anxiety – sexual or racial – as an underlying cause. The separation also allows those fears and anxieties not to be confronted. Similarly, in the past the separation of boys from girls was about their perceived differences and ensuring male control. In Victorian times, girls and boys were educated differently based on their separate roles and spheres in life. Women were in the home and men in the marketplace because 'Men, who were strong and powerful, were capable of long, earnest thought; women were not. Lack of depth, which flightiness of thought implied, made women naturally inferior to men' (Burstyn 1980: 70). Other arguments, including that education would harm women's reproductive organs, were used to justify educational difference between boys and girls (Burstyn 1980; Purvis 1980; Sayers 1982). Such arguments, like modern-day ones, concentrated on perceived differences between the sexes to 'justify' separation. These differences have also been to do with class and gender. Plummer (2000) highlights how working-class girls come to be positioned as an inferior group. In all cases, difference is emphasized over similarity to 'justify' separation and control. The process of separating could in effect, even if not intended, reinforce power differences and increase the underlying anxieties that led to the feeling for the need to separate. The exaggerated differences can become generalizations based on gender and enter the psyche as reasons for treating and acting in different ways towards different people. This is the reverse of some feminist arguments that hold that when together girls learn a social construction of gendered identity that renders them unequal. Rather, as shown in Chapters 5 and 7, there is theoretical and

practical research that supports that presence enables challenges to power through decreasing the perception of difference, reinforcing similarity, showing ambiguity and experiencing different power positions. Hence girls and boys, within a suitably constructed classroom, are allowed the freedom to develop a wider range of possible identities.

3 *Separation implies that what is good for one sex is* not *good for the other sex.* For example, that different curricula and learning styles are needed for each sex (Kruse 1992; Sax 2005). On the other hand, co-education implies that what is good for one is good (maybe in different ways) for the other. There is also a hidden curriculum in separation. Girls and boys must have an idea of why they are being separated. These would include: it helps girls to work harder (implying that boys don't); boys are aggressive (implying girls are submissive), more active (implying girls are passive) and have different learning styles. It would also suggest to boys and girls that this was a matter of biology rather than culture. Single-sex schooling can reinforce 'male' and 'female' as a binary opposition that emphasizes difference over similarity. More complex and overlapping subjectifications of masculinity and femininity are possible in suitably structured co-educational schools (see Chapter 7) through the multiple and contradictory discourses the boys and girls hold with each other (Davies 1993). In the single-sex environment, stereotyped 'genderizations' can go unchallenged due to the lack of presence of the other sex, and ambiguous genderizations go unnoticed. The single-sex environment 'narrows the range of available student perspectives' (Simpson 2005: 454).

Separation and stereotypical behaviour

A key question is how will separation help solve the problems of sexism? We have seen above that difference is exaggerated to establish a reason for separation in the first place. In the case of sex it is explicit, in the case of class it is usually implicit. I will now look at one case to illustrate another difficulty. Some argue for single-sex schools on the basis that girls work better when they are together and there is a better working environment than in co-educational schools. Carolyn Jackson (2002: 39–40) states that:

> Although a range of factors clearly is important in assessing the benefits of single sex classes within mixed schools, there is an increasing tendency amongst educational researchers with an interest in gender to focus almost exclusively upon attainment, and to neglect classroom issues . . . [and it is essential that they do not] ignore pupils' experiences and perceptions of classroom environments.

Jackson then focuses on the pupils' perceptions of single-sex and co-education groups and how they felt and achieved in those settings. There was some evidence in this article that an increase in stereotyping may occur in the single-sex situation, and it is to this I now turn.

Jackson (2002) reports that:

> In contrast to the more relaxed and supportive environment of the girls' groups, the climate of the boys' groups was reported to be more competitive and aggressive than the climate of mixed classes.
>
> (p. 44)

> evidence from the research presented in this article . . . suggests that these hard, macho masculine attitudes may actually be exacerbated in such classroom settings.
>
> (p. 45)

The point being made, therefore, is that single-sex classrooms are unlikely to be the way to enhance the levels of achievement among boys, as macho values are not conducive to achieving well in schools (Willis 1977; Salisbury and Jackson 1996; Parry 1997; Head 1999). On the other hand, it could be argued that the greatest problem is the increase in stereotypical behaviour rather than that it would not lead to greater academic success. Jackson points out that other research has produced the same results (Askew and Ross 1990; Kenway and Willis 1990; Kenway *et al.* 1998). The result of such research is to argue that girl-only classes have benefits for girls but that 'curriculum-as-usual classes may do nothing to challenge the macho or "laddish" cultures inherent in schools; indeed, it may be the case that they actually exacerbate them' (Jackson 2002: 46).

Why is this a cause for concern? It is wrong because in the long term we want to counter stereotypes and the assumptions that go with them, and the more that people act them out, the less likely they are to change. This is not to say that the sexes will ever do anything other than define themselves differently (Connell 1987; Schnarch 1991). Boys and girls, men and women, have differences, but acceptance should be based on the variations that exist in people, and not on stereotypes that hinder development and limit potential. In other words, if boys do become more sexist, then girls are not benefiting either! Pupils benefit from relating to each other as whole people. If either sex behaves in exaggerated ways that reinforce a set of assumptions about how boys and girls are different, it demeans both sexes. To challenge stereotypes involves the development of empathy and acceptance of difference based on understanding and tolerance. For this to happen, boys and girls would benefit from developing together provided suitable strategies, such as those detailed in Chapters 6 and 7, are being adopted.

It is interesting that while it is noted that boys become more macho (that is, more aggressive, 'lively' and difficult to teach) and are implicitly or explicitly criticized for it, there is comparatively little analysis of how girls change although they are easier (more compliant) to teach. However, it is possible to analyse this in a different way. Table 9.1 shows how, if one accepts a gender binary, stereotypically boys and girls are supposed to behave (Stanworth 1981; Salisbury and Jackson 1996; Francis 1998).

Table 9.1 Stereotypical behaviour

Boys' stereotypical behaviour	Girls' stereotypical behaviour
aggressive	cooperative
bad behaviour	good behaviour
lack of work	work harder
low concentration	good concentration
competitive	supportive atmosphere
male bravado	girls bonding
	take on 'caretaker' role
against school ethos	with school ethos

Now, it is possible that *both* boys and girls are behaving in more stereo-typical ways in that the girls in the girl-only groups are also exhibiting greater stereotypical behaviour (similar principles can be applied to differences based on 'race' or social class). However, the girls are praised for this (because their behaviour is within the school ethos and produces better academic results), while boys are criticized for it. In fact, if one looks at only the social and emotional aspects of their behaviour, both boys and girls could be criticized. What masks this is the implicit focus on academic work. It is possible to argue that girls work too hard and are too focused on school. Maybe they can, like boys, lower their priority on homework and put more energy into other things, like 'doing nothing', playing games and exercising. If this were the view (and I realize this goes against the whole emphasis in schools at the moment), then boys could be regarded less on a deficit model and more as having something to contribute when they mix with girls. At present, it is common to see girls as positive role models, and boys as deficits (i.e. that boys should be more like girls, and that boys have little positive to contribute). The point here is that separation appears to produce greater stereotyped behav-iours in both boys *and girls*. This cannot be positive. A greater focus on how pupils can learn through interactions to improve their social and emotional relationships, including how to understand each other and empathize, could lay the roots of decreasing sexism (see Chapters 3 and 4). People would be more likely to be valued for what they are and what they bring to a situation.

Different perspectives, knowledges and understandings become positive. People are not the same and difference can be celebrated and accepted. In saying this, I want to reiterate that similarity and difference are important and the varied femininities and masculinities that are available to be drawn on can lead to what Samuels (2001: 38–45) calls a positive 'gender confusion', such that certainties over gender categorization are dissolved. As a result, gender boundaries become fluid and less threatening and, so difference is more likely to be celebrated. For such a fluidity to be achieved, the aims of schooling need to be changed and have a greater focus on the emotional development of pupils. However, these social and emotional aspects of co-educational schools can cause concern, and I now turn to this.

Social interactions in co-educational schools

Another set of arguments put forward to support single-sex schools concerns the social interactions of boys and girls. Supporters of single-sex schooling argue that co-educational schools are not good places for girls to be as they suffer harassment from boys. The girls' self-esteem and how much they feel in control can be affected (Stanworth 1981; Deem 1984; Mahony 1985; Kenway and Willis 1990; AAUW 1998; Shmurak 1998; Epstein and Johnson 2000; Skelton 2001; Datnow and Hubbard 2002; Salomone 2003; NASSPE 2004).

Self-esteem

Research into self-esteem has shown that both boys and girls experience a decrease in self-esteem as they enter and move through adolescence, but that there is a greater drop for girls (Orenstein 1994). However, self-esteem can be measured globally, or split into different parts – social, cognitive, athletic and general – which are shown to vary, sometimes with boys being greater and sometimes girls (Cairns 1990). Pamela Haag (1998: 18), in a book supportive of co-education, reviewed the research evidence and said 'neither school type has been shown in these studies to generate a greater quantity of overall self-esteem for girls, although a specific source of esteem – for example appearance or athletic skill – may differ for girls in single-sex and co-ed schools'. Similarly, Salomone (2003), who supports single-sex schools, also reviewed the research on girls having a voice, self-esteem and inner confidence, and indicated the complexity of the findings, especially when 'race' and class are included. Salomone stated that the reported large decline in girls' self-esteem had been found by one study to be small for both boys and girls, and that this was made up in adulthood (Kling *et al.* 1999). Salomone (2003: 211) also reported that while some research indicated that self-esteem was favoured in single-sex schools (Lee and Bryk 1986), another report found that this was only true for academically orientated schools (Cairns 1990), and other research found no differences for girls in either type of schooling (Foon 1988). Haag's and Salomone's overviews indicate the complexity of the educational situation, and that self-esteem and similar measures do not provide a sound basis for deciding on one type of schooling or the other. Indeed, it is interesting to note that Salomone does not refer to self-esteem in her conclusion, which supports the introduction of single-sex schooling.

A complicating factor, which is generally not separated out as a variable, is the effect of setting or streaming. Some research into streaming has indicated that the self-esteem and self-concept of boys is greater than that of girls when they are about 13 years old (Year 9), but that they are the same two years later (Year 11) (Ireson *et al.* 1999, 2001). However, pupils can have lower self-esteem in schools that set pupils by ability (Ireson *et al.* 2001: 9). Similarly, it has been found that grouping by ability disadvantages academically the least able students, while having little impact on high attainers (Venkatakrishnan and William 2003); it can negatively affect progress and that misplacement can affect a child's self-concept (Boaler 1997; Boaler *et al.* 2000; MacIntyre and Ireson 2002; William and Bartholomew 2004). Hence reducing setting and streaming, or moving completely to mixed-ability teaching, may have a larger effect on academic achievement and maintain self-esteem than changing to single-sex schooling.

The complexities of gender

Another line of argument is that girls suffer at the hands of boys in co-educational schools who use a variety of techniques to maintain male dominance. The techniques include the use of sexual language like 'slut', and hogging teacher time so that teachers pay more attention to boys than to girls (Deem 1984; Mahony 1985). Evidence was gathered that showed that teachers viewed boys and girls differently, with boys being seen as more active, creative (or having greater natural ability), troublesome and speaking more than girls; while girls were harder working (and so received less attention and instruction), conforming and passive (Measor and Woods 1984; Darling and Glendinning 1996). This focus on how girls suffered at the hands of boys was important in raising pedagogic issues that have to be resolved. This early research tend to see boys and girls as distinct categories and further research uncovered the complexity of gender identity and indicated that there were multiple masculinities and femininities – as well as sexualities – that pupils could, and did, draw on (Epstein 1988; Mac an Ghaill 1994; Connell 1995; Skelton 2001). These studies also explored how power was situated and some of the mechanisms involved (Paechter 1998). Much of this work focused on masculinities, and how male power was exercised over females, rather than researching the interplay of power between the two. One aspect the research revealed was that there were intersections of 'race', class and sexuality within any formulation of masculinities or femininities (Epstein 1988; Connell 1995, 2002; Mac an Ghaill 1997; Paechter 1998; Skelton 2001). Sewell (1997: xiii) wrote about 'race' and:

> the need to balance a theoretical rejection of essentialism, objectivism and universalism with a commitment to non-aggressive, democratic and pluralistic values. Therefore 'living identity through difference' recognises that we are all composed of multiple social identities, and thus any attempt to organise people in relation to their diversity of identification has to be a struggle that is constructed positionally.

Similarly, the complexity of identity is also reinforced by Creese *et al.* (2004: 191):

> We are mindful of the need to avoid cultural essences and absolutism when discussing gender. Indeed, at the centre of our argument is the belief that identity is socially constructed, highly contextualised, fluid and variable. Masculinities and femininities are hugely diverse as are the relations between and within each gender. Indeed, we do not wish to argue that boys speak in one way and girls in another across all contexts. We agree . . . that gender identity is an ongoing process.

Gender, ethnic, sexual and class identities are an ongoing process that is affected by the experiences, communications and dialogue that are encountered. It is through participation, and being part of a varied group, that we can come to an essence, a communal identity and recognize the 'we' in the 'I', and the 'I' in the 'we'. This cannot occur to the degree that significant others are not present. The multiple nature of identity makes separating out pupils on the basis of sex, 'race' or class to some extent arbitrary. In particular, the problem of separating pupils by sex for single-sex schooling is basically essentialist, as it is based entirely on biological sex. If one were to separate out pupils because of social reasons, why not do it on the basis of how well they get on together, so those boys and girls who could relate well were in one school, and those who could not in another? Or it could be based on who got on well across ethnic divides, or social divides? If one took these suggestions seriously, one would also have to ask if the separation would help any of the fears, projections, anxieties or prejudices that pupils have. The act of separation, on grounds of sex, 'race' or class, hides these and provides fewer opportunities for confronting them. Also, ambiguity and ambivalence are less visible.

Change in co-education settings

Clearly, though, if we are to keep pupils together, it is incumbent upon teachers to help pupils with their relationships. There is research that indicates that this is possible. Creese *et al.* (2004: 204) showed that the explicit teaching of collaborative skills created a respect for difference. Children were taught how to be tolerant of one another and build on group ideas. Children did not ignore 'the other'.

Allard and Cooper's (2001) research involved three primary schools where pupils, about 8 years old, worked in collaborative groups that were varied by the teacher. Allard and Cooper discuss gender power relations and indicate that when the teacher makes the expectation that boys and girls will work together cooperatively, then 'working together becomes "normalised" within this classroom culture because of specific techniques used by the teacher to help children understand and achieve such co-operation . . . How power is exercised in constructing classroom cultures plays a very important part in bringing about more productive gender relations in the classroom' (p. 167). One aspect that is stressed is the importance of making clear why the pupils are made to work with a variety of pupils.

Little research has looked positively at boy–girl relationships in schools. Allard and Yates's (2001) study is an exception. They found that boys and girls in Year 10 had different agendas; the boys were more concerned with competitive judgements, while the girls were concerned with the pressures of intimacy with other girls. However, these gendered differences and pressures were not a source of mutual misunderstanding, but instead provided a bridge to enjoyment of friendship with each other. In other words, gender difference was constituted as a source of pleasure among the Year 10 students. These findings are consistent with my own research (Matthews 2003a) that indicates pupils think it is very important the sexes learn about each other and appreciate the interactions (see Chapter 7). I would emphasize that acceptance of gendered differences are essential to the formation of identity. Similarly, Skelton (2001) found at Deneway School that sexism does not have to be a defining aspect of the relationship between boys and girls. This indicates, along with my own research, that co-educational schools can have an impact on gender and other relationships (Matthews 1996, 2004; Matthews and Sweeney 1997). We need to move beyond the gender wars so that inter-sex relationships are debated in schools, so they are acknowledged as interdependent and accepted for the pleasures as well as the difficulties they can bring (Haag 1999; AAUW 2001). Creese *et al.* (2004: 204) show the complexities of gender and pedagogy in the classroom and write, 'It is not just that this [fixating on the variable of gender] homogenises what are actually internally diverse groups; it is also that it becomes a way of not talking about other key variables'.

Co-education and the difficulties of change

In previous chapters, several reasons have been proposed for why pupils being together could possibly help them become less discriminatory. In essence, these are that:

1　Pupils will be less likely to project their anxieties onto 'others' to promote difference and power differentials.
2　Power differentials can more easily be made visible.
3　It is possible to help pupils to experience how it can feel to have less of a power differential.
4　Pupils can become less anxious over difference because it will be more familiar and not so 'foreign'.
5　Sameness and difference can be explored to bring out the overlap in masculinities and femininities.
6　Emotional literacy can be developed through the use of dialogue with 'others'. Emotions can be experienced and so pupils become more able to use them and to realize how others feel.
7　Concrete experiences can be used to make explicit that there are many masculinities and femininities (and variations of ethnicity, class, etc.) that can be drawn on.
8　It is possible for pupils to experience and internalize the politics of presence with 'others'. They can be enabled to consider, through practice, forms of deliberative democracy.

Being in co-educational and multi-ethnic schools can provide pupils with more knowledge, empathy and understanding of the 'other'. Pupils can interact in ways that develop their social skills and allow them to experience how boys and girls could interact. Chapters 6 and 7 have shown how pupils can help each other to learn and appreciate each other for their differences. These are clear theoretical arguments for co-educational multi-ethnic schools; I have yet to find any theoretical arguments to support separating the sexes will strengthen these processes. In general, there is the assumption that if the sexes are kept apart, then when they are older they will be able to deal with difference better. However, most psychological evidence refutes this and indicates that the earlier anxieties are confronted, the greater the chance that positive change will occur.

As we have seen, gender (un)consciousness is a central feature affecting change. We all have a cultural lens, which operates at a conscious level, so that we know how to behave towards each other and the other sex. However, much is actually unconscious and means that we interpret situations to fit into our beliefs and so reinforce that that is the way things should be. To change our beliefs about gender is not a simple process. People are unlikely to change if simply made aware (as in the single-sex situation) of gender issues. To give a simple example. When I train PGCE science students to become teachers, we discuss the importance of them asking questions and interacting with all the pupils, both boys and girls. To aid the processes the students, when they are teaching, are monitored on the positive and negative interactions they have with the pupils. The vast majority of students – male and female – are initially *unaware* of how much they over-interact with the boys in comparison with the girls, even though they are aware it should be equal, and know they are being monitored when I come in to observe. Both experience and practice are necessary to bring the unconscious into consciousness and then change the behaviour. Those students who go to single-sex schools have to complete a similar exercise on the distribution of questions and interactions. When these students move to a co-educational school, we find that learning the skills of distribution in a single-sex setting is only a partial help when the co-educational experience is then encountered. Schmuck *et al.* (2002: 206) emphasize that gender awareness is important, but not sufficient, and say it is important that 'Individuals recognize the unspoken assumptions that privilege, which is determined by the valued position in the society (sex, social class, and ethnicity), provides some individuals with access to social rewards'. They argue for a critical transformation of gender attitudes and stress that schools can help pupils 'question issues of privilege and dominance in the society', and that curricula could enable this. If boys and girls are together in these processes, each is there to express their views and make them felt. One aspect is that one cannot give power to others, it has to be taken. Schools can most effectively empower pupils (and this includes both boys and girls, as it is not the case that all boys are powerful and all girls are not) through placing them in situations where they can:

1   Make visible the power *exchanges* that are occurring.
2   Discuss and reflect on how those exchanges felt, and who had the most control and privilege, and in which areas of the interactions.
3   Make conscious their feelings to each other.
4   Be placed so they can experience how it feels to have a different power relationship – to the extent that it is possible.
5   Consider a critical transformation of relationships and how everyone benefits.
6   Engage in these processes with a sense of agency.

Clearly, the co-educational situation offers greater possibilities for raising these points than single-sex schooling.

Viewing sexuality positively

Gender is always with us and 'emotions play a central role in schooling and have many implications for learning, change and gender reform ... [we] do not sufficiently understand the complexities of the emotions involved, their psycho-dynamics and their social role, hence they are rather innocent about the gendered politics of emotion' (Kenway *et al.* 1998: 163). This means that gender pervades everything both consciously and unconsciously. Becky Francis (1998), in her study of primary pupils, found different constructions of gender were held by the pupils but most saw it as oppositional. Because most of the girls and boys held the latter views, Francis argues against masculinity and femininity being defined as relational and says: 'A *pro-equality* perspective should be offered to children, which actively attacks discrimination and con-structs the genders as *not different*' (p. 176). This approach is important as it recognizes similarities, but can be problematic because clearly genders (includ-ing different sexualities) *are* different. Sexuality, including heterosexuality, is a source of wonder, joy and affirmation, and provides one meaning to life – despite its difficulties and anguishes. As Connell (1987: 288) says:

> What would be our loss if they [current gender regimes/relations] went down the gurgle-hole of history?
> It has to be said that a great deal of our culture's energy and beauty, as well as its barbarism, has been created through and around gender relations ... Much of the fine texture of everyday life, from the feel of our own bodies, through the lore of running a household, to popular songs and everyday humour, are predicated on gender. Our eroticism and our imagination seem to be both limited and fuelled by gender. To discard the whole pattern does seem to imply a way of life that would be seriously impoverished by comparison with the one we know. At best it would be so different from the world of our experience that we can hardly know whether it would be desirable or not.

It seems to me that, while relationships, of all forms, bring our greatest pleasures and heartaches, the joys of desire, sexual pleasure and companion-ship are understated in schools. In many sexual relationships, difference is a key element in desire and, however lived out, masculine and feminine will have significant differences. They are also relational in the sense that 'mascu-linity' has no meaning outside an understanding of 'femininity'; the two are interdependent (Matthews 1998). The issue is one of appropriateness rather than gender. It is not appropriate to use gender differences when discussing who should or should not take up mathematics or English. The real problem is that different genders (used in the widest sense) are ascribed differences that do not exist and these are used to discriminate and allocate unwarranted privilege. It seems to me that one way forward is to work with the pleasures of difference. If we don't, we will find it difficult to justify 'difference-as-normal' and that difference, be it sexual or cultural, is to be celebrated. This includes all cultures, sexualities, and sexual and non-sexual relationships. In these encounters, ambiguity and ambivalence can surface over sameness and difference to help counter stereotypes.

Sexual relationships and power balances

An underplayed aspect that could be used in schools to help boys and girls is the area of desire. It is during their period of schooling that most pupils feel the first stirrings of desire and sexual pleasure. Yet schools, mainly because of unresolved adult fears and anxieties, put their collective heads in the sand and try to ignore that up to half of the adolescents in schools are engaged in sexual activity in one form or another (Kirby 2001; Wellings 2001). As Carol Lee (1983: 149) puts it:

> In a world as complex as ours it is . . . necessary that young people have the means to express their feelings and thoughts and of relating these to themselves and others. This way they may enter into relationships which sustain them and which in turn sustain others . . . Unless we do this young people are being sold dreadfully short, and for that we all pay . . . the ostrich position is tragic for both adult and child. It makes inconsolable adults and leaves children to fend for themselves.

This is not to say that schools do not cover sex education at all, but often the provision is limited. What they do not do, partly because of the pressures for cognitive success, is to integrate centrally emotional literacy between the sexes, and enable them to communicate. Schools cannot change their pupils' lives and experiences, but they can, through mixed-sex collaborative group work, using the types of strategies described in Chapter 6, enable pupils to experience good inter-gender dialogue, which involves power exchanges and not domination. Pupils need to experience what good communication between the sexes looks and feels like. Within relationships between the sexes, deliberative democracy is important. According to Giddens (1993: 188): 'The possibility of intimacy means the promise of democracy . . . We can envisage the development of an ethical framework for a democratic personal order, which in sexual relationships and other personal domains conforms to a model of confluent love'.

Discussions of sexual relationships in schools could be motivational for change because they involve caring, sharing, trust, communication, pleasure and power-sharing (Schnarch 1991). Giddens argues that the erotic can be vitalized as:

> a generic quality of sexuality in social relations formed through mutuality rather than through unequal power. Eroticism is the cultivation of feeling, expressed through bodily sensation, in a communicative context; and art of giving and receiving pleasure. Shorn of differential power, it can revive . . . aesthetic qualities.
>
> (Giddens 1993: 202)

While it is not evident in many relationships, intimacy, power sharing, democracy – and therefore equality – can all be linked. This is a powerful point for change as most pupils are concerned with forming sexual relationships and want to gain pleasure from them. If schools can cue into this, and make the connections between intimacy, equality and pleasure, they have a chance of accomplishing a change in pupils' attitudes to each other. This is not to deny the real difficulties involved in relationships, but to argue that the potential benefits from equal relationships could be worked out with pupils. And even better, schools can have their cake and eat it, since study after study has shown that the better and deeper the sex education that pupils experience, the later they are likely to engage in sex and the lower the teenage pregnancy rates (Baldo 1993; Kane and Wellings 1999; Kirby 2001; Swann *et al.* 2003; HDA 2004). The health and happiness of pupils as they grow into adulthood is centrally affected by their ability to forge good relationships. A happy marriage adds five years to a person's life, and more friends and better social networks improve one's immune system and can add up to nine years to life (and a positive personality seven and a half years) (Dobson 2004). These figures restore the balance to what I am saying: what really matters are *relationships of all forms*, of which the sexual is only one. It is in friendships that one hopes the basics of relationships like caring, sharing and trust are built up, rather than seeing relationships as about what you can get out of other people (Dweck 2000). Clearly, all these points can be made in single-sex schools as well as co-educational ones, but if both sexes are present the chances of understanding and change are greater.

The above discussion links with the importance of power being seen as a positive life force. At present power is commonly portrayed as negative (how men have power over women, how governments control the population, how multi-nationals use their power to exploit). This emphasis could change and power be analysed for the pleasure it can provide for both the giver and the receiver – but this requires that power is shared or it distorts the relationship. There are many aspects to positive power: the power to help, to bring relief, to make people laugh, the power of the pleasure bringer. Positive power applies to all relationships – in this section I have over-emphasized sexual relationships.

It also applies to same-sex relationships, but single-sex schooling, by the very nature of separation, can emphasize the negative aspects of power. Sex-separation says 'we are keeping you apart because otherwise you will suffer'. It does not say, 'the pleasure to be gained from boys and girls being together is vital for life!' In saying 'boys and girls' in this sentence, I do not mean just heterosexual, but include all sexualities and cultural backgrounds.

Girls need emotional development as well as boys

One generalization based on gender is that it is often accepted that girls are far more mature than boys and discuss their feelings more. This generalization may have truth in it, but it can mask that boys do discuss feelings, and that some girls are emotionally immature. Boys have emotionally difficult times and do carry out emotional work with feelings, even if they do not have the range of emotional languages that many girls have (Lee 1989, 1993; Kenway *et al.* 1998; Head 1999). The emphasis on boys can hide the fact that girls also need emotional development. For example, a young girl had gone on holiday with her parents, met a boy and then ran away to Turkey and married him. An article about this incident (which I cannot trace) argued that the assumption that girls are mature and good at handling relationships can be detrimental, as it can cover up how insecure they really are. This leads adults to overlook what would otherwise be suspicious behaviour, and lets girls get into situations that should be avoided. Now, I agree that girls are generally more mature than boys, talk a lot more about relationships, and are generally more able to discuss their emotions. However, this does not mean that they are mature or good at forming relationships. Female friendships are pervaded with similar problems as male ones; with like and dislike, and aggression (Hey 1997; George and Browne 2000; George 2004). For example, anorexia in girls can be an indication that they are not ready to become adult, and not a sexual adult, and can also mean that they do not want to be like their mothers (Williams 1997; Lee 2004). Also, girls can be over-emotional; it is often commented how boys can often get over arguments quickly, but girls can ruminate over incidents for ages. Similarly, in adult relationships it is often 'six of one and half-a-dozen of the other' when break-ups occur. Some women can be over-protective of their children and not aid their children in their passage to adulthood and leaving home. These instances illustrate how girls can need to develop emotionally. I have drawn attention to this *not* to get at girls, but to indicate that both boys *and* girls need to work at forming relationships. In the single-sex situation, it can be assumed that girls are socially and emotionally developed, and so schools can focus on the academic. To the extent to which we hold the stereotypes, girls may not be helped to develop their relationships in the way they need.

To me, the overriding issue is how to get pupils to recognize their communality (across ethnicity, sex and class) while accepting and celebrating their differences: ways of approaching this have already been suggested in earlier chapters. This brings the pleasure of power and everyone benefits from the attendant equality and democracy (Hofkins 2004).

Power, separation and violence

We can see conflicts all over the world. Many of these are cultural or religious as well as economic. To take concrete examples, there is the Israel–Arab conflict, the Catholic–Protestant conflict in Ireland, and the Balkan wars. Now I do not want to present these as simple cultural, religious or ethnic struggles; the roots are more complex and include economic ones. These conflicts are about one group of people having power, and the others wishing to take that power away. In this sense, power is taken as being oppositional. The power is overlaid with issues of mistrust, misunderstanding and violence of an emotional and physical nature. The underlying issues are not simply about personal prejudice, which if it was implies it would be possible to resolve the problems through learning about each other at a distance. It is much deeper, about psychological fears, anxieties, discriminations and a felt lack of justice. The problems are compounded as those with most power can undergo minimal self-reflection. Projection and misunderstanding play a part in maintaining hatred. There can be a fear of mixing and that the 'other's' views will contaminate one, let alone a fear of loss of economic resources. However, most people would agree that in the end the only way for the conflicts to be resolved is by dialogue between all parties. Violence will continue until, through interactions, peace becomes possible via understanding *and* a change in power. If the power situation can become seen as an exchange, that is liberational, then perhaps difference can be celebrated and everyone benefit. Power becomes part of pleasure, not just oppression (although power has the two possibilities of oppression and pleasure closely allied).

Now I realize that supporters of single-sex education could say that this discussion has no bearing on the single-sex/co-educational debate. I accept that the situations are entirely different, but believe that some principles apply; that contact and dialogue are essential to gain understanding and to change the nature of power. If for no other reason than that power has to be taken rather than given. In some cases, for example when some religious groups want single-sex education, it can be to preserve difference and to maintain male power. Against this I realize that when some feminists argue for single-sex education it is because they see it as a way of increasing female power and of gaining equality. While I agree with their aims, I do not, for the reasons given above, think that it is the way to do it.

The comprehensive ideal

Finally, I would like to turn to the comprehensive ideal (Benn and Chitty 1997; Chitty 2004) and that compulsory schooling should be organized around the principle of neighbourhood schools. Further, Benn and Chitty (1997: x) argue for a comprehensive *education* that aims to encompass everyone. A necessary precondition for a comprehensive education would be to have co-educational schools that cut across gender, ethnic, religious, sexual persuasion and class divides. It would be based on the importance of equal rights, social justice and equality. Further, the establishment of comprehensive education is seen by some as part of a democracy (Benn and Chitty 1997; Hillcole Group 1997). At present, although one hopes that this will change, full comprehensive education is impossible in many geographical areas due to the economic and cultural segregation of the population. However, it is possible for schools to be co-educationally comprehensive.

In many co-educational schools in Britain there are more boys than girls. This is partly because there are more single-sex girls' schools. The existence of single-sex schools undermines the potential of co-educational schools. It also calls into question the statistics that compare single-sex with co-educational schools. For it to be valid, the co-educational schools should have roughly equal numbers of boys and girls.

Conclusion

I would argue that the case for co-education is sound, especially when the focus of the arguments changes from simple considerations of academic performance to include the social dimension of human interactions. At present, girls generally outperform boys academically, so this does not seem to be a sound reason to argue for single-sex girls' schools. I believe that co-educational schools offer the greatest choice of possible futures for pupils and society. As indicated in Chapters 3 and 4, equity issues can be raised and tackled while developing emotional literacy. One aspect is that pupils of both sexes are in attendance and so have a voice of representation. The importance of discussing power and how projection can hide similarities and exaggerate differences was discussed in Chapter 5, while Chapters 6 and 7 indicated approaches to enabling boys and girls to appreciate each other through recognizing similarities and difference, while being taught strategies that enable them to collaborate, surmount conflict and help each other learn. Hence, the development of the whole child is focused on, rather than mainly academic performance. This is not to say that co-educational schools will be easy to teach in; indeed, because of gender issues and allowing anxieties to surface, they will be challenging. To realize the true potential of co-educational schools they need to change to promote the emotional literacy and power exchanges of the pupils, and this requires considerable change in our education system.

Note

1   This debate reminds me of the old arguments that brain differences meant that women were not as intelligent as men (Sayers 1982).

10 Broadening the emotional context

I have argued that it is important for schools to integrate emotional literacy into the curriculum. I believe that schools should be enabling pupils to become emotionally responsive, able to form peer and adult relationships, and to make the transition to a responsive and responsible adulthood, including cognitive progression. Some of the difficulties in deciding the best ways of achieving pupils' emotional progress have been indicated. However, there are wider influences from society that may act as a brake on emotional development. In this chapter, I will look at some of the ways in which societies may be changing and how that might affect people's emotions and discuss how schools can unwittingly act to exacerbate the pressures these changes can bring.

Emotions and control

Meštrović (1997) argues that we are entering a post-emotional society. He contends that there is now an attempt to bring emotions under control: 'I argue that western societies are entering a new phase of development in which synthetic, quasi-emotions become the basis for the widespread manipulation of self, others, and the culture industry as a whole' (Meštrović 1997: xi). Meštrović believes that individuals are becoming emotionally uninvolved. Further, that for people to be involved in action there has to be a connection between the emotions and intellect, and that this connection is decreasing. He argues that the emotions are being 'mechanized' through the forms of industrialization that place efficiency before feeling. People are becoming more isolated from each other, and in the workplace it can be difficult to maintain a strong sense of community and collegiality. In these ways, people become more emotionally controllable. In other words, people can be taught to be compliant rather than passionate. One could argue that Meštrović is wrong and that people are more engaged with their emotions as evidenced by the numbers of people engaged in counselling and psychotherapy. It could be argued that this emotional engagement is at a personal level and could be a response to the wider societal level that Meštrović is concerned with. I will now consider four possible threats to the achievement of emotional well-being that make people more controllable, and how schools might counter or exacerbate them: emotional anxiety, emotional attachments, surveillance, and emotional control in employment.

Emotional anxiety

There has been an increase in anxiety in society (Leary and Kowalski 1995; James 1998; de Botton 2004a, 2004b; Hamilton 2004; SP/SAA 2005). James (1998) and de Botton (2004b) point out that many societies have increased their economic wealth so one would expect people to be happier, yet in fact there has been an increase in depression and anxiety. Although there are many factors involved, both writers forefront the idea of 'status anxiety'. We worry about how others view us and how well we are doing in comparison with them. The extent to which we do this, how we do it, and how it affects us, is dependent on many factors but the main ones include family socialization processes and the way society encourages us to make these comparisons. These comparisons can *help* us with self-esteem, or be *maladaptive* in that they increase status anxiety. What James (1998) and de Botton (2004b) argue is that we may make comparisons with people who are above us. For example, if we are learning to drive a car and compare our performance with a professional driver, we will feel inadequate and suffer from status anxiety. Similarly, we can compare our income with very rich people. In each case, the deprivation we feel is *relative*. We can also compare ourselves with less well off people. However, our self-esteem and confidence requires that we feel that we are noticed and valued by those around us. Hence it is possible to compare ourselves with those of a similar status, and to focus on being well regarded by those people we know. These processes are of particular importance in childhood in all societies.

Do schools help or hinder pupils' anxiety?

James (1998: 63) reviews evidence that children who have had demands for high performance placed on them are more likely to develop self-destructive comparisons with others. Similarly, if a child is made to feel unattractive or worthless through being labelled 'bad' or 'stupid', he or she can feel subordinated and suffer depression. James argues that at the moment we are encouraged to compare a great deal: he calls it 'Death by a 1000 comparisons' and points out how present educational policies are responsible for an increase in anxiety because of the pressure placed on pupils (Slater 2004). We can see how the constant testing of pupils, culminating in exams and SATs, invoke constant comparison. These comparisons can result in competition between pupils and can contribute to an emotional distancing, which can increase anxiety and is evident in many countries around the world. For example, although figures are not certain, it appears that in Britain teenage depression has doubled in the last ten years (Holt 2004). One factor specifically mentioned was 'not being able to keep up with peers'. Similarly, there has been a 50 per cent increase, in a year, in young people phoning help lines 'because they are struggling to cope with the pressure of exams' (Childline 2004). There is concern over the mental health of children, with the incidences of bullying, self-abuse and suicide all increasing (Goodchild 2004a; Shaw 2004).

There are multiple causes of the increase in anxiety, including family breakdown, but school pressures are adding to it, and exam stress is sometimes the last straw. James (1998) indicates how the competitive nature of schooling has led to greater social comparison and insecurity for pupils, whether or not they are academically able. Anxiety fuels fears and acts to inhibit performance; pupils with high anxiety do not perform so well in exams. The pressure also leads pupils to increase their status anxiety and emotionally accept social hierarchies. The development of instrumental testing can have a profound impact to slow the growth of inner life and vitality. Because of the emphasis on the measurable, children can become seen as objects to be controlled, surveyed and even criminalized (Kelly 2003; Goodchild 2004b). In this way, pupils are 'other' to adults.

One way that schools can help decrease the anxiety that children experience is through increasing cooperation between pupils, reducing the amount of competition, especially through reducing the frequency of, and emphasis on, testing and examinations, and finding other ways to reduce social comparisons. Anxiety is debilitating and usually makes people easier to control. Hence schools can contribute to status anxiety, but could counter it through building pupil–pupil and pupil–adult cooperation, and a sense of community, through developing their emotional literacy. Achieving these will increase teachers' workload in the short term, but in the long term will decrease pressure as pupils' anxieties are reduced.

Emotional attachments

The second area is the need for emotional attachments. These include 'care giving and receiving, affiliation (the desire for emotional and physical contact) and altruism' (James 1998: 46). There is some evidence that young children are not developing socially as much as in the past (Basic Skills Agency 2003, 2005; Christakis *et al.* 2004; Literacy Trust 2004; Ward 2004) and that social phobia – which is a fear of meeting people – is increasing (Feldman 1999; SP/SAA 2005). Social anxiety is the fear of social situations that involve interactions with other people, and the fear and anxiety of being *judged* and *evaluated* by other people (SP/SAA 2005). There are several reasons for the increase in social phobia, like the present emphasis on the individual in society, combined with new technologies like TV and ICT, which make it easier for people to avoid social situations rather than having to confront their fears. Anxieties over meeting socially, or the lack of development of social skills, is an indication that emotional attachments of all forms are not being sufficiently made in society and school.

Do schools help or hinder the development of emotional attachments?

The introduction of social and emotional learning programmes should help pupils to mature and develop emotional attachments of all forms. However, schools can undermine this development to a certain degree through focusing on the individual pupil. At present, it can be argued that there is, throughout society, a focus on the individual at the expense of relationships. Clearly, the main place that we experience and learn about emotions is in the family, and then with friends. However, schools are important because of the influence they can exert. James (1998: 335) states that: 'From a social-comparison standpoint, the key issue is whose interests are best served by the present system, which starts formal teaching too young and is too intensive and exam-orientated. From a clinical psychological standpoint it is difficult to see many benefits to the children and a great many destructive consequences'.

The problem is that an education system can be so focused on assessing each pupil individually that it reinforces a separation between pupils and does not sufficiently recognize the importance of the social aspects of learning. Teacher-centred whole-class teaching focuses on individual pupils learning from the teacher, and so separates pupils socially. Social separation is also reinforced with the idea of individualized learning materials for each pupil. For example, in England the Minister for School Standards stated that decisive progress in educational standards occurs when careful attention is paid to each child and their individual learning styles, motivations and needs. He called for a rigorous use of individual pupil target setting linked to high-quality assessment (Milliband 2004). All of these located ability in an individual, and imply that factors like learning styles are comparatively fixed. In Dweck's terms, the non-social entity model, rather than the social incremental model, is reinforced. The concentration on the individual reduces the importance of the group, and the recognition of dependence and interdependence on each other for learning and support goes largely unrecognized. It separates pupils from their communal culture. On the other hand, pupils can be helped to recognize the importance of group effort when they support each other in the class.

The emphasis on individual learning also leads to a non-social view of learning, and an isolation from feelings; social interaction concretizes feelings (Vygotsky 1978). Similarly, it is possible to treat pupils' emotions and self-esteem as if they could be individualized through, for example, the acceptance of the concept of EQ. While individually experienced emotions are important, there is an interplay between the cultural setting of the individual and how emotions are experienced. For example, suppose a pupil is experiencing racism in a class. This will not only affect how they feel and their capacity to learn, it will also influence their self-esteem. Griffiths (1998) argues that self-esteem is usually seen as an independent variable, can therefore be correlated with other factors like achievement, and so avoids the discourses of social justice that raise power relationships and the way that culture produces discriminations that affect self-esteem. If individualistic ideas of EQ and self-esteem are rejected, then it is possible, through the inclusion of the cultural dimensions of emotions, that difference-as-normal can be accepted (Chetcuti and Griffiths 2002). Accepting that all people are different, and using this as a positive, enables pupils and teachers to argue that people should be valued for their differences. So self-worth can be built on valuing yourself without comparison with others, or at least, less comparison. This would help decrease status anxiety, as engaging in difference-as-normal encourages dialogue and promotes the development of emotional attachments.

The greater the individualization and social separation of peer from peer, the more difficult it is to form grounded emotional attachments. This is because anxieties over relationships will be hidden rather than be allowed to surface so that they can be confronted. One key aspect that I am going to focus on briefly is sexual emotional attachments. Children are aware of sexuality from an early age. Throughout primary and secondary schooling, pupils engage in play about sex-roles. During adolescence the world changes as boys and girls perceive and relate to each other differently – irrespective of their sexuality. Rich and varied interactions can take place as friendship is occasionally permeated with desire. Sexuality is viewed and experienced as a private part of our lives, and it is often fraught with tension and anxiety. Surveillance and judgements, rather than sympathetic emotional support, hinder facing up to and dealing with these anxieties and can increase a sense of internal chaos. It is partly because of these tensions that adults can find it difficult to talk openly with children to help them with their passage to sexual maturity. The silence over sex and different sexualities does not help pupils come to terms with their anxieties, especially if they are gay or lesbian, but rather encourages them to deny them. This disavowal that pupils are undergoing sexual feelings and require sincere help is a denial of eroticism, which does not help young people to be authentically in touch with their feelings. Pupils need encouragement and support to make the transition to being self-determining and moving away from the authority of the parent. Dealing and discussing fully with issues around love and sex enables pupils to have authentic emotions that enable them to connect with their desires and to go on to make positive decisions. This is part of the reason why there are lower teenage pregnancy rates in countries that have full sex education programmes (Kane and Wellings 1999; Kirby 2001). In other words, pupils need to have social and emotional help to develop and schools can help in this through emphasizing the social, emotional and collaborative nature of learning.

Finally, if adults feel their own sexual relationships are not good, they can be envious of adolescents' emerging sexuality and their capacity to explore. Rather than recognize this, adults can project their discontentments onto the adolescents, who are then in 'need' of strict supervision. Similarly, if adults feel over-controlled at work, they can transfer these feelings onto children.

Surveillance

In this section, I discuss surveillance and pupils, but to begin I need to review surveillance in society at large. Surveillance is a contested area of research and it is beyond the scope of this book to give proper discussion. I will therefore cover the basic ground required for the purposes of this section, and provide references for the interested reader to follow up.

Surveillance of people in society has always occurred and can be both positive and negative; the data held on medical records can save our lives as well as being used as a source of information on us. At present, the techno-logical surveillance of people is increasing. There are many concerns about the possible attendant decrease in civil liberties and the effects it could have on society (Davies 1996; Graham and Wood 2003; Lyon 2003; Liberty 2004; O'Harrow 2005). There are many forms of information collected on us, which give us an electronic identity or persona (Norris and Armstrong 1999). As there are a variety of sources, some less secure than others, it can give criminals an opportunity for identity theft (Hunter 2002).

What concerns most people is the oppressive nature of surveillance and that it invades our privacy; we may not know what information is being col-lected on us, if it is accurate, and who it is passed on or sold to. A further worry is that, since information is power, it can be used to control us: 'We should not be seduced by the myth of benevolent government for, while it may only be a cynic who questions the benign intent of their current rulers, it would surely be a fool who believed that such benevolence is assured in the future' (Norris and Armstrong 1999: 230).

As more information is gained, so there is a bureaucratization that results in people becoming objects of surveillance. The worst scenario being that 'Big Brother' society is created and our privacy will vanish (Garfinkel 2001; Parker 2001; Hunter 2002). However, Lyon (1994) argues that it is the loss of personhood that is the real concern, and I have argued that acceptance of rational bureaucratic management, together with the suggestion that computers can be 'intelligent', can lead to a de-humanized view of people (Matthews 1991, 1992). In the end, we can lose our identity as we self-censor our behaviour, especially creative and spontaneous aspects, because we never know if we are being watched (Jensen and Draffan 2004). Of course, cameras do not watch us; there is always 'someone' who decides who is going to be the object of the gaze. This 'someone' has perceptions of who needs to be spied on that they bring to the observations. Their conscious and unconscious views may be discriminatory, which will result in some people being scrutinized more than others: 'CCTV operators selectively target those social groups they believe most likely to be most deviant. This leads to the over-representation of men, particularly if they are young or black' (Norris and Armstrong 1999: 196).

Certain geographical areas are under surveillance more than others and this is often to protect the property of those people with wealth, which is why there are so many cameras in shopping malls: 'As space becomes subservient to the interests of business and defined by an "ecology of fear" difference is not something to be celebrated but to be managed, segregated and excluded' (Norris and Armstrong 1999: 23).

As a result, society and people become divided. Also, since knowledge is power, and the data collected through information technology generally goes to the wealthy, it can serve to increase social class divides. There is evidence that at present surveillance is a form of social sorting and is a powerful means of creating and reinforcing social differences (Lyon 2002). In particular, under the fears generated over the threat of terrorism, people of certain ethnic and religious backgrounds are being kept under observation. Fear is being used to push through acts against civil liberties, even though it is disputed that security and surveillance go hand in hand (Lyon 2003; Peissi 2003). One way of alleviating people's fears about surveillance is to have openness and yet:

> in the current climate it is hard to see how calls for democratic accountability and ethical scrutiny of surveillance systems will be heard as anything but liberal whining. Yet democratic accountability starts with a willingness to listen to the voice of the other. And ethical scrutiny begins with care for the other, to relieve and to prevent suffering.
>
> (Lyon 2001: 5)

Openness, two-way communication and trust are essential in generating social capital and a feeling of community. They are the basis of relationships between people and democracy. Yet any closed system of surveillance, where people do not know what information is held on them and how it may be used, invokes social distrust between people, especially if one person is 'different' (Lyon 2003). One aspect of having a community is that people feel responsible for and look after each other. The more they feel the all-seeing eye will do it for us, the more emotional distance may result and social participation and trust become undermined. At any rate, a feeling of responsibility for each other is not generated.

Lyon (1994) warns against pessimistic attitudes and argues that while electronic surveillance represents a threat to social participation and personhood, 'The prominent paradox is that surveillance simultaneously represents both a means of social control and a means of ensuring that citizens' rights are respected' (p. 219). For example, through data collection incidences of racism can be evidenced and so acted upon, and police databases can help solve crimes. We are willing participants in our own surveillance through the use of debit cards, store cards, internet banking and caller ID phones because we find them useful and liberating. Surveillance is always with us; think of the teacher in the classroom who has 'eyes in the back of their head'. What matters, Brin (1999) argues, is the balance between freedom, privacy and surveillance, and that this is best served by openness and accountability. Accountability must work both ways; the transparent society is a call for reciprocal transparency so we know what the government, the wealthy and techno-elite are doing, and that they, in turn, can be watched.

There are complex debates about surveillance and I have only had space to discuss some briefly. I want to pose the question, 'How can we move forward and help pupils as they move into society as adults?' Lyon argues that we must hold onto the ideal of a 'good society' if we are to move forward and not become so pessimistic that inaction results. He argues: 'Imaginative analysis, informed by constructively critical theory based on notions of participation, personhood and purpose . . . would create space for genuine alternatives' (Lyon 1994: 225). We can note that the first two of these, participation and personhood, both require emotional development of the individual. Pupils should also have sufficient knowledge to be able to be constructively critical so that they can discuss alternatives. I do not know of any schools that fully engage pupils in the above social, moral and political debates. Indeed, it appears that if anything pupils are being prepared to accept surveillance rather than consider its impact.

Surveillance of pupils

I am aware that the surveillance of pupils is limited and that this reflects what is happening in society. However, there are indications that surveillance in schools may grow substantially and I wish to discuss some of the possible negative effects of this on pupils' emotional and social development. I believe that if the surveillance of pupils were to increase, it could slow down their ability to develop emotional attachments. To explain this, I first need to cover some key points on how adults can treat children. Children can be treated as growing adults who are continually changing and maturing. In other words, as they grow older they are already engaged in practical adulthood – similar to the view of citizenship in Chapter 1. For pupils to make the transition to adulthood, they need to develop an integrated and coherent identity while forging relationships with peers. They are helped in this project by having emotional support from adults who will listen and take their views into account. They need to be trusted and given responsibility to explore the world and themselves. This requires time to themselves, time to play and to have 'nothing to do', in the constructive sense, without supervision or surveillance. They can then learn to become street-wise and independent. The passage to adulthood marks a gradual change in the nature of authority, from control to self-control: from choices being made for children to making their own decisions. When treated in this way, childhood and adulthood are seen as a continuum and so children are not seen as 'other' to adults, while differences are acknowledged. On the other hand, adults can treat children in ways that focus on the child–adult differences, and on the need to control them. This implies being emotionally distant and, as a result, keeping them childish. With discussion in the background I will now look at what I consider to be three linked disturbing aspects of surveillance.

The first aspect is that under the guise of 'progress' – pupils are constantly monitored not only for their academic work, but also behaviour. Some schools have CCTV in the playgrounds, mainly to watch pupil behaviour and instances of bullying, while some have even introduced them into the classroom (Hagan 2003). In some cases, pupils control the camera to watch what is happening in the school. In Texas, 28,000 students are being fitted with electronic badges so their movements on and off buses can be monitored (Richel 2004), although some parents are opposing such surveillance (Bailey 2005). The main reason given for the monitoring in Texas is in case the children are kidnapped, yet no child in the region has been kidnapped. In Japan, students are given electronic chips and tracked when they leave school, and parents can be sent a message informing them when this happens (Associated Press 2004). Parents can now track their children via their mobile phones, find out if they go outside a specific area, track their speed when they drive and be sent an alarm if they go over the speed limit, check exams and homework grades without talking to the child or seeing their homework, and check the child's use of their computers and messages sent (Goodman 2004). It is probable that the effects of surveillance will encourage emotional distance as information can be gained electronically rather than through personal communication. For example, the parent should be talking to their child about homework, how well they are doing, and so on. It is difficult to see why schools would release such information electronically because teachers should request to see parents to discuss any problems. Similarly, bullying is a whole-school issue that requires policies on pupil relationships and conflict resolution programmes. By itself, CCTV can make the bullying become more hidden and teachers think that it has decreased. The surveillance also keeps the hierarchy of control as adult over child, rather than transferring control to the child. Psychologically, if children are not helped to take self-control, they can feel insecure unless adults tell them what to do and are supervising them. It promotes a culture of dependency, which children either can remain in or rebel against. Children need help to make the transition to self-determination, to forge relationships and to make mistakes. Surveillance polices the borders of freedom and imagination while undermining trust. My intuition is that there will be long-term psychological damage to children if there is increasing surveillance, as the purpose of surveillance is control from above. This is not to deny that parents and teachers have to control children, but this should be done with emotional connectedness and the development of trust. The use of surveillance technology enables both over-control and emotional distance. If children are stunted in their emotional growth and not guided to become independent self-determined people, they will be more likely to grow to become adults with the ungrown child in them. When Stubbs (2005: 29) said 'The tyranny of curricula, exams and league tables compels schools to rear battery students, when we all know free-range is best', she intuitively combined both forms of control: control through the curriculum, and that children need to be able to roam (free-range) without supervision.

Also, both children and adults need to 'horse around', play and take risks. Under the surveillance of cameras, both children and adults start to self-moderate their behaviour. The idea that 'You have nothing to worry about if you are not doing anything wrong' is a red herring. When you grew up you would have minded if your parents had been in your room when you had friends round because it would have been a gross invasion of privacy. You would know that all your actions would constantly have been judged (and found wanting or silly even by the best of parents). Everyone needs privacy to do things without any judgements. Hence the constant monitoring can put a break on spontaneous vivacity and on the development of 'self' while promoting instead continued adult control, with a lack of communication and emotional dialogue.

Second, surveillance also undermines the sense of community where people help and take responsibility for each other because technology is being used to 'solve' problems that at root have social and emotional causes. Technology only provides a short-term control answer. Also, there is always a person behind the camera and certain groups of people are monitored more than others – usually from the ethnic minorities and young men – hence creating division (Norris and Armstrong 1999). There is no reason to assume that the same would not happen in schools. Who is observed tends to be based on beliefs about behaviour, not natural justice. Hence a sense of community is undermined as some pupils will be watched more than others. Also, always observing pupils who, say, are badly behaved will not necessarily make them better, as the underlying social causes need to be addressed. To the extent that surveillance may be successful in controlling behaviour, it can mask the real social and emotional causes that should be addressed for successful change. Hence it can make effective social change less likely, undermine community and a sense of shared responsibility for each other.

Third, surveillance can prevent schools from preparing pupils to think critically about the problems of surveillance in the society in which they live. Schools are increasingly preparing pupils to accept surveillance, rather than be open to question it. As a person during an interview stated: 'But, with the presence of CCTV everywhere, I suppose this [cameras in schools] is an inevitable step in modern culture' (Hagan 2003). As a result, they are more likely to accept surveillance in society. Technology is being used to alleviate social problems instead of focusing on the root causes like poverty and inequality. We are going through a period where governments are increasingly using the threat of terror to control their populations, and increasingly children and adults accept this view, even though it is open to question (Curtis 2004). Civil liberties in many countries are under threat (Liberty 2004). People need an emotional maturity to be able to question governments and not give in to fear. It is difficult to see how pupils can be prepared to contribute fully to a deliberative democracy if constantly kept under surveillance.

Surveillance of pupils is in its infancy, and here I have speculated on what might happen. It is an aspect of education and society worthy of deep reflection before any further decisions are made on introducing technological surveillance, despite the climate of increasing surveillance in society.

However, we can also see that, together with moves to individualization in education, surveillance could operate to decrease the quality of emotional attachments and spontaneity that pupils can build up with peers and adults. To reverse these trends could also help pupil–teacher relationships and so make teaching easier.

Emotional control in employment

An important aim for schools is to enable pupils to promote economic growth in a competitive world (DES 1985; Labour Party 1996; Chitty 2004). This requires individuals who have a range of skills and abilities; hence the present stress on passing exams. However, to compete effectively it is often crucial that managers and entrepreneurs have an emotional distance from their workers (Chodorow 1978). Also, the workplace is changing and in many countries more people are becoming involved in service industries. With this shift, according to Hochschild (1983, 2003), comes a new danger to the emotional well-being of many of the population. Hochschild argues that in the service industries the employees have to do 'emotional labour'. That is, they have to manage their feelings; for example, flight attendants have to smile, be nice and always cheerful. This is actually an important part of the job, as no one wants to have a surly stewardess! But to do this the attendants have to hide their real feelings. To act in this sort of way requires that they know how they 'should' feel – Hochschild calls this a 'feeling script', and is an important part of life. We all have to control our feelings and behave appropriately in certain situations, like when at a funeral or birthday party. Feeling scripts are also intertwined with gender. To accept the stereotypes for a moment, girls (and gay men) are supposed to express their emotions, and boys hold them in. These gendered emotions, Boler (1999: xxi) argues, are part of a way of organizing access to power in our culture: 'The emotional rules are not arbitrary; they are systematically designed to enforce our acceptance of gendered divisions of "private" and "public", of women as emotional and men as rational. These divisions justify social stratifications and maintaining power in the hands of an elite few'. In this case, people are controlled through their emotions and the degree to which some groups can express certain emotions, and others not. What concerns Hochschild is what happens when industry demands the management of feelings through training and supervision. This commercialization of human feeling has costs: 'It affects the degree to which we listen to feeling and sometimes our capacity to feel' (Hochschild 2003: 21). Flight attendants can feel emotionally exhausted at the end of a flight and be emotionally dead for a while. In more extreme cases, because they are expected to draw on both their parental and sexual roles, they can suffer a loss of sexual interest. The point is not that flight attendants should not be nice and relaxed to help the tensions of the flight; it is about the emotional boundaries expected and the extent to which employees are in control of the boundary. Hochschild is concerned about the way managers in industry are controlling people's emotions, which makes employees, and the population, more susceptible to social anxiety:

> If rapid periods of change induce status anxiety, they also lead to anxiety about what, after all, the feeling rules are. In times of uncertainty, the expert rises to prominence. Authorities on how a situation ought to be viewed are also authorities on how we should feel. The need for guidance felt by those who must cross shifting social sands only adds importance to a more fundamental principle: in the matter of what to feel, the social bottom usually looks for guidance to the social top. Authority carries with it a certain mandate over feeling rules.
>
> (Hochschild 2003: 75)

The implication of Hochschild's research is that increasingly emotions, rather than being personal and private, are being seen as a commodity that can be a 'product' for the benefit of corporations. It can also be argued that businesses are using emotional labour to force through controls of all forms. There is concern over control and what happens when feeling becomes a commodity. Hochschild concludes: 'And how, in this realm [of marketized private life] do we manage our attachments to – and detachments from – one another? What do we feel? I don't know yet. But stay tuned' (Hochschild 2003: 207).

Teachers and emotional labour

Teachers are also an example of the cost of emotional labour. They have to control their emotions all the time. They always have done, there is nothing new in this. However, because of the present pressures of exams and testing, teachers are less able to relate to pupils as they might like. This is one way of emotionally controlling people. When I began teaching, the main emphasis was on pupils gaining understanding, and time was available to deviate from the curriculum or to spend time addressing pupils' emotional needs. Progression was taken to mean that pupils would gain a greater understanding with more complex depth. Teachers knew that this occurred over time and was neither predictable nor consequential. The same linear teaching did not produce understanding in all pupils, and one would not generally know what particular combination of factors would lead to the response 'Oh yes, now I understand it'. This has changed and now in England and many other countries performance-orientated goals are specified. Progression becomes defined as achieving these performance goals, so teachers are under pressure to think of their pupils through the lens of cognitive testing and adapt their teaching in ways that contradict what they believe is good pedagogy (Pedulla 2003). This results in emotional stress (Adams 2001). Hence teachers can increase their internal conflicts and become separated emotionally from their pupils; see them instrumentally, and so reinforce an 'us/them' split.

Teachers are aware that their professional responsibilities include being responsible for the pupils' social, emotional, moral, ethical and physical dimensions and that these require time, but have to accept the 'feeling script' put on them by the demands of curricular coverage and SATs. It is damaging to force people to teach and think about something in ways that do not match their beliefs. To be forced to think of pupils through the veil of mainly cognitive achievement masks thinking of children as competent learners who make uneven, unpredictable progress through ideas. Hence time is *not* spent on thinking of them as children with needs for creativity, self-expression and physical and emotional growth. The outcome is that teachers now have to do a great deal more emotional labour as they are forced to teach and relate to pupils in ways that do not correspond to the emotional demands of children's education or of the teacher's job. For teachers to keep their emotions 'in order' (emotional self-censorship) is hard work that drains energy. Teachers can come to accept the feeling rules and be more emotionally distant with their pupils than they wish to. Hence there can be a silence over emotional matters when pupils need time for discussion with an adult. The teachers can be unaware of the energy this denial requires. Curriculum demands and workload, when combined with the pressure to get pupils through exams, are causing a great deal of teacher stress (Michelson and Harvey 2000; Wilson 2002). This emotional stress makes teachers more controllable in the sense that they have less energy to respond to or challenge dictates from above with which they do not agree. Some people can accept the dictates more than others, and because there has been no discussion to air different views, a distance from colleagues can be created, which has been cited as one of the causes of stress (Wilson 2002).

Hamilton (2004) voices another concern about the importance attached to economic development. The general thrust of government policy is to be competitive in the marketplace to ensure economic growth. Emotional labour is only one part of that push for growth. However, Hamilton (2004: x), echoing James and de Botton, states that:

> despite several decades of sustained economic growth, our societies are no happier than they were. Growth not only fails to make people contented; it destroys many of the things that do. Growth fosters empty consumerism, degrades the natural environment, weakens social cohesion and corrodes character.

Hamilton argues that we should not be trying to get ever increasing amounts of economic growth, but rather focus on leading rich lives and developing those things that will make us more contented and happy. These include having emotional ties and friendships, and feeling control over one's life. Hamilton (2004) produces evidence that income and wealth only accounts for 10 per cent of personal happiness (p. 34), which indicates that their pursuit is over-valued and more attention should be paid to developing relationships. If there is any truth in the arguments of Hochschild and Hamilton, there are implications for schools. Teachers have a very difficult task in both preparing pupils for work and alerting them to its problems.

Hence, it can be argued that, in different ways, the workplace and education are becoming a site of struggle for the control of emotions. It is uncertain how much industry will change, and educational policy alter, to try to control emotional labour, but it is significant that Hochschild's book was reissued in 2003, 20 years after it was first published. I feel that it is important that educators are alerted to the discussion on how industry may be changing so that they can consider how best to prepare pupils *emotionally* to be able to contribute, and be constructively critical, in the world of work. Clearly, schools can be organized to develop emotional literacy programmes, for both pupils and teachers, so that they can understand the mechanisms that can lead to emotional control. We can also note, though, that CCTV in the classroom will further increase teachers' emotional and professional self-censorship and decrease the creative risks they are likely to take.

Social anxiety, inequality and health

Several issues have been raised above: the extent to which education makes pupils aware of the problems and benefits of industry, the problems of anxiety, and the extent to which schools should be about enabling pupils to lead happy, fulfilled lives. Most people would add that pupils should also be brought up to be physically healthy. Wilkinson (1996, 2000) brings many of these threads together. He has studied the socio-economic factors that make societies and groups within them healthy. He found that people were healthier, had less illness and lived longer in societies where there was more equality, and this was largely independent of gross national product. Rich countries were not necessarily healthier. Similarly, if one takes two cities in America, one with greater inequalities in wealth of the people living in it than the other, the more equal city will have fewer health problems (Wilkinson 1996). Wilkinson establishes that this is probably because 'more equal societies are less stressful: people are more likely to trust each other and are less hostile and violent towards each other' (Wilkinson 2000: 3) and that social anxiety is a factor. Social anxiety is due to a fear of negative social evaluation by others, but the quality of friendships and relationships is a factor in decreasing anxiety:

> social status and supportive social relationships are linked not only because they both exert a powerful influence on health but also because of the strong tendency for social relationships to weaken as the social structure hierarchy becomes more hierarchical. In an important sense, social status and friendship are the opposite sides of the same coin. Social hierarchy . . . is based on power, coercion and access to resources regardless of the needs of others. In contrast, reciprocity, mutuality, sharing and recognition of others' needs mark friendship.
>
> (Wilkinson 2000: 21–2)

Patterns of dominance that are associated with inequality and low socio-economic status *undermine* a sense of mutuality and trust which help make a person's immune system stronger and so promotes health. As James and de Botton also point out, it is maladaptive social comparisons that are crucial. Socially anxious people can often disaffiliate from society and are more prone to depression, smoking and alcoholism. Hence Wilkinson brings together the work on status and social anxiety, inequality, class and health. Being wealthy may not make people happy, but as sure as eggs are eggs, lacking wealth makes poor people anxious, unhappy and ill. This leads me to believe that education should be for pupils to lead rich lives, not a life of riches.

Summary

We can see that schools have a prime responsibility to develop pupils' emotional literacy so that they can be responsive to their own feelings, without being at their mercy. Pupils should also be able to control their emotions, while also feeling passionately about people, causes and inequalities. A realization of the common humanity and ambiguity of people is a component of this. Pupils need educating to be comfortable socially, be happy, form friendships and close sexual relationships. As Lee and Robbins (1998) found, people with good social connectedness correlated with them having fewer anxieties. Pupils should grow up healthily and be able to balance their need to express their individuality with their regard for the common values and beliefs that are required for a sense of communality. Through this balance they can develop trust, mutuality and the recognition of interdependence and a gradual transition from the authority of the adult. The hierarchy of pupil and adult has to change to help the formation of emotional attachments: 'At every level, hierarchies are characterized by social exclusion rather than inclusion. That is why greater inequality is associated with deterioration in the quality of social relations' (Wilkinson 2000: 76).

For schools to help in all of the above areas is going to be difficult, and while in the short term developing the ideas will increase pressures on teachers, in the long term it should reduce them. In this chapter, I have outlined some of the pressures that may exacerbate the problems. If schools enable pupils to develop their emotional literacy, it will help them take their place in society, irrespective of whether or not the issues identified continue or not. If teachers and policy makers have these issues in mind, they will be more likely to produce an environment that will aid pupils' social and emotional development rather than make them susceptible to outside emotional control.

11 Ways forward

The aim of this chapter is to review some of the issues covered in the book and indicate their importance to schools. There will be many complexities and variations depending on the particular context of the schools in which teachers work. Consequently, this chapter does not contain a list of what teachers or schools could or could not do. The processes that the teachers, managers, support and technical staff all go through are as important as school policies that emerge. Within each school, teachers and other staff will need to work out what policies to implement, how these may be accomplished and develop strategic plans for the short or long term. This will require sensitivity and awareness to the type of school and the community in which it is set. Although this book has focused on pupils, nearly all the areas covered also apply to teachers.

Our emotions are constantly changing and are the source of all our pleasures and pains and shape how we relate to others. This book has argued that we cannot afford to undervalue pupils' emotional development in schools. Our children need and deserve more from us. One theme running through the book has been the importance of emotional development, which is intimately connected to issues of equity and social justice. A second theme has been the importance of equity and the associated power relationships. These are forged at the individual psychic level and at societal levels, although in this book the former has been focused on to the exclusion of the latter. Power is maintained by emotional distance, certainties, rigidities and setting up psychic boundaries that emphasize difference over similarity. All of these are used as 'justifications' for separating people physically, psychologically or socially. Hence, I have argued, to move to a more democratic and equitable society schools can concentrate on pupils' emotional literacy to forge emotional inclusion, ambiguity and fluidities. These will help pupils set up fluid psychic boundaries that emphasize similarities while celebrating difference and seeing it as a source of pleasure. Power exchanges, and the pleasure that comes from sharing power, can be focused on. The *processes* of communication and getting to know and accept each other should be emphasized alongside developing cognitive learning. However, there are real dangers in an emotional literacy curriculum; it can be seen as something to be taught rather than experienced, it can be used to exert more surveillance and control over pupils rather than liberate them.

In this book, I suggest ways of developing integrated practices and policies to meet the emotional needs of pupils within socially diverse contexts. I appreciate that teachers can feel that these suggestions mean that they have even more to do, but in the longer term the implementations should result in less pressure, greater enjoyment in teaching and a supportive school atmosphere.

I will start by looking at (1) General issues and then consider (2) emotional literacy and cognitive skills, (3) pedagogies, (4) equity and social justice and (5) continuity and transformation.

1. General issues

Schools exist for many purposes, one of which is to enable pupils to learn academically so that they can in turn make a contribution to society. Schools can also attend to pupils' needs and desires. To do this, schools need to consider a wide range of approaches that ensure excellence and equity for all students. A too narrow and rigid view of the curriculum can lead to an overemphasis on narrowly defined achievement that loses touch will be the real needs of equipping pupils for a changing world. All curricula are based on knowledge that has already been discovered, and so form only one aspect of preparing pupils for the future. Since the technological world is changing fast, we require an education system that will encourage acceptance of self, and difference, with vitality and the confidence to face change. These are social and emotional issues that speak to ethical and moral values as well as cognitive ones. Pupils will be more prepared to be active democratic citizens if they are enabled to mature, accept difference and be self-critical (see Chapters 1 and 2).

Here are some points about general approaches in the school that teachers may wish to consider:

A social view of learning and relationships. In principle, pupils are helped if they are encouraged to accept all abilities, including intelligence, as cultivated through effort, experience and learning, what Dweck (2000) calls the incremental view of learning. Pupils will then be more able to face difficulties and setbacks, have growth and transformability (Hart *et al.* 2004) beliefs and a relaxed view of others. Teachers can ask themselves how can:

- a cooperative classroom atmosphere be generated where pupils work in mixed collaborative groups to help each other, and where effort rather than achievement is praised?

- pupils be encouraged to look at the strategies they use to learn and realize that if they do not achieve, they can try another strategy, rather than thinking they cannot do it?
- we ensure a whole range of assessment techniques are used so avoiding overemphasizing academic achievement through formal tests? This could include discussing progress and results with pupils rather than putting up or reading out lists of grades that encourage comparison and competition.
- mixed-ability teaching be developed so pupils are *learning-within-relationships* (Chapter 1)?
- we avoid a culture of comparison and anxiety (Chapter 10)?

Supportive classroom atmosphere. One key element in the teacher–pupil relationship is that a classroom atmosphere is generated in which individual differences are celebrated and pupils feel valued (Noble and Bradford 2000). The uniqueness of each individual can be seen to contribute to the classroom. One part is to recognize that personal experiences are valid. This is a counter to the objective reality usually stressed in academic subjects. Open-mindedness for both pupils and teachers is an asset. This can be generated through accepting ambiguity rather than teaching for certainties.

Trust and adulthood. One aspect of enabling children to develop socially is to see them as already having aspects of adulthood within them, and to gradually trust them more. Avoiding a culture of dependency with greater surveillance of all forms is a key element (Chapter 10). Not undermining trust with greater use of surveillance, but instead building the social atmosphere where difficulties are discussed in a spirit of exploration with pupils and, when relevant, parents.

Overall school atmosphere. A general democratic atmosphere will be more likely to generate ideas and involvement. Staff can be more involved if they are engaged in the development of ideas and considering what constitutes good practice and why it would benefit pupils. In many cases, good pedagogic practice will arise from discussion, and is helped through classroom observations or videos of lessons. However, staff need to feel secure to be able to do this and feel strong collegiate support rather than judgement. Books are now available that argue for the importance of a collaborative, emotionally open leadership in schools (Sharp 2001; Antidote 2003a, 2003b; Elias *et al.* 2003; Weare 2003). The more that staff are supported emotionally, the greater the chance they can support each other and the pupils.

2. Emotional literacy and cognitive skills

In many educational matters, one has to balance competing demands, for example the emphasis on cognitive learning and emotional development. At present, schools focus on cognitive skills to the exclusion of emotional development and pastoral care of pupils. If these can be integrated, it reduces the problems of time considerably. With the background of the previous chapters I will now define emotional literacy as I use it. *Emotional literacy involves factors such as people understanding their own and others' emotional states; learning to manage their emotions and to empathize with others. It also includes the recognition that emotional literacy is both an individual development and a collective activity and is both about self-development and the building of community so that one's own sense of emotional well-being grows along with that of others', and not at their expense. Emotional literacy involves connections between people and working with their differences and similarities while being able to handle ambiguity and contradiction. It is a dynamic processs through which the individual develops emotionally and involves culture and empowerment. For example, it includes understanding how the nature of social class, 'race' and gender (sexism and homophobia) impinge on people's emotional states to lead to an understanding of how society could change. Hence it incorporates an understanding of power exchanges between people and a challenging of power differentials.* Some of the key aspects of introducing emotional literacy into schools could include:

- Placing an emphasis on the centrality of dialogue, since emotional development is acquired through communication (Antidote 2003b). To what extent can collaborative group work be at the centre of pedagogy in your school? Emotional literacy for *all* pupils is helped by being pupil-centred as well as teacher-led. The advantages of pupils having some control are that they can respond to their own needs, evolve at a pace and in areas where they are ready.
- Encouraging pupils to be reflective about their interactions and develop their meta-social and meta-emotional skills. Pupils can be encouraged to use collaborative strategies to develop their emotional responsiveness and to socially connect with others (see 'Principles for developing emotional literacy', p. 96).
- Debating 'How can we avoid viewing emotional literacy as *just* a property of the individual and open to objective measurement?' Concepts like self-esteem, self-confidence and knowing feelings should not be separated from their social context in order to be measured. When school and class policies on assessment and learning are considered, the extent to which all assessments – but in particular emotional literacy – can be developed as *a balance between individual and group* characteristics could be contemplated (see Chart 4.1). Chapter 7 provides some ideas on what can be included in an *individual-in-group* evaluation in emotional literacy, while Chapter 4 indicates that pupils benefit from having some control over the assessment processes.
- Finding ways to decrease the extent to which pupils can project their

anxieties onto the 'other'. This involves recognition of similarity and difference (Chapter 5) and the overlap of masculinities and femininities (Chapter 9) (Salisbury and Jackson 1996). Teachers can consider how they can enable pupils to recognize and confront anxieties. These could include the techniques described in Chapters 6 and 7 on classroom interactions, although teachers can invent and develop better ways.

• Asking 'What mechanisms could be available when pupils interact and how to make *visible* the exchanges of power (Chapters 5 and 7)? How can stereotypical behaviour be made more visible and then reflected upon by pupils? One key aspect is for pupils to reflect meta-socially and meta-emotionally. These strategies could be used occasionally and enable pupils to experience what a change in power feels like. One aspect of engendering change is to focus on the pleasures that can be obtained from power exchanges.

• Debating and working out strategies to raise issues about those groups not present in the school; for example, in all 'White' or all 'Black' schools, how is inclusion with other ethnic groups tackled? Schools vary enormously in the variety of pupils they contain. The pupils who come to any school, irrespective of their social and cultural backgrounds, can all benefit from emotional literacy programmes. There will always be some pupils who are experiencing violence, emotional deprivation or abuse and so are especially in need. Hence, teachers can consider their schools' priorities.

• Helping pupils in secondary schools to acknowledge and develop the erotic dimension to their lives and relationships. Teachers can investigate ways of accomplishing this, and consider what strategies might help in discussing openly the nature of all types of sexualities and relationships, and lay out guidelines for helping pupils face up to their anxieties.

Achieving the above should make schools happier places and reduce the pressures on teachers. The following are policy decisions that teachers may wish to consider:

• Having a non-competitive atmosphere where there is less anxiety over status derived from tests, exams and SATs will enhance emotional development. To change to a less competitive situation, teachers as a body could consider challenging governmental and state policies that focus so much on academic attainment.

• If pupils' emotional needs are met, and they progress emotionally, then it is highly likely that behaviour in classrooms will improve and academic results get better. It is possible that schools and administrators will accept this and go no further. However, even though academic results are very important for pupils, policies that tackle the societal problems of inequality in terms of economics, health, gender, sexuality, class and ethnicity could be pursued.

- All types of schools can contribute to developing pupils' emotional literacy. But greater opportunities can arise in co-educational and multi-ethnic schools. Policies could be pursued so that there would be equal numbers of boys and girls in co-educational schools.
- For teachers to equip pupils to meet the demands of a fast changing world, and to respond to pupils' needs, we need professionally trusted teachers who are trained to be able to think on their feet and have the confidence to 'make it up as they go along'. In turn, this requires a curriculum that is flexible. People at all levels of education could promote policies that work towards removing restrictive curricula that do not allow for creative and innovative approaches to education.
- Address the social and emotional upset that pupils can experience when changing schools, especially during the primary to secondary transfer.

3. Pedagogies

One difficulty facing many teachers is the tension that exists in pedagogy because of the differing demands. On the one hand, especially in academic subjects, the emphasis is on pedagogy to produce cognitive learning so that pupils can pass exams. This pedagogy can emphasize narrow accepted knowledge, specialization and stratification. Certainty of knowledge is often the goal. On the other hand, to address the pupils' social and emotional needs requires a more open pedagogy. The emphasis is more on broad experiences and interactions, openness, expansion and equality. Ambiguity and acceptance of individual differences are often the goals. If this dichotomy is preserved, the teacher is placed in an impossible situation and the solution at present is often to focus on the traditional, closed, pedagogy.

You might consider the extent to which the following pedagogical features are present in your school:

- How do teachers bring the human dimension into lessons, especially in the sciences and mathematics? What proportion of work in a school has a clear social dimension and could be open to investigation and multiple answers? A test of this would be to ask the pupils the extent to which they saw themselves working towards fixed answers as opposed to answering open questions.
- Are there clear boundaries between the academic and the pastoral,

leading to a reinforcement of different pedagogies? Will it help to merge the academic and emotional curriculum experiences, while also having separate times for them? An issues-based approach is one way of facilitating this merger. Dialogue has been identified (Chapters 3 and 4) as a key pedagogical strategy. Group work has been shown to be very valuable in academic learning, and is part of the constructivist classroom (Brookes and Brookes 1993). In each case, the pupil is seen as an active learner who has ideas/frameworks that should be made visible to both the learner and the teacher. Teachers can consider how much they can incorporate group work discussions into lessons, using the strategies outlined in Chapter 5, p. 85 and in Chapter 6. The same pedagogic strategies can be used to integrate the academic and the pastoral.

- In what ways does the teacher have authority? This can be achieved in different ways but there is evidence that the most important job for a teacher is to build up a relationship with his or her pupils based on honesty, trust and valuing pupils. This moves away from the teacher–pupil relationship being seen primarily as a hierarchy. Building up relationships is easier in primary schools but more difficult in secondary schools where pupils can have short lessons. Secondary schools could consider reviewing the length of their lessons. For emotional development, the teacher has often to be a facilitator. Discussion of a whole-school policy on classroom management can help individual teachers achieve a more communal shift.

Implementation of the above should make for easier teacher–pupils relationships.

4. Equity and social justice

Many of the ideas outlined above under 'Emotional literacy and cognitive skills' also apply to approaching equity. Teachers can enable pupils to understand and question some of the hierarchies like those ascribed to gender, 'race' and class. In this case, it is due to perceived group differences. The power differences that exist can be deconstructed so that they are not seen as natural and that the similarities can be identified. Hierarchical power will always exist, and in some respects is essential for the running of any large society. However, many hierarchies are unwarranted. Pupils could be encouraged to visualize a more deliberative democratic power exchange that values difference rather than finding it a threat. The deliberation can include voices of representation as well as 'recognition' (Chapter 2). It is the balance between the hierarchical control and democracy in the classroom that could be changed. Teachers could ask themselves the extent to which the following could be addressed in their schools:

- Does your school make visible the ways that pupils interact with each other? In all school subjects, the ways that pupils interact with each other could be made visible. The differences and assumptions, which will vary from subject to subject, can be used to deconstruct the way that power works to maintain separation. For example, in science boys may be constructed as being more 'able' than girls and a range of conscious and unconscious strategies used to undermine girls' confidence. The reverse, in different ways, can happen in music or drama, where girls may be constructed as being 'naturally better' than boys, and this used to undermine boys' confidence in their ability to sing or dance. Teachers could work together in a cross-curricular way to make these constructions open to challenge through comparison. In this way, the 'other' can be better recognized and their voices heard. The boys and girls can make comparisons about how they feel in each subject.
- How does your school enable pupils to celebrate difference-as-normal across gender and other differences? Since many variations cut across accepted gender, ethnic and class lines, the similarities and ambiguities can be explored (see Table 5.1) (Lynch and Lodge 2002; Griffiths 2003).
- What strategies can be used to enhance deliberative democracy in pupil–pupil interactions and in the school in general? An understanding of what participating in a deliberative democracy might feel like can be suggested through the pleasure that can be obtained from power exchanges. Pupils helping each other learn can be contrasted with control and negative power. This is not simple, as raw power, like taking someone's pocket money, is pleasurable to the bully.
- What strategies are used during collaborative work so that pupils can be encouraged to understand that friendships develop and require work over time – that is, a *growth belief* (Dweck 2000)? Within this they can come to understand that working through friendships and relationships involves deliberative power exchanges rather than domination. The elements of desire within some friendships can also be debated, and the ways in which intimacy in relationships can be a basis for democracy (Giddens 1993) (Chapter 9).

The ways in which power is made visible links directly to the types of pedagogy used and is a whole-school issue (Lynch and Lodge 2002; Griffiths 2003; Vincent 2003).

5. Continuity and transformation

This book started with a discussion of the main aim of schools, which is to enable pupils to develop their cognitive abilities. This aim is part of preparing pupils to obtain jobs and to join society. Another theme was that education could engage pupils in critical thinking so that they could contribute to democracy. The two elements of transforming society and accepting the *status quo* are both key. Teachers could audit the ways they approach pupils' critical thinking skills, their ability to reflect on the way that society is developing, as well as how pupils are involved in decision making in the school. O'Sullivan (1999: 281) ends his book on transformative learning with:

> The inability to express our sense of ecstasy and gratitude for the *gift of life* constitutes a loss of meaning about our vocation and place in the larger life processes. We live in an incredible time in earth history and we must capture the sense of our purpose through celebrating the fullness of our existence in both time and space. Celebration is an essential part of the ritual of existence.

Much of *Engaging Education* is about enabling pupils to gain a sense of the possible joys of life, a central part of which is to have a vision of how their lives and society could be different. As they are more able to make connections with other people, discuss and engage in life and learning, so they may be happier and healthier. It is to this vision that this book is devoted.

Appendix 1
Details of the Improving Science and Emotional Development (ISED) project[1]

The research was completed with 82 pupils in three Year 7 (11–12 years old) classes, with one male and two female teachers. Another three parallel Year 7 classes were used as controls. The schools were typical inner-city state co-educational multi-ethnic comprehensives and the pupils were achieving under the national average in their end of primary school Standard Assessment Tasks (SATs). A further 80 Year 7 pupils acted as a control group. The classes involved resulted from the timetabling of the school; no groups were pre-selected (Table A1). The one-year project set out to test the hypothesis that pupils in co-educational schools could be helped to develop their emotional literacy using collaborative group work with feedback mechanisms.

Pupils worked in mixed-sex groups where they self-monitored how well they worked together. They made written comments on their cognitive and emotional interactions, knowing that both listening and talking skills were regarded as important. Having both aspects of development on the agenda, the pupils were able to discuss issues, engage their emotions and so, hopefully, mature. An outline of the pattern of research is given in Chart A1 overleaf.

Table A1   Numbers of pupils involved

	Research	Control	Total
Boys	45	46	91
Girls	37	37	74
Total	82	83	165

Instruments of assessment and procedures

Pre- and post-questionnaires

Two questionnaires were administered to the pupils at the beginning and end of the research period. The first was called the **Survey**, which was filled in by the pupils in the research and control groups. It included: (i) opinion

---

Chart A1   Summary chart of the phases of the research

Phase 1: Beginning of Year 7 (aged 11–12 years), when pupils have just started secondary school

Data collection
Pupils in three research classes and three parallel control classes were given two Lickert type questionnaires; the **Survey** and **How are you feeling?** Pupils filled in the **Survey**, which had questions on what they thought about science, science lessons and how well they got on with boys and girls. The **Survey** was also given to pupils in both an all-girls' and an all-boys' school.
How are you feeling? asked questions about how they felt about (a) themselves, (b) other pupils, (c) school and (d) aspects of their science lessons. The data collected were analysed using a statistical package.

Phase 2: During the first 6 weeks of Year 7: group activity to raise issues on social and emotional factors involved in learning

Intervention
Pupils put into groups of two boys and two girls, usually by teachers. Another pupil was appointed as an observer.

1   Pupils put into groups of four do some science activity for 10 minutes or more. The pupil-observer filled in the **Discussion assessment** sheet, which indicated how much the pupils talked, listened, supported each other and learnt.
2   Pupils in the group filled in, by themselves, how well they and the other members of the group learnt, talked, listened, helped each other and learnt.
3   Led by the observer, the pupils discussed the results of the sheets to raise cognitive and emotional factors. Through comparing the sheets, they could also learn to realize how the different members of the group felt. This contributed to them learning to empathize.

Data collection
Discussion assessment sheets collected and analysed.

Phase 3: Week 6 onwards: collaborative learning

Intervention
The observer was removed.
Once the pupils were used to the procedures, they all worked in groups of four so that all the class was involved in learning science. Only **Opinion** sheets were used. There are different sheets, each one with a different focus. These include ones on: group learning; getting on with others in the group; group work and science; teaching and learning in groups; conflict; and social skills.
The same procedures as above were used, except the group organized its own discussions.

Data collection
Data from the **Opinion** sheets were put in a specially written data-analyser.

Phase 4: Main research period

Intervention
Collaborative learning tasks with **Opinion** sheets used every three weeks throughout the year.
Homeworks and class tasks set.

Data collection
Opinion sheets analysed.
Further data were collected through homeworks and class tasks. These were open-ended questions to cross-check other data sources and to elicit:

(a) how pupils were **Getting on with each other** and the other sex.
(b) how the pupils felt about learning with each other and the other sex called **Learning with other pupils**.
(c) aspects of their learning, called **Thinking about your learning**.

Another task was a ranking exercise on **Why do mixed-sex collaborative work in science?** and the questions were on: (a) learning science, (b) inter-gender social skills, (c) life social skills.

Phase 5: End of Year 7 Questionnaires and interviews

Data collection
The research and control pupils were given the **Survey** and **How are you feeling?** again. Forty per cent of the pupils interviewed by independent evaluator. Data analysis of the **Survey, How are you feeling?, Opinion** sheets, interviews and all other data.

statements with an 8-point Likert scale response, (ii) bipolar adjectives on a 8-point scale, and (iii) short answer questions. Eight-point scales were chosen so that pupils were unable to select a neutral option. The **Survey** was given at the beginning and end of the academic year. On each question the pupils could choose answers on a scale of 1 to 8, where the most negative answers (e.g. I do not understand science lessons at all) were scored 1, and the most positive answers (e.g. I understand science lessons very well) were scored 8. This questionnaire covered three main areas: (1) how pupils got on with each other, (2) what they thought of science and scientists, and (3) how they viewed science lessons. The **Survey** was also given to equivalent pupils in an all-girls' school and an all-boys' school.

The second questionnaire, '**How you are feeling?**', was given to the research and control groups and was designed to elicit data on statements about the (i) interpersonal, (ii) intrapersonal, (iii) school in general and (iv) science lessons. It contained statements on a 6-point Likert scale response. The data were obtained and treated in the same way to that of the **Survey** but with the scores being given from 1 to 6. It is worth stressing here that **How are you feeling?** was *not* used like an EQ test to study how individual pupils reported that they had changed over the year. It was only used to gain information about the cohort as a whole.

The data from both the **Survey** and **How are you feeling?** were analysed statistically using a matched-sample *t*-test to establish whether any changes in the beginning and end of year scores were significant.

Measures and procedures during classroom interventions

The classroom strategies developed for the research involved the use of questions on pro-formas, followed by discussions around the pupil responses to those questions. The discussions were to help the pupils become more self-aware and so have the potential for changing gender interactions and attitudes to science education (Matthews and Sweeney 1997). The intervention materials used with the research groups are explained in Chapter 6 and were called **Discussion, Guesses** and **Opinion** sheets. Each pupil filled in a sheet, so provided them with data from different perspectives on how well they had learnt and got on together in the groups. In the research, the data obtained were put into a spreadsheet for analysis of the monitoring criteria. Additionally, the **Opinion** sheets were administered about every three weeks through the rest of the research period. The pupils' responses were looked over by the teacher taking the class, and any particular points noted. A researcher analysed the replies and put them into three categories:

1   Positive (or supportive of the question) where one, two or more positive statements were being made.

2 Neutral, or contradicted itself.

3 Negative where one, two or more negative points were made in response to the question.

The data were then put into a spreadsheet that calculated the percentages of responses in each category. The class teacher then reviewed the data entry and results.

The research and control classes were taught using the same schemes of work and so experienced very similar scientific content and practical work. Thus the only difference between the two groups was the research intervention of collaborative group work. Boys and girls, as they engaged in collaborative group work while learning, were regularly monitored for their learning. Typical activities for the group work are described in the main text.

Note

1 The appendix is based on Matthews (2004).

Appendix 2
Sample sheet for use in the classroom

Name: Caroline Herschel	Class:	Date:	6

Members of group:
~~Da~~ Me, Arundati Roy, Mick Jagger, Albert Einstein

In each of the questions below write the person's names in order in the boxes.

1. Who do you think spoke:

the most	next most		the least
Arundati	Mick	Me	Albert

2. Who do you think listened:

the most	next most		the least
Me	Arund	Alb	Mick

3. Who do you think suggested useful things to do:

the most	next most		the least
Bert	Mick	Me	Arund

4. Who do you think disrupted the group:

the least	next least		the most
all	the same		

5. When I was working in my group I felt ....

good

because .... I was part of it and they listened to me. Everyone took part

6. Working in a group was useful because......... you have other peoples opinions as well to help you. Get to know them better

7. How does group work help you, or stop you, from learning? Helps.

Sometimes you get more ideas. If I feel like I'm wrong the others say the same and I feel definate.

Appendix 3
Sample sheet for use in the classroom

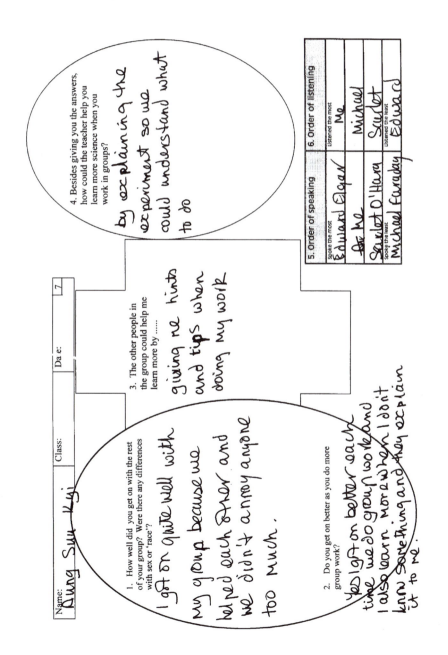

Name: Aung Sun Kyi   Class: Date: 7

1. How well did you get on with the rest of your group? Were there any differences with sex or 'race'?

I got on quite well with my group because we helped each other and we didn't annoy anyone too much.

2. Do you get on better as you do more group work?

Yes I get on better each time we do group work and I also learn more when I don't know something and they explain it to me.

3. The other people in the group could help me learn more by ......

giving me hints and tips when doing my work

4. Besides giving you the answers, how could the teacher help you learn more science when you work in groups?

By explaining the experiment so we could understand what to do

5. Order of speaking	6. Order of listening
Spoke the most	Listened the most
Edward Elgar	Me
Me	Michael
Scarlet O'Hara	Scarlet
Spoke the least	Listened the least
Michael Faraday	Edward

Appendix 4
Sample sheet for use in the classroom

| Name: Isaac Newton | Class: | Date: | 11 |

1. When I worked in this group I found that working with the girl(s) was ..... *fine* *because I got to know them*

Next time we work in a group I would like her/them to .... *stay the same but talk less*

2. When I worked in this group I found that working with the boy(s) was ..... *good* *because we get on good*

Next time I would like him/them to .... *Work a bit harder*

3. Ring **one** statement below to say how you prefer to work:

| only on my own | mostly on my own | sometimes on my own | don't mind | sometimes in groups | (mainly in groups) | always in groups |

4. How important do you think it is to develop the social skills so that you can get on with others?

Important

The advantages of developing social skills are .... *that when your older and have a job you need to work with other people. Have friends.*

| 5. The skills **I** need to develop to get on well with everyone in the group are ...... | 6. I could get better at **my** skills by .... |
| *to listen more to what they are saying even if you dont like them try to get along with them.* | *help out more* |

7. Order of speaking	8. Order of listening
Spoke the most	Listened the most
Mary Shelley	*Rosalind*
Gengis khan	*Mary*
me	*me*
Spoke the least	Listened the least
Rosalind Franklin	*Gengis*

9. Who did you enjoy working with? Write down their name(s):
Mary Gengis

References

AAUW (1998) *Separated by Sex: A Critical Look at Single-sex Education for Girls.* Washington, DC: American Association of University Women Educational Foundation.

AAUW (2001) *Beyond the Gender Wars: A Conversation About Girls, Boys and Education.* Washington, DC: American Association of University Women Educational Foundation.

Ackerman, B. and Fishkin, J. (2003) Deliberation day, in J. Fishkin and P. Laslett (eds.) *Debating Deliberative Democracy.* Oxford: Blackwell.

Adams, E. (2001) A proposed causal model of vocational teacher stress, *Journal of Vocational Education and Training,* 53(2): 223–46.

Adorno, T., Frenkel-Brunswik, E., Levinson, D. and Sandford, R. (1982) *The Authoritarian Personality.* London: Norton.

Alderson, P. (2000) Citizenship in theory and practice: being or becoming citizens with rights, in D. Lawton, J. Cairns and R. Gardner (eds.) *Education for Citizenship.* London: Continuum.

Allard, A. and Cooper, M. (2001) 'Learning to cooperate': a study of how primary teachers and children construct classroom cultures, *Asia-Pacific Journal of Teacher Education,* 29(2): 153–69.

Allard, A.C. and Yates, L. (2001) Exploring positive cross-gender peer relations: year 10 students' perspectives on cross-gender friendships, *International Journal of Inclusive Education,* 5(1): 33–46.

Allport, G.W. (1979) *The Nature of Prejudice.* Reading, MA: Addison-Wesley (originally published 1954).

Alwyn, R. (2004) *American Virgins: This World.* British Broadcasting Corporation, 25 January.

Amit, V. (ed.) (2002) *Realizing Community: Concepts, Social Relationships and Sentiments.* London: Routledge.

Antidote (2003a) www.antidote.org.uk (accessed April 2005).

Antidote (2003b) *The Emotional Literacy Handbook: Promoting Whole-school Strategies.* London: David Fulton in association with Antidote.

Antidote (2005) *SEELS.* http://www.antidote.org.uk/seels/s18.html (accessed April 2005).

Apter, T. (2004) *You Don't Really Know Me: Why Mothers and Daughters Fight and How Both Can Win.* London: Norton.

Arnot, M., Gray, J., James, M. and Rudduck, J. (1998) *Recent Research on Gender and Educational Performance.* London: Ofsted.

Aronson, E. (1997) Back to the future: a retrospective review of Leon Festinger's *A theory of cognitive dissonance*, *American Journal of Psychology*, 110(1): 127–57.

Aronson, E., with Blaney, N., Stephan, C., Sikes, J. and Snapp, M. (1978) *The Jigsaw Class-room*. Beverly Hills, CA: Sage.

Aronson, E. and Yates, S. (1983) Co-operation in the classroom: the impact of the jigsaw method of inter-ethnic relations, classroom performance, and self-esteem, in H. Blumberg, A. Hare, V. Kent and M. Davies (eds.) *Small Groups and Social Interaction*, Vol. 1. New York: Wiley.

Asher, S. and Rose, A. (1997) Promoting children's social-emotional development with peers, in P. Salovey and D. Sluyter (eds.) *Emotional Development and Emotional Intelligence: Educational Implications*. New York: Basic Books.

Askew, S. and Carnell, E. (1998) *Transforming Learning: Individual and Global Change*. London: Cassell.

Askew, S. and Ross, C. (1990) *Boys Don't Cry: Boys and Sexism in Education*. Buckingham: Open University Press.

Associated Press (2004) Japan schools tracking students by radio, *The Boston Globe* (http://www.boston.com/news/education/k_12/articles/2004/09/28/ japan_schools_tracking_students_by_radio/ [accessed March 2005]).

Bacon, R. and Eltis, W. (1976) *Britain's Economic Problem: Too Few Producers*. London: Macmillan.

Bailey, E. (2005) Flap forces halt to student-tracking experiment, *Los Angeles Times* (http://www.latimes.com/news/local/la-me-tracking17feb17,1,7192936. story?ctrack=1&cset=true [accessed April 2005]).

Baldo, M. (1993) Does sex education lead to earlier or increased sexual activity in youth? Paper presented to the *Ninth International Conference on Aids*, Berlin, 6–19 June.

Ball, S. (2003) *Class Strategies and the Education Market: The Middle Classes and Social Advantage*. London: RoutledgeFalmer.

Barab, S. and Plucker, J. (2002) Smart people or smart contests? Cognition, ability and talent development in an age of situated approaches to knowing and learning, *Educational Psychologist*, 37(3): 165–82.

Barash, D. (1978) *Sociobiology and Behaviour*. London: Heinemann.

Barker, M. (1982) *The New Racism*. London: Junction Books.

Bar-on, R. (1997) *The Emotional Quotient Inventory (EQ-i): Technical Manual*. Toronto: Multi-Health Systems.

Bar-on, R. and Parker, J. (eds.) (2000) *The Handbook of Emotional Intelligence: Theory, Development, Assessment and Application at Home, School, and in the Workplace*. San Francisco, CA: Jossey-Bass.

Baron-Cohen, S. (2003) *Essential Difference: Men, Women and the Extreme Male Brain*. London: Penguin.

Basic Skills Agency (2003) *Too many children not well prepared for starting school* (http://www.basic-skills.co.uk/site/page.php?p=986 [accessed March 2005]).

Basic Skills Agency (2005) *Talking with your children can make all the difference* (http://www.basic-skills.co.uk/site/page.php?p=1433 [accessed March 2005]).

Bay-Cheng, L. (2003) The trouble of teen sex: the construction of adolescent sexuality through school-based sexuality education, *Sex Education*, 3(1): 61–74.

BBC (2003) *Girls top of the class worldwide* (http://news.bbc.co.uk/2/hi/uk_news/education/3110594.stm [accessed January 2005]).

Belbin, R. (1993) *Team Roles at Work*. Oxford: Butterworth-Heinemann.

Benn, C. and Chitty, C. (1997) *Thirty Years On: Is Comprehensive Education Alive and Well or Struggling to Survive?* London: Penguin.

Best, R. (ed.) (1996) *Education, Spirituality and the Whole Child*. London: Cassell.

Biesta, G. and Miedema, S. (2002) Instruction or pedagogy? The need for a transformative conception of education, *Teaching and Teacher Education*, 18: 173–81.

Bigger, S. and Brown, E. (eds.) (1999) *Spiritual, Moral, Social and Cultural Education: Exploring Values in the Curriculum*. London: David Fulton.

Bleach, K. (ed.) (1998) *Raising Boys' Achievement in Schools*. Stoke on Trent: Trentham Books.

Block, N.J. and Dworkin, G. (1977) *The I.Q. Controversy: Critical Readings*. London: Quartet Books.

Bly, R. (1990) *Iron John: A Book About Men*. Reading, MA: Addison-Wesley.

Boaler, J. (1997) *Experiencing School Mathematics: Teaching Styles, Sex and Setting*. Buckingham: Open University Press.

Boaler, J., Wiliam, D. and Brown, M. (2000) Students' experiences of ability grouping – disaffection, polarisation and the construction of failure, *British Educational Research Journal*, 26(5): 631–48.

Boler, M. (1999) *Feeling Power: Emotions and Education*. New York: Routledge.

Bone, A. (1983) *Girls and Girl-only Schools*. Manchester: Equal Opportunities Commission.

Bray, R., Gardner, C., Parsons, N., Downes, P. and Hannan, G. (1997) *Can Boys do Better?* Leicester: SHA.

Brin, D. (1999) *The Transparent Society: Will Technology Force Us to Choose Between Privacy and Freedom?* New York: Basic Books.

Brookes, J. and Brookes, M. (1993) *In Search of Understanding: The Case for Constructivist Classrooms*. Alexandria, VA: Association for Supervision and Curriculum Development.

Brown, P. (2000) Globalisation of positional competition, *Sociology*, 34(4): 633–45.

Bullough, R. and Krudel, C. (2003) Adolescent needs, curriculum and the Eight-Year Study, *Journal of Curriculum Studies*, 35(2): 151–69.

Burstyn, J. (1980) *Victorian Education and the Ideal of Womanhood*. London: Croom Helm.

Cabinet Office (2005) *Strategic audit: progress and challenges for the UK*, Prime Minister's Strategy Unit (http://www.strategy.gov.uk/files/pdf/strategic_audit2.pdf [accessed April 2005]).

Cairns, E. (1990) The relationship between adolescent perceived self-competence and attendance at single-sex secondary school, *British Journal of Educational Psychology*, 60: 210–18.

Casel (2003) *Safe and Sound: An Educational Leader's Guide to Evidence-based Social and Emotional Learning Programs.* Chicago, IL: University of Chicago Press (available at: www.casel.org/downloads/Safe%20and%20Sound/1A_Safe_&_Sound.pdf).

Casel (2005) *Casel website for academic learning* (http://www.casel.org/sel_resources/SEL%20and%20Academics.php [accessed April 2005]).

CBS (2002) *Bush push for single-sex schools* (www.cbsnews.com/stories/2002/05/09/politics/ [accessed February 2003]).

Chetcuti, D. and Griffiths, M. (2002) The implications for student self-esteem of ordinary differences in schools: the cases of Malta and England, *British Educational Research Journal*, 28(4): 529–50.

Childline (2004) *Major rise in exam stress calls to Childline* (www.childline.org.uk/majorriseinexamstress.asp [accessed May 2005]).

Chitty, C. (1996) *Generating a National Curriculum*, Block 4, Unit 2. EU208. Milton Keynes: Open University Press.

Chitty, C. (2004) *Education Policy in Britain.* Basingstoke: Palgrave.

Chodorow, N. (1978) *The Reproduction of Mothering: Psychoanalysis and the Sociology of Gender.* Berkeley, CA: University of California Press.

Christakis, D., Zimmerman, F., DiGiuseppe, D.L. and McCarty, C.A. (2004) Early television exposure and subsequent attentional problems in children, *Pediatrics*, 113(4): 708–13.

Coffield, F., Moseley, D., Hall, E. and Ecclestone, K. (2004) *Should We Be Using Learning Styles? What Research Has to Say About Practice.* London: Learning and Skills Research Centre.

Cohen, J. (ed.) (1999) *Educating Minds and Hearts: Social and Emotional Learning and the Passage into Adolescence.* New York: Teachers College.

Cole, M. (1996) *Cultural Psychology: A Once and Future Discipline.* Cambridge, MA: Harvard University Press.

Cole, M. (2005) Introduction, in M. Cole (ed.) *Professional Values and Practice: Meeting the Standards.* London: David Fulton.

Colley, A. (1994) School subject preferences of pupils in single-sex and co-educational secondary schools, *Educational Studies*, 20(3): 381–5.

Connell, R.W. (1987) *Gender and Power.* Cambridge: Polity Press.

Connell, R.W. (1995) *Masculinities.* Cambridge: Polity Press.

Connell, R.W. (2002) *Gender.* Oxford: Polity Press.

ContractorUK (2005) *IT skills shortage to crash UK economy* (http://www.contractoruk.com/news/001792.html [accessed April 2005]).

Cook, S.W. (1985) Experimenting on social issues: the case of school desegregation, *American Psychologist*, 40: 452–60.

Cooke, B. and Kothari, U. (eds.) (2001) *Participation, the New Tyranny?* London: Zed Books.

Cooper, R. and Sawaf, A. (1997) *Executive EQ: Emotional Intelligence in Business*. London: Orion Business Books.

Cornwell, T. (1997) Sex division in classes in San Francisco, *Times Educational Supplement*, 21 November, p. 18.

Creese, A., Leonard, D., Daniels, H. and Hey, V. (2004) Pedagogic discourses, learning and gender identification, *Language and Education*, 18(3): 191–206.

CSEE (Centre for Social and Emotional Education) (2005) http://www.csee.net/resources/readings.aspx (accessed April 2005).

Curry, L. (1990) A critique of the research on learning styles, *Educational Leadership*, 48(2): 50–6.

Curtis, A. (2004) *The Power of Nightmares*, British Broadcasting Corporation, 20 and 27 October, 3 November.

Dalal, F. (1998) *Taking the Group Seriously: Towards a Post-Foulkesian Group Analytic Theory*. London: Jessica Kingsley.

Dalal, F. (2002) *Race, Colour and the Process of Racialization: New Perspectives from Group Analysis, Psychoanalysis and Sociology*. Hove: Brunner-Routledge.

Dale, R.R. (1971) *Mixed or Single-sex School? Vol. 2: Some Social Aspects*. London: Routledge & Kegan Paul.

Dale, R.R. (1974) *Mixed or Single-sex School? Vol. 3: Attainment, Attitudes and Overview*. London: Routledge & Kegan Paul.

Damasio, A. (1996) *Descartes' Error: Emotion, Reason and the Human Brain*. London: Papermac.

Daniels, H. (2001) *Vygotsky and Pedagogy*. London: RoutledgeFalmer.

Darling, J. and Glendinning, A. (1996) *Gender Matters in Schools: Pupils and Teachers*. London: Cassell.

Datnow, A. and Hubbard, L. (2002) *Gender in Policy and Practice: Perspectives on Single-sex and Coeducational Schooling*. London: RoutledgeFalmer.

Davidson, A. and Edwards, C. (1998) A different style of learning, in K. Bleach (ed.) *Raising Boys' Achievement in Schools*. Stoke on Trent: Trentham Books.

Davies, B. (1993) *Shards of Glass: Children Reading and Writing Beyond Gendered Identities*. Sydney, NSW: Allen & Unwin.

Davies, S. (1996) *Big Brother: Britain's Web of Surveillance and the New Technological Order*. London: Pan.

Dawkins, R. (1976) *The Selfish Gene*. Oxford: Oxford University Press.

de Botton, A. (2004a) *Status Anxiety*, British Broadcasting Corporation, 6 March.

de Botton, A. (2004b) *Status Anxiety*. London: Hamish Hamilton.

Deem, R. (ed.) (1984) *Co-education Reconsidered*. Milton Keynes: Open University Press.

DES (1985) *Better Schools*, Cmnd 9469. London: HMSO.

Deuchar, R. (2003) Preparing tomorrow's people: the new challenges of citizenship education for involving Scottish pupils and teachers in participative decision-making processes, *Scottish Educational Review*, 35(1): 27–37.

DfES (2003) *Developing Children's Social, Emotional and Behavioural Skills: Guidance.* London: Department for Education and Skills (available at: www.standards. dfes.gov.uk/primary/pdf/pns075903_sebsguide.pdf?version=1).

DfES (2005) *Excellence and Enjoyment: Social and Emotional Aspects of Learning. Guidance.* Primary National Strategy. London: Department for Education and Skills.

Dhingra, D. (2005) *The skills gap*, iVillage (http://www.ivillage.co.uk/workcareer/ findjob/jobseek/articles/0,,184_171821,00.html [accessed April 2005]).

Dobson, R. (2004) Secrets to a longer life: buy a cat, avoid main roads, get married (and stay married), *Independent on Sunday*, 15 August, p. 15.

Dorman, P. and Hudson, J. (2003) Welfare governance in the surveillance society, *Social Policy and Administration*, 37(5): 468–82.

Duffy, M. (2002) Achievement gap, *Times Educational Supplement*, 15 November, pp. 15–18.

Duvall, L. (1994) *Respecting our Differences: A Guide to Getting Along in a Changing World.* Minneapolis, MN: FS Publishing.

Dweck, C.S. (2000) *Self-theories: Their Role in Motivation, Personality, and Development.* Philadelphia, PA: Psychology Press.

Elias, M. (2003) *Academic and social-emotional learning.* Paris: UNESCO (available at: http://www.ibe.unesco.org/International/Publications/EducationalPractices/ EducationalPracticesSeriesPdf/prac11e.pdf).

Elias, M., Zins, J., Weissberg, R. and Frey, K. (1997) *Promoting Social and Emotional Learning.* Alexandria, VA: Association for Supervision and Curriculum Development.

Elias, M.J., Arnold, H. and Hussey, C.S. (2003) *EQ + IQ = Best Leadership Practices for Caring and Successful Schools.* Thousand Oaks, CA: Corwin Press.

Elias, N. (1978) *What is Sociology?* New York: Columbia University Press.

Elias, N. (1991) *The Symbol Theory.* London: Sage.

Elias, N. (1994) *The Civilising Process.* Oxford: Blackwell.

Epstein, C.F. (1988) *Deceptive Distinctions: Sex, Gender and the Social Order.* New Haven, CT: Yale University Press.

Epstein, D. and Johnson, R. (2000) Schooling sexualities, *British Journal of Educational Studies*, 48(2): 204–5.

Epstein, D., Elwood, J., Hey, V. and Maw, J. (eds.) (1998) *Failing Boys: Issues in Gender and Achievement.* Buckingham: Open University Press.

Epstein, S. (1998) *Constructive Thinking: The Key to Emotional Intelligence.* London: Praeger.

Erikson, E. (1950) *Childhood and Society.* New York: Norton.

Erikson, E. (1985) *The Life Cycle Completed.* New York: Norton.

Erricker, C., Erricker, J., Sullivan, D., Ota, C. and Fletcher, M. (1997) *The Education of the Whole Child.* London: Cassell.

Faupel, A. (ed.) (2003a) *Emotional Literacy: Assessment and Intervention. Ages 7 to 11.* London: NFER/Nelson.

Faupel, A. (ed.) (2003b) *Emotional Literacy: Assessment and Intervention. Ages 11 to 16.* London: NFER/Nelson.

Feldman, M. (1999) Is shyness catching? Social phobia, *Utne Reader,* November/December, pp. 16–17.

Festinger, L. (1962) *A Theory of Cognitive Dissonance.* London: Tavistock.

Festinger, L. (1964) *Conflict, Decision and Dissonance.* London: Tavistock.

Foon, A. (1988) The relationship between school type and adolescent self-esteem, attribution styles and affiliation needs: implications for educational outcome, *British Journal of Educational Psychology,* 58: 44–54.

Foulkes, S.H. (1948) *Introduction to Group Analytic Psychotherapy.* London: Karnac Books.

Foulkes, S.H. (1990) *Selected Papers.* London: Karnac Books.

FPA (Family Planning Association) (2003) *Sexual behaviour* (http://www.fpa.org.uk/about/PDFs/Factsheet6.pdf [accessed April 2005]).

Francis, B. (1998) *Power Plays: Primary School Children's Constructions of Gender and Power.* Stoke on Trent: Trentham Books.

Fraser, N. (1997) *Justice Interruptus: Critical Reflections on the 'Postsocialist' Condition.* London: Routledge.

Fraser, N. and Honneth, A. (2003) *Redistribution or Recognition? A Political-Philosophical Exchange.* London: Verso.

Fraser, S. (ed.) (1995) *The Bell Curve Wars: Race, Intelligence, and the Future of America.* New York: Basic Books.

Freeman, C. (2004) *Trends in Educational Equity of Girls and Women: 2004* (NCES 2005-016), US Department of Education, National Centre for Statistics. Washington, DC: US Government Printing Office (available at: http://nces.ed.gov/pubs2005/2005016.pdf).

Freire, P. (1972a) *Cultural Action for Freedom.* Harmondsworth: Penguin.

Freire, P. (1972b) *Pedagogy of the Oppressed.* Harmondsworth: Penguin.

Freire, P. (1997) *Education for Critical Consciousness.* New York: Continuum.

Furedi, F. (2004) Should teachers be therapists?, *The Daily Telegraph,* 21 January, p. 19.

Gadamer, H.-G. (1989) *Truth and Method.* London: Sheed & Ward.

Gaine, C. and George, R. (1999) *Gender, 'Race' and Class in Schooling: A New Introduction.* London: Falmer.

Gallagher, K. and Rivière, D. (2004) Pink . . . with shades of grey: mediating moments of diversity in urban secondary classrooms, *Westminster Studies in Education,* 27(2): 127–41.

Galton, M., Morrison, I. and Pell, T. (2000) Transfer and transition in English schools: reviewing the evidence, *International Journal of Educational Research,* 33: 341–63.

Gamarnikow, E. and Green, A. (2000) Citizenship, education and social capital, in D. Lawton, J. Cairns and R. Gardner (eds.) *Education for Citizenship.* London: Continuum.

Garfinkel, S. (2001) *Database Nation: The Death of Privacy in the 21st Century.* London: O'Reilly.

George, R. (2004) The importance of friendship during primary to secondary school transfer, in C. Benn and C. Chitty (eds.) *A Tribute to Caroline Benn: Education and Democracy.* London: Continuum.

George, R. and Browne, N. (2000) 'Are you in or are you out?' An exploration of girl friendship groups in the primary phase of schooling, *International Journal of Inclusive Education*, 4(4): 289–300.

Gewirtz, S. (1998) Conceptualizing social justice in education: mapping the territory, *Journal of Education Policy*, 13(4): 469–84.

Gewirtz, S., Ball, S. and Bowe, R. (1995) *Markets, Choice and Equity in Education.* Buckingham: Open University Press.

Giddens, A. (1993) *The Transformation of Intimacy: Sexuality, Love and Eroticism in Modern Societies.* Cambridge: Polity Press.

Goleman, D. (1996) *Emotional Intelligence: Why it Can Matter More than IQ.* London: Bloomsbury.

Goleman, D. (1999) *Working with Emotional Intelligence.* London: Bloomsbury.

Goodchild, S. (2004a) 'Army of therapists' to tackle huge rise in child depression, self-harm and suicide, *Independent on Sunday*, 12 September, p. 8.

Goodchild, S. (2004b) A generation of troubled youngsters 'criminalised', *Independent on Sunday*, 31 October, p. 8.

Goodman, C.K. (2004) *High-tech devices can spy on kids 24/7, but what about trust?*, Knight Ridder Newspapers (http://www.azcentral.com/families/articles/1029fam_spyteens.html [accessed March 2005]).

Gould, C. (1996) Diversity and democracy: representing difference, in S. Benhabib (ed.) *Democracy and Difference: Contesting the Boundaries of the Political.* Princeton, NJ: Princeton University Press.

Graham, S. and Wood, D. (2003) Digitizing surveillance: categorization, space inequality, *Critical Social Policy*, 23(2): 227–48.

Grant, C. and Hodgson, N. (1913) *The Case for Co-education.* London: Grant Richards.

Greenfield, S., Peters, J., Lane, N., Rees, T. and Samuels, G. (2002) *Set Fair: A Report on Women in Science, Engineering and Technology.* London: Department of Trade and Industry (available at: http://www.dti.gov.uk/).

Greenhalgh, P. (1994) *Emotional Growth and Learning.* London: Routledge.

Griffiths, M. (1998) The discourses of social justice in schools, *British Educational Research Journal*, 28: 301–16.

Griffiths, M. (2003) *Action for Social Justice in Education: Fairly Different.* Buckingham: Open University Press.

Haag, P. (1998) Single-sex education in Grades K12: what does research tell us?, in AAUW (ed.) *Separated by Sex: A Critical Look at Single-sex Education for Girls.* Washington, DC: American Association of University Women Educational Foundation.

Haag, P. (1999) *Voices of a Generation*. Washington, DC: American Association of University Women Educational Foundation.

Hagan, J. (2003) Classroom CCTV alarms teachers, *The Guardian* (http://education. guardian.co.uk/schools/story/0,5500,902114,00.html?=rss [accessed March 2005]).

Hall, K., Collins, J., Benjamin, S., Nind, M. and Sheehy, K. (2004) SATurated models of pupildom: assessment and inclusion/exclusion, *British Educational Research Journal*, 30(6): 801–17.

Hall, S. (2000) Multicultural citizens, monocultural citizenship?, in N. Pearce and J. Hallgarten (eds.) *Tomorrow's Citizens: Critical Debates in Citizenship and Education*. London: Institute for Public Policy Research.

Hamilton, C. (2004) *Growth Fetish*. London: Pluto.

Hannan, D.F., Smyth, E., McCullagh, J., O'Leary, R. and McMahon, D. (1996) *Co-education and Gender Equality: Exam Performance, Stress and Personal Development*. Dublin: Oak Tree Press/Economic and Social Research Institute.

Hanson, T. and Austin, G. (2002) *Resilience & Youth Development Module: Aggregated California Data, Fall 1999–Spring 2002*. Los Alamitos, CA: West Ed. (available at: http://www.wested.org/chks/pdf/rydm_aggregate.pdf).

Harding, J. (1986) *Perspectives on Gender and Science*. London: Falmer Press.

Harré, R. (1991) *Physical Being*. Oxford: Blackwell.

Hart, S., Drummond, M.J., Dixon, A. and McIntyre, D. (2004) *Learning Without Limits*. Buckingham: Open University Press.

Hassan, R. (2001) What if . . . information technology were to hinder learning and undermine democracy?, *Information, Technology, Education and Society*, 2(1): 89–102.

Haynes, N., Ben-Avie, M. and Ensign, J. (eds.) (2003) *Getting Results in Math and Science Education*. New York: Teachers College.

Haywood, C. and Mac an Ghaill, M. (1995) The sexual politics of the curriculum: contesting values, *International Studies in Sociology of Education*, 5(2): 221–36.

HDA (Health Development Agency) (2004) *Teenage pregnancy and sexual health interventions* (http://www.hda-online.org.uk/Documents/CHB4-sexualhealth-14–7.pdf [accessed April 2005]).

Head, J. (1997) *Working with Adolescents: Constructing Identity*. London: Falmer Press.

Head, J. (1999) *Understanding the Boys: Issues of Behaviour and Achievement*. London: Falmer Press.

Heather, N. (1976) *Radical Perspectives in Psychology*. London: Methuen.

Henderson, J. and Wellington, J. (1998) Lowering the language barrier in learning and teaching science, *School Science Review*, 79(228): 35–46.

Herrnstein, R.J. and Murray, C.A. (1996) *The Bell Curve: Intelligence and Class Structure in American Life*. New York: Simon & Schuster.

Hessel-Mial, M. (2004) Teaching beyond abstinence, *Kansas City Star* (http://www.kansascity.com/mld/kanascity/10515997.htm?1c [accessed February 2005]).

Hey, V. (1997) *The Company She Keeps: An Ethnography of Girls' Friendship.* Buckingham: Open University Press.

Hilgard (1953) *An Introduction to Psychology.* New York: Harcourt Brace.

Hillcole Group (1997) *Rethinking Education and Democracy.* London: Tufnell Press.

Hochschild, A.R. (1983) *The Managed Heart: The Commercialization of Human Feeling.* Berkeley, CA: University of California Press.

Hochschild, A.R. (2003) *The Managed Heart: Commercialization of Human Feeling,* Twentieth Anniversary Edition. Berkeley, CA: University of California Press.

Hodson, D. (1998) *Teaching and Learning Science: Towards a Personalised Approach.* Buckingham: Open University Press.

Hoff Sommers, C. (1996) Where the boys are, *Education Weekly,* 12 June (http://edweek.org/ew/vol-15/38sommer.h15 [accessed February 2003]).

Hofkins, D. (2004) Democrats all the way from the cradle, *Times Educational Supplement,* 7 May, p. 22.

Holt, A. (2004) *Teen depression on the increase,* BBC News, 3 August (available at: http://news.bbc.co.uk/go/pr/fr/-/1/hi/health/3532572.stm).

Hunter, R. (2002) *World Without Secrets: Business, Crime and Privacy in the Age of Ubiquitous Computing.* New York: Wiley.

Illich, I. (1973) *Tools for Conviviality.* London: Calder & Boyars.

International Idea (1999) *Youth Voter Participation: Involving Today's Young in Tomorrow's Democracy.* Stockholm: International Institute for Democracy and Electoral Assistance.

Ireson, J., Hallam, S., Mortimer, P., Hack, S., Clarke, H. and Plewis, I. (1999) *Ability Grouping in Schools: Practices and Consequences,* London. Institute of Education.

Ireson, J., Hallam, S. and Hurley, C. (2001) *Ability Grouping in the Secondary School: Effects at Key Stage 4,* Final Report. London: Nuffield Foundation/Institute of Education.

Jackson, C. (2002) Can single-sex classes in co-educational schools enhance the learning experiences of girls and/or boys? An exploration of pupils' perceptions, *British Educational Research Journal,* 28(1): 37–48.

Jacoby, R. and Glauberman, N. (eds.) (1995) *The Bell Curve Debate: History, Documents, Opinions.* New York: Times Books.

James, O. (1998) *Britain on the Couch: Why We're Unhappier than We Were in the 1950s – Despite Being Richer.* London: Arrow.

Jensen, D. and Draffan, G. (2004) *Welcome to the Machine: Science, Surveillance, and the Culture of Control.* White River Junction, VT: Chelsea Green.

Johnson, M. (2005) *Developmental Cognitive Neuroscience* (2nd edn). Oxford: Blackwell.

Johnson, D. and Johnson, R. (2000) The three Cs of reducing prejudice and discrimination, in S. Oskamp (ed.) *Reducing Prejudice and Discrimination.* Mahwah, NJ: Lawrence Erlbaum Associates.

Kamin, L., Lewontin, R. and Rose, S. (1984) *Not in Our Genes: Biology, Ideology and Human Nature.* Harmondsworth: Penguin.

Kane, R. and Wellings, K. (1999) *Reducing the Rate of Teenage Conceptions – An International Review of the Evidence: Data from Europe.* London: Health Education Authority (http://www.hda-online.org.uk/documents/ pregnancyinternationalpt1.pdf and 2.pdf [accessed April 2005]).

Karst, K. (1990) Boundaries and reasons: freedom of expression and the subordination of groups, *University of Illinois Law Review*, 1990(1): 95–149.

Kegan, R. (1982) *The Evolving Self: Problem and Process in Human Development.* London: Harvard University Press.

Kelly, A. (1985) The construction of masculine science, *British Journal of Sociology of Education*, 8(4): 399–412.

Kelly, A. (1996) Comparing like with like, *Education*, 187(1): 13–15.

Kelly, P. (2003) Growing up as risky business? Risks, surveillance and the institutionalized mistrust of youth, *Journal of Youth Studies*, 6(2): 165–80.

Kenway, J. and Willis, S. (1990) *Heart and Minds: Self-esteem and the Schooling of Girls.* London: Falmer Press.

Kenway, J., Willis, S., with Blackmore, J. and Rennie, L. (1998) *Answering Back: Girls, Boys and Feminism in Schools.* London: Routledge.

Kessler, R. (2000) *The Soul of Education.* Alexandria, VA: Association for Supervision and Curriculum Development.

Kirby, D. (2001) *Emerging Answers: Research Findings on Programs to Reduce Teen Pregnancy.* Washington, DC: National Campaign for the Prevention of Teen Pregnancy (http://www.teenpregnancy.org/resources/data/pdf/emeranswsum. pdf [accessed April 2005]).

Kirby, D. (2002) *Do Abstinence-only Programs Delay the Initiation of Sex Among Young People and Reduce Teen Pregnancy?* Washington, DC: National Campaign for the Prevention of Teen Pregnancy (http://www.teenpregnancy.org/resources/ data/pdf/abstinence_eval.pdf NCPTP [accessed April 2005]).

Kirsta, A. (1994) *Deadlier than the Male.* London: HarperCollins.

Kitcher, P. (1985) *Vaulting Ambition: Sociobiology and the Quest for Human Nature.* Cambridge, MA: MIT Press.

Klein, M. (1988) *Envy and Gratitude and Other Works 1946–1963.* London: Virago.

Kling, K., Hyde, J., Showers, C. and Buswell, B. (1999) Gender differences in self-esteem: a meta-analysis, *Psychological Bulletin*, 125(4): 470–500.

Kreml, W. (1977) *The Anti-authoritarian Personality.* London: Pergamon.

Kruse, A.-M. (1992) '. . . We have learnt not just to sit back, twiddle our thumbs and let them take over'. Single-sex settings and the development of a pedagogy for girls and a pedagogy for boys in Danish schools, *Gender and Education*, 4(1/2): 81–103.

Kruse, A.-M. (1996) Single-sex settings: pedagogies for girls and boys in Danish schools, in P. Murphy and C. Gipps (eds.) *Equity in the Classroom: Towards Effective Pedagogy for Girls and Boys.* London: Falmer Press/UNESCO.

Kukathas, C. and Pettit, P. (1990) *Rawls: A Theory of Justice and its Critics.* London: Polity Press.

Kutnick, P. and Rogers, C. (eds.) (1994) *Groups in Schools*. London: Cassell.

Kutnick, P., Blatchford, P. and Baines, E. (2002) Pupil groupings in primary school classrooms: sites for learning and social pedagogy?, *British Educational Research Journal*, 28(2): 187–206.

Labour Party (1996) *Lifelong Learning at Work and in Training*. London: Labour Party.

Laitsch, D., Lewallen, T. and McCloskey, M. (2005) *The Whole Child: A Framework for Education in the 21st Century*. Alexandria, VA: Association for Supervision and Curriculum Development (http://www.ascd.org/portal/site/ascd/menuitem.bfaa683e7841320fb85516f762108a0/ [accessed April 2005]).

Lamb, W.W.H. (2001) The 'whole child' in education, *Journal of Philosophy of Education*, 35(2): 203–17.

Lambert, A. (2003) Sex remains the great taboo between generations, *The Independent*, 20 November, p. 37.

Lankshear, C. (1997) *Changing Literacies*. Buckingham: Open University Press.

Lawton, D., Cairns, J. and Gardner, R. (eds.) (2000) *Education for Citizenship*. London: Continuum.

Leary, M. and Kowalski, R. (1995) *Social Anxiety*. New York: Guilford Press.

LeDoux, J. (1998) *The Emotional Brain*. London: Weidenfeld & Nicolson.

Lee, C. (1983) *The Ostrich Position: Sex, Schooling and Mystification*. London: Writers & Readers.

Lee, C. (1989) How we hurt our sons, *Sunday Times*, 21 October, pp. 54–8.

Lee, C. (1993) *Talking Tough: The Fight for Masculinity*. London: Arrow.

Lee, C. (2004) *To Die For: A Young Woman's Battle with Anorexia*. London: Century.

Lee, M. (2003) Engaging the whole person through the practice of collaborative learning, *International Journal of Lifelong Education*, 22(1): 78–93.

Lee, R. and Robbins, S. (1998) The relationship between social connectedness and anxiety, self-esteem, and social identity, *Journal of Counseling Psychology*, 45(3): 338–45.

Lee, V. and Bryk, A. (1986) The impact of school size and single-sex education on performance, *Journal of Educational Psychology*, 78(5): 381–95.

Lewis, J. (1998) Deadlier than the male? Women, knowledge and power, *Africa*, 68(2): 284–93.

Lewis, J. (2000) Spiritual education as the cultivation of qualities of the heart and mind: a reply to Blake and Carr, *Oxford Review of Education*, 26(2): 263–83.

Lewontin, R. (1987) Are the races different?, in D. Gill and L. Levidow (eds.) *Anti-racist Science Teaching*. London: Free Association Books.

Liberty (2004) www.liberty-human-rights.org.uk (accessed January 2004).

Literacy Trust (2004) *Research claims infants weaned on TV 'cannot concentrate'* (http://www.literacytrust.org.uk/Database/TV.html [accessed March 2005]).

Little, A. (2002) *The Politics of Community: Theory and Practice*. Edinburgh: Edinburgh University Press.

Lynch, K. and Lodge, A. (2002) *Equality and Power in Schools: Redistribution, Recognition and Representation*. London: RoutledgeFalmer.

Lynch, O. (ed.) (1990) *Divine Passions: The Social Construction of Emotions in India.* Berkeley, CA: University of California Press.

Lyon, D. (1994) *The Electronic Eye: The Rise of Surveillance Society.* Cambridge: Polity Press.

Lyon, D. (2001) Surveillance after September 11, *Sociological Research Online*, 6(3) (http://www.socresonline.org.uk/6/3/lyon.html [accessed April 2005]).

Lyon, D. (ed.) (2002) *Surveillance as Social Sorting: Privacy, Risk and Automated Discrimination,* London: Routledge.

Lyon, D. (2003) *Surveillance After September 11.* London: Blackwell.

Mac an Ghaill, M. (ed.) (1994) *Making of Men: Masculinities, Sexualities and Schooling.* Buckingham: Open University Press.

Mac an Ghaill, M. (ed.) (1997) *Understanding Masculinities: Social Relations and Cultural Arenas.* Buckingham: Open University Press.

MacGeorge, E., Graves, A., Feng, B., Gillihan, S. and Burleson, B. (2004) The myth of gender cultures: similarities outweigh differences in men's and women's provision of and responses to supportive communication, *Sex Roles*, 50(3/4): 143–75.

MacIntyre, H. and Ireson, J. (2002) Within-class ability grouping: placement of pupils in groups and self-concept, *British Educational Research Journal*, 28(2): 249–64.

Mahony, P. (1985) *Schools for Boys?* London: Hutchinson.

Malecki, C. and Elliott, S. (2002) Children's social behaviours as predicators of academic achievement: a longitudinal analysis, *School Psychology Quarterly*, 17(1): 1–23.

Mansell, W. (2004) They'd feel lost without the Sats, *Times Educational Supplement*, 23 January, p. 2.

Marans, S. and Cohen, J. (1999) Social and emotional learning: a psychoanalytic- ally informed perspective, in J. Cohen (ed.) *Educating Minds and Hearts: Social and Emotional Learning and the Passage into Adolescence.* New York: Teachers College.

Marx, G. (2002) What's new about the 'New Surveillance'?, *Surveillance and Society*, 1(1): 9–29.

Maslen, G. (2001) Mixed classes fail both sexes, *Times Educational Supplement*, 7 September, p. 20.

Matte-Blanco, I. (1988) *Thinking, Feeling and Being.* London: Routledge.

Matthews, B. (1992) Towards an understanding of the social issues in information technology: concerning computers, intelligence and education, *Journal of Information Technology for Teacher Education*, 1(2): 201–13.

Matthews, B. (1991) *Who Controls Whom? The Social Implications of Information Technology.* Coventry: National Council for Educational Technology.

Matthews, B. (1996) Peacemakers in the battle of the sexes, *Times Educational Supplement*, 17 May, p. 18.

Matthews, B. (1998) Co-education, boys, girls and achievement, in K. Bleach (ed.) *Raising Boys' Achievement in Schools.* Stoke on Trent: Trentham Books.

Matthews, B. (2002) Why is emotional literacy important to science teachers?, *School Science Review*, 84(306): 97–103.

Matthews, B. (2003a) *Improving Science and Emotional Development (The ISED Project): Emotional Literacy, Citizenship, Science and Equity*, 2nd edn. London: Goldsmiths.

Matthews, B. (2003b) Making science more popular through group work and emotional literacy: a possible contribution to internationalism?, *Science Education International*, 14(2): 12–20.

Matthews, B. (2004) Promoting emotional literacy, equity and interest in KS3 science lessons for 11–14 year olds: the 'Improving Science and Emotional Development' project, *International Journal of Science Education*, 26(3): 281–308.

Matthews, B. (2005) Emotional development, science and co-education, in S. Alsop (ed.) *Beyond Cartesian Dualism: Encountering Affect in the Teaching and Learning of Science*. Dordrecht: Kluwer Academic.

Matthews, B. and Sweeney, J. (1997) Collaboration in the science classroom to tackle racism and sexism, *Multi-cultural Teaching*, 15(3): 33–6.

Matthews, B., Kilbey, T., Doneghan, C. and Harrison, S. (2002) Improving attitudes to science and citizenship through developing emotional literacy, *School Science Review*, 84(307): 103–14.

Mayer, J.D. and Salovey, P. (1997) What is emotional intelligence?, in P. Salovey and D. Sluyter (eds.) *Emotional Development and Emotional Intelligence. Educational Implications*. New York: Basic Books.

Mayer, J., Salovey, P. and Caruso, D. (1999) Emotional intelligence meets traditional standards for an intelligence test, *Intelligence*, 27(4): 267–98.

Mayer, J., Salovey, P. and Caruso, D. (2000) Models of emotional intelligence, in R. Sternberg (ed.) *Handbook of Intelligences*. Cambridge: Cambridge University Press.

Mayer, J., Salovey, P. and Caruso, D. (2003) *Mayer-Salovey-Caruso Emotional Intelligence Test*. Toronto: Multi-Health Systems.

McGregor, D. (2004) Interactive pedagogy and subsequent effects on learning in science classrooms, *Westminster Studies in Education*, 27(2): 237–61.

McIntosh, P. and Style, E. (1999) Social, emotional and political learning, in J. Cohen (ed.) *Educating Minds and Hearts: Social and Emotional Learning and the Passage into Adolescence*. New York: Teachers College.

McLaughlin, T.H. (1996) Education of the whole child?, in R. Best (ed.) *Education, Spirituality and the Whole Child*. London: Cassell.

Measor, L. and Woods, P. (1984) *Changing Schools*. Milton Keynes: Open University Press.

Meštrović, S. (1997) *Postemotional Society*. London: Sage.

Michelson, W. and Harvey, A. (2000) Is teachers' work never done? Time-use and subjective outcomes, *Radical Pedagogy*, 2(1): 1–5 (available at: http://radicalpedagogy.icaap.org/content/issue2_1/02Michelson.html).

Miller, A. (1987) *For Your Own Good: Hidden Cruelty in Child-rearing and the Roots of Violence*. London: Virago.

Miller, A. (1990) *Thou Shalt Not be Aware: Society's Betrayal of the Child*. London: Pluto Press.

Milliband, D. (2004) *Personalised learning: building a new relationship with schools* (www.teachernet.gov.uk/growingschools/downloads/Milliband%20speech. doc [accessed March 2005]).

Moore, H. (2005) *Intolerance and Fundamentalism*. London: London School of Economics (http://www.lse.ac.uk/collections/sociology/pdf/Intolerance-Moore.pdf).

Murphy, P. and Elwood, J. (1998) Gendered learning outside and inside school: influences on achievement, in D. Epstein, J. Elwood, V. Hey and J. Maw (eds.) *Failing Boys: Issues in Gender and Achievement*. Buckingham: Open University Press.

Murphy, P. and Gipps, C. (eds.) (1996) *Equity in the Classroom: Towards Effective Pedagogy for Girls and Boys*. London: Falmer Press/UNESCO.

Nagda, B., Gurin, P. and Lopez, G. (2003) Transformative pedagogy for democracy and social justice, *Race, Ethnicity and Education*, 6(2): 163–91.

NASSPE (National Association for Single Sex Public Education) (2004) *Single sex education* (http://www.singlesexschools.org/ [accessed October 2004]).

National Advisory Committee on Creative and Cultural Education (2001) *All Our Futures: Creativity, Culture & Education*. London: Department for Education and Employment.

NCPTP (National Campaign to Prevent Teen Pregnancy) (2002) *Not just another single issue: teen pregnancy prevention's link to other critical social issues* (http:// www.teenpregnancy.org/resources/data/pdf/notjust.pdf [accessed April 2005]).

Nicholson, J. (1984) *Men and Women: How are They Different?* Oxford: Oxford University Press.

Nitsun, M. (1998) *The Anti-group: Destructive Forces in the Group and their Creative Potential*. London: RoutledgeFalmer.

Noble, C. and Bradford, W. (2000) *Getting it Right for Boys. . . and Girls*. London: Routledge.

Norris, C. and Armstrong, G. (1999) *The Maximum Surveillance Society: The Rise of CCTV*. Oxford: Berg.

O'Harrow, R. (2005) *No Place to Hide*. New York: Free Press.

O'Leary, J. (1999) Girls' schools fill top 8 places for GCSEs., *The Times*, 4 September, p. 12.

Orenstein, P. (1994) *SchoolGirls*. New York: Doubleday.

Oskamp, S. (ed.) (2000) *Reducing Prejudice and Discrimination*, Mahwah, NJ: Lawrence Erlbaum Associates.

O'Sullivan, E. (1999) *Transformative Learning: Educational Vision for the 21st Century*. London: Zed Books.

Paechter, C. (1998) *Educating the Other: Gender, Power and Schooling*. London: Falmer Press.

Parker, J. (2001) *Total Surveillance: Investigating the Big Brother World of E-spies, Eavesdroppers and CCTV*. London: Piatkus.

Parry, O. (1997) Schooling is fooling: why do Jamaican boys underachieve in school?, *Gender and Education*, 9: 223–31.

Pearce, N. and Hallgarten, J. (eds.) (2000) *Tomorrow's Citizens: Critical Debates in Citizenship and Education*. London: Institute for Public Policy Research.

Pedulla, J. (2003) State-mandated testing – what do teachers think?, *Educational Leadership*, 61(3): 42–6.

Peissi, W. (2003) Surveillance and security: a dodgy relationship, *Journal of Contingencies and Crisis Management*, 11(1): 19–24.

Perlman, D. and Cozby, P.C. (2000) *Social Psychology*. New York: Holt, Rinehart & Winston.

Pettit, P. (2003) Deliberative democracy, the discursive dilemma, and republican theory, in J. Fishkin and P. Laslett (eds.) *Debating Deliberative Democracy*. Oxford: Blackwell.

Phillips, A. (1993) *Democracy and Difference*. Cambridge: Polity Press.

Phillips, A. (1995) *The Politics of Presence*. Oxford: Oxford University Press.

Phillips, A. (1999) *Which Equalities Matter?* Cambridge: Polity Press.

Phillips, S. (2004) Schools lie about sex to pupils, *Times Educational Supplement*, 24/31, p. 11.

Plummer, G. (2000) *Failing Working Class Girls*. Stoke on Trent: Trentham Books.

Postman, N. and Weingartner, C. (1971) *Teaching as a Subversive Activity*. London: Penguin.

Prentice, R. (1996) The spirit of education: a model for the twenty-first century, in R. Best (ed.) *Education, Spirituality and the Whole Child*. London: Cassell.

Pring, R. (1994) *Personal and Social Education in the Curriculum*. London: Hodder & Stoughton.

Print, M. and Coleman, D. (2003) Towards understanding of social capital and citizenship education, *Cambridge Journal of Education*, 33(1): 123–49.

Purvis, J. (1980) Working class women and adult education in nineteenth century Britain, *History of Education*, 9(3): 193–212.

Ranson, S. (1984) Towards a tertiary tripartism: new codes of social control and the 17+, in P. Broadfoot (ed.) *Selection, Certification and Control: Social Issues in Educational Assessment*. London: Falmer Press.

Rawls, J. (1971) *A Theory of Justice*. Cambridge, MA: Harvard University Press.

Reynolds, M. (1997) Learning styles: a critique, *Management Learning*, 28(2): 115–33.

Richel, M. (2004) In Texas, 28,000 students test an electronic eye, *New York Times* (http://www.nytimes.com/2004/11/17/technology/17tag.html?ex=1107493200&en=55adb5ae569d544d&ei=5070&oref=login [accessed February 2005]).

Riordan, C.H. (1990) *Girls and Boys in School: Together or Separate?* New York: Teachers College Press.

Riordan, C.H. (2002) What do we know about the effects of single-sex schools in the private sector?, in A. Datnow and L. Hubbard (eds.) *Gender in Policy and Practice: Perspectives on Single-sex and Coeducational Schooling.* London: RoutledgeFalmer.

Robinson, P. and Smithers, A. (1999) Should the sexes be separated for secondary education – comparisons of single-sex and co-educational schools?, *Research Papers in Education,* 14(1): 23–49.

Rodger, A. (1996) Human spirituality: towards an educational rationale, in R. Best (ed.) *Education, Spirituality and the Whole Child.* London: Cassell.

Rowe, K., Turner, R. and Lane, K. (2002) Performance feedback to schools of students' Year 12 assessments: the VCE Data Project., in A.J. Visscher and R. Coe (eds.) *School Improvement Through Performance Feedback.* Lisse, The Netherlands: Swetz & Zeitlinger.

Rubsamen-Waigmann, H., Sohlberg, R., Rees, T. *et al.* (2003) *Women in Industrial Research: A Wake Up Call for European Industry.* Brussels: European Commission Directorate-General for Research (available at: http://europa.eu.int/comm/research/science-society/women/wir/report-en.html).

Salisbury, J. and Jackson, D. (1996) *Challenging Macho Values: Practical Ways of Working with Adolescent Boys.* London: Falmer Press.

Salomone, R. (2003) *Same, Different, Equal: Rethinking Single-sex Schooling.* New Haven, CT: Yale University Press.

Salovey, P. and Sluyter, D. (eds.) (1997) *Emotional Development and Emotional Intelligence: Educational Implications.* New York: Basic Books.

Salusbury, M. (2003) The police paparazzi, *Independent on Sunday,* 19 October, pp. 36–7.

Samuels, A. (2001) *Politics on the Couch: Citizenship and the Internal Life.* London: Profile Books.

Samuels, A. (2005) *Fundamentalism.* London: London School of Economics (http://www.lse.ac.uk/collections/sociology/pdf/IntoleranceSamuels.pdf   [accessed April 2005]).

Sandel, M. (1982) *Liberalism and the Limits of Justice.* Cambridge: Cambridge University Press.

Sandler, J. (ed.) (1987) *Projection, Identification, Projective Identification.* New Haven, CT: International Universities Press.

Sax, L. (2005) *Why Gender Matters: What Parents and Teachers Need to Know About the Emerging Science of Sex Differences.* New York: Doubleday/Random House.

Sayers, J. (1982) *Biological Politics: Feminist and Anti-feminist Perspectives.* London: Tavistock.

Scales, P. and Roehlkepartain, E. (2003) Boosting student achievement, *Insights and Evidence,* 1(1): 1–10 (available at: http://www.search-institute.org/research/Insights/IE–10–03-Achievement.pdf).

Scarberry, N.C., Ratcliff, C.D., Lord, C.G., Lanicek, D.L. and Desforges, D.M. (1997) Effects of individuating information on the generalization part of Allport's contact hypothesis, *Personality and Social Psychology Bulletin*, 23(12): 1291–9.

Schmuck, P., Nagel, N. and Brody, C. (2002) Studying gender consciousness in single-sex and coeducational high schools, in A. Datnow and L. Hubbard (eds.) *Gender in Policy and Practice: Perspectives on Single-sex and Coeducational Schooling*. London: RoutledgeFalmer.

Schnarch, D. (1991) *Constructing the Sexual Crucible: An Integration of Sexual and Marital Therapy*. New York: Norton.

Sewell, T. (1997) *Black Masculinities and Schooling: How Black Boys Survive Modern Schooling*. Stoke on Trent: Trentham Books.

Sharma, Y. (2000) Racial mix leads to greater tolerance (Reporting the research of Dr Rainer Dollase), *Times Educational Supplement*, 20 October, p. 5.

Sharp, P. (2001) *Nurturing Emotional Literacy*. London: David Fulton.

Shaw, M. (2004) Calls to Childline from bully victims rocket, *Times Educational Supplement*, 27 August, p. 10 (available at: http://www.childline.org.uk).

Sheerman, B. (2004) Have we got our priorities right?, *The Guardian* (http://education.guardian.co.uk/egweekly/story/0,5500,1121193,00.html [accessed April 2005]).

Shmurak, C. B. (1998) *Voices of Hope: Adolescent Girls at Single Sex and Coeducational Schools*. New York: P. Lang.

Shriver, T., Schwab-Stone, M. and DeFalco, K. (1999) Why SEL is the better way: the New Haven Development Program, in J. Cohen (ed.) *Educating Minds and Hearts: Social and Emotional Learning and the Passage into Adolescence*. New York: Teachers College.

Sidanius, J. and Veniegas, R. (2000) Gender and race discrimination: the interactive nature of disadvantage, in S. Oskamp (ed.) *Reducing Prejudice and Discrimination*. Mahwah, NJ: Lawrence Erlbaum Associates.

Simpson, G. (2005) *Separate but Equal and Single-sex Schools*. Cornell Law School Research Paper #05–001 (available at: http://ssrn.com/abstract=646961 [accessed April 2005]).

Singh, B. (2001) Dialogue across cultural and ethnic differences, *Educational Studies*, 27(3): 343–55.

Skelton, C. (2001) *Schooling the Boys: Masculinities and Primary Education*. Buckingham: Open University Press.

Slater, J. (2004) Exam fears haunt pupils, *Times Educational Supplement*, 23 January, p. 9.

Smith, J. (2003) *Education and Public Health: Natural Partners in Learning for Life*. Alexandria, VA: Association for Supervision and Curriculum Development.

Smith, S. (1984) Single-sex setting, in R. Deem (ed.) *Co-education Reconsidered*. Milton Keynes: Open University Press.

Smithers, A. and Robinson, P. (1995) *Co-educational and Single-sex Schooling.* Manchester: Centre for Education and Employment Research.

SP/SAA (Social Phobia/Social Anxiety Association) (2005) http://www. socialphobia.org/ (accessed February 2005).

Spielhofer, T., O'Donnell, L., Benton, T., Schagen, S. and Schagen, I. (2002) *The Impact of School Size and Single-sex Education on Performance.* Slough: NFER

Stables, A. (1990) Differences between pupils from mixed and single-sex schools in their enjoyment of school subjects and in their attitudes to science and school, *Educational Review*, 42(3): 221–30.

Stangor, C. (2000) *Stereotypes and Prejudice: Essential Readings.* Philadelphia, PA: Psychology Press.

Stanworth, M. (1981) *Gender and Schooling: A Study of Sexual Divisions in the Classroom.* London: Women's Research and Resources Centre Publications.

Steiner, C. with Perry, P. (1997) *Achieving Emotional Literacy.* London: Bloomsbury.

Sternberg, R. (ed.) (2000) *Handbook of Intelligences.* Cambridge: Cambridge University Press.

Stubbs, I. (2005) Quotes, *The Independent on Sunday*, 30 January, p. 29.

Swan, B. (1998) Teaching boys and girls in separate classes at Shenfield High School, Brentwood, in K. Bleach (ed.) *Raising Boys' Achievement in Schools.* Stoke on Trent: Trentham Books.

Swann, C., Bowe, K., McCormick, G. and Kosmin, M. (2003) *Teenage Pregnancy and Parenthood: A Review of Reviews.* London: Health Development Agency (http://www.hda-online.org.uk/documents/teenpreg_evidence_briefing.pdf [accessed April 2005]).

Taylor, C. (1994) The politics of recognition, in A. Gutman (ed.) *Multiculturalism: Examining the Politics of Recognition.* Princeton, NJ: Princeton University Press.

Thompson, S. and Hoggett, P. (2001) The emotional dynamics of deliberative democracy, *Policy and Politics*, 29(3): 351–64.

Thompson, T. and Mintzes, J. (2002) Cognitive structure and the affective domain: on knowing and feeling in biology, *International Journal of Science Education*, 4(6): 645–60.

Tomlinson, S. (2001) *Education in a Post-welfare Society.* Buckingham: Open University Press.

Tooley, J. (2002) *The Miseducation of Women.* London: Continuum.

Traianou, A. (2005) Teachers' adequacy of subject knowledge in primary science: assessing constructivist approaches from a sociocultural perspective, *International Journal for Science Education*.

Tsagarousianou, R., Tambini, D. and Bryan, C. (1998) *Cyberdemocracy: Technologies, Cities and Civic Networks.* London: Routledge.

Venkatakrishnan, H. and William, D. (2003) Teaching and mixed-ability grouping in secondary school mathematics classrooms: a case study, *British Educational Research Journal*, 29(2): 189–204.

Vincent, C. (ed.) (2003) *Social Justice, Education and Identity*. London: RoutledgeFalmer.

Vygotsky, L. (1978) *Mind in Society: The Development of Higher Psychological Processes*. Cambridge, MA: Harvard University Press.

Vygotsky, L. (1997) *Educational Psychology*. Boca Raton, FL: St Lucie Press.

Walkerdine, V., Lucey, H. and Melody, J. (2001) *Growing Up Girl: Psychosocial Explorations of Gender and Class*. Basingstoke: Palgrave.

Walzer, M. (1983) *Spheres of Justice*. Oxford: Blackwell.

Ward, H. (2004) From grunting to greeting, *Times Educational Supplement*, 30 January, p. 10.

Warschauer, M. (2000) Speculations: does the Internet bring freedom?, *Information, Technology, Education and Society*, 1(2): 93–101.

Watkins, C., Lodge, C. and Best, R. (eds.) (2000) *Tomorrow's Schools – Towards Integrity*. London: RoutledgeFalmer.

Weare, K. (2003) *Developing the Emotionally Literate School*. London: Paul Chapman.

Weare, K. and Gray, G. (2003) *What Works in Developing Children's Emotional and Social Wellbeing?* London: Department for Education and Skills.

Wegerif, R., Littleton, K., Dawes, L., Mercer, N. and Rowe, D. (2004) Widening access to educational opportunities through teaching children how to reason together, *Westminster Studies in Education*, 27(2): 143–56.

Weisinger, H. (1998) *Emotional Intelligence at Work*. San Francisco, CA: Jossey-Bass.

Wellings, K. (2001) Sexual behaviour in Britain: early heterosexual experience, *Lancet*, 385(9296): 1843–50.

Wentzel, K. (1991a) Relations between social competence and academic achievement in early adolescence, *Child Development*, 62(3): 1066–78.

Wentzel, K. (1991b) Social competence at school: relation between social responsibility and academic achievement, *Review of Educational Research*, 61(1): 1–24.

Wentzel, K. (1993) Does being good make the grade? Social behavior and academic competence in middle school, *Journal of Educational Psychology*, 85:357–64.

Wheatley, J. (1996) Outclassed, *The Times Magazine*, 30 March, pp. 17–19.

Wigfield, A., Eccles, J., MacIver, D., Reuman, D. and Midgely, C. (1991) Transitions during early adolescence: changes in children's domain-specific self-perceptions and general self-esteem across the transition to junior high school, *Developmental Psychology*, 27(4): 552–65.

Wilkinson, R. (1996) *Unhealthy Societies: The Afflictions of Inequality*. London: Routledge.

Wilkinson, R. (2000) *Mind the Gap: Hierarchies, Health and Human Evolution*. London: Weidenfeld & Nicolson.

William, D. and Bartholomew, H. (2004) It's not which school but which set you're in that matters: the influence of ability grouping practices on students' progress in mathematics, *British Educational Research Journal*, 30(2): 279–93.

Williams, G. (1997) *Internal Landscapes and Foreign Bodies: Eating Disorders and Other Pathologies*. London: Duckworth.

Willis, P. (1977) *Learning to Labour: How Working-class Kids Get Working-class Jobs.* Aldershot: Gower.

Willis, S. and Kenway, J. (1986) On overcoming sexism in schooling: to marginalize or mainstream, *Australian Journal of Education*, 30(2): 132–49.

Wilson, E.O. (1978) *On Human Nature.* Cambridge, MA: Harvard University Press.

Wilson, V. (2002) *Feeling the Strain.* Glasgow: The Scottish Centre for Research in Education (http://www.scre.ac.uk/resreport/pdf/109.pdf [accessed April 2005]).

Yeatman, A. (1994) *Postmodern Revisionings of the Political.* London: Routledge.

Yorks, L. and Kasl, E. (2002) Towards a theory and practice for whole-person learning: reconceptualizing experience and the role of affect, *Adult Education Quarterly*, 52(3): 176–92.

Young, I. (1990) *Justice and the Politics of Difference.* Princeton, NJ: Princeton University Press.

Young, I. (1996) Communication and the Other: beyond deliberative democracy, in S. Benhabib (ed.) *Democracy and Difference: Contesting the Boundaries of the Political.* Princeton, NJ: Princeton University Press.

Young, I.M. (2000) *Inclusion and Democracy.* Oxford: Oxford University Press.

Zeidner, M., Roberts, R. and Matthews, G. (2002) Can emotional intelligence be schooled? A critical review, *Educational Psychologist*, 37(4): 215–31.

Zins, J.E., Weissberg, R.P., Wang, M.C. and Walberg, H.J. (eds.) (2004) *Building Academic Success on Social and Emotional Learning: What Does the Research Say?* New York: Teachers College.

Zittleman, K. and Sadker, D. (2003) The unfinished gender revolution, *Educational Leadership*, 60(4): 59–63.

Zsolnai, A. (2002) Relationship between children's social competence, learning motivation and school achievement, *Educational Psychology Review*, 22(3): 317–29.

Index

Schnarch, D., 144, 154
science, 1, 4, 13, 62, 68, 71, 95, 96, 97, 102,
   105, 107, 109, 114, 119, 120, 121,
   124, 125, 136, 138, 139, 151, 182,
   184–7
SEAL (Social and Emotional Aspects of
   Learning), 52, 53, 70
security, 19, 28, 39, 48, 75, 165
SEL
   see also Social and Emotional Learning, 51,
   52, 53, 56, 60, 68
'self', 28, 30, 45, 47, 48, 50, 62, 63, 66, 74, 75,
   76, 86, 87, 96, 97, 120, 126, 135, 168
self-control, 38, 55, 67, 167, 168
self-determining, 163
self-esteem, 21, 24, 33, 45, 46, 50, 54, 56, 58,
   59, 60, 92, 93, 116, 130, 146, 147, 160,
   163, 178
self-identity, 24, 30, 34
separation, 30, 49, 78, 137, 138, 139, 140,
   141, 142, 143, 145, 148, 155, 156, 162,
   163, 182
Sewell, T., 148
sex
   (*as sexual activity*) , 55, 76, 77, 154, 163, 164
   (*biological*), 24, 26, 45, 46, 63, 66, 72, 77,
   80–6, 92, 94, 95, 97, 98, 102, 105,
   108–13, 118, 119, 120, 121–3, 124, 126,
   135–40, 143, 144, 146, 148, 150, 151,
   153, 156, 157, 164, 184, 186
   -power, 73
   -roles, 73, 163
sex education, 137, 153, 154, 156, 164
sexism, 37, 54, 60, 61, 62, 72, 77, 79, 87, 94,
   98, 117, 118, 139, 140, 141, 143, 145,
   149, 178
sexual, 15, 45, 49, 52, 55, 75, 87, 88, 129, 130,
   139, 142, 147, 148, 152, 153, 154, 155,
   163, 164, 170, 174
sexualities, 3, 44, 46, 65, 83, 124, 128, 135,
   147, 152, 153, 155, 163, 179
sexuality, 27, 32, 36, 42, 45, 55, 76, 77, 148,
   152, 154, 157, 163, 164, 180
Shmurak, C., 136, 146
shoes, 74, 75
similarity, 26, 29, 60, 61, 74, 75, 80, 81, 82,
   83, 84, 87, 107, 122, 123, 124, 135, 142,
   143, 146, 175, 179
single-sex, 1, 26, 49, 61, 112, 135–41, 148,
   151, 154, 156–7
Skelton, C., 73, 86, 87, 146, 147, 148, 149

social and emotional learning, 51, 52, 54, 69,
   96
social anxiety, 162, 170, 173, 174
social capital, 19, 52, 130, 165
social class, 22, 32, 39, 46, 57, 60, 78, 85, 136,
   151, 165, 178
social justice, 3, 6, 22–5, 26, 31–2, 34, 59, 67,
   71, 86, 129, 130–1, 135, 138, 139, 157,
   163, 175, 176, 181
social reflexivity, 130
spiritual, 16, 17, 18, 74
splitting, 47, 49–50, 75, 97, 126, 141
spontaneity, 169
status anxiety, 160, 161, 163, 170
Steiner, C., 43, 44, 51, 69
stereotype, 49, 72, 81, 87, 92, 110, 123, 143,
   144, 145, 179
surveillance, 19, 70, 160, 163, 164–9, 176,
   177
Survey, 111, 112, 185–7
symmetric logic, 74, 75, 80, 81

Taylor, C., 24, 25, 30
teacher-centred, 51, 56, 66, 162
teacher-curriculum, 52
teacher-led, 52, 54, 66, 70, 178
technology, 168, 169
teenage
   see also adolescence, 154, 161, 164
'them', 74, 75, 76, 78, 171
Thompson, S., 28, 30
tolerant, 14, 20, 24, 31, 34, 41, 43, 53, 60, 86,
   144, 149
traffic lights, 17, 27
transference, 47, 48, 50
transformation, 14, 16, 17, 18, 21, 31, 67, 92,
   115, 120, 127, 151, 176, 183
trust, 16, 19, 123, 130, 153, 154, 165, 166,
   168, 173–4, 177, 181

United Nations, 11
'us', 29, 74, 75, 76, 78

voices of representation, 130, 135, 181
Vygotsky, L., 57, 68, 79, 91, 163

Walkerdine, V., 29
Watkins, C., 14
Weare, K., 35, 44, 52, 62, 63, 64, 68, 69,
   177
whine, 121

Related books from Open University Press

Purchase from www.openup.co.uk or order through your local bookseller

---

LEARNING WITHOUT LIMITS

Susan Hart, Annabelle Dixon, Mary Jane Drummond and Donald McIntyre

- Why do some teachers insist on teaching without recourse to judgements about ability?
- What are the key principles on which they draw as they organize and provide for learning?
- What is the significance of their alternative approach for classrooms in the 21st century?

This book explores ways of teaching that are free from determinist beliefs about ability. In a detailed critique of the practices of ability labelling and ability focused teaching, *Learning without Limits* examines the damage these practices can do to young people, teachers and the curriculum.

Drawing on a research project at the University of Cambridge, the book features nine vivid case studies (from Year 1 to Year 11) that describe how teachers have developed alternative practices despite considerable pressure on them and on their schools and classrooms. The authors analyze these case studies and identify the key concept of transformability as a distinguishing feature of these teachers' approach. They construct a model of pedagogy based on transformability: the mind-set that children's futures as learners are not pre-determined, and that teachers can help to strengthen and ultimately transform young people's capacity to learn through the choices they make. The book shows how transformability-based teaching can play a central role in constructing an alternative improvement agenda.

This book will inspire teachers, student teachers, lecturers and policy makers, as well as everyone who has a stake in how contemporary education and practice affect children's future lives and life chances.

Contents
Part one: The problem in context – Why learning without limits? – What's wrong with ability labelling? – Researching teachers' thinking and practices – Part two: The case studies – nine teachers in action – Part three: Towards an alternative model – The principle of transformability – From principle to practice – The contexts of teaching for learning without limits – Pupils' perspectives on learning without limits – An alternative improvement agenda – Conclusion – Index.

192pp   0 335 21259 X (Paperback)   0 335 21260 3 (Hardback)

UNIVERSITY OF WOLVERHAMPTON
LEARNING & INFORMATION SERVICES